"*Unstoppable Women* is an invaluable tool for any wo1. ͏
her dream." —Jack Canfield, co-author, *New York Times* #1
best-selling *Chicken Soup for the Soul* series

"*Unstoppable Women* is an exceptional book. The program Cynthia has developed is extremely practical—and it's easy to incorporate the process into your life. In no time, you'll be speeding along the path of your dreams."
—Robert G. Allen, author of the *New York Times* bestsellers
Nothing Down, Creating Wealth, Multiple Streams of Income,
Multiple Streams of Internet Income, and co-author of *The One Minute Millionaire*

"*Unstoppable Women* is a must-read for anybody serious about making their dreams come true!" —Les Brown, author of *Live Your Dreams,*
It's Not Over Until You Win, and *Up Thoughts for Down Times*

"Cynthia Kersey has created a foolproof process to ensure that every single woman who reads this marvelous book will find the courage, confidence, and determination to reach her life's goal—one unstoppable moment at a time. You can't read this book and not move forward."
—Gail Blanke, executive coach, motivational speaker, and author of *Between Trapezes: Flying into Your Next Life with the Greatest of Ease*

"I love this book! *Unstoppable Women* is a practical and hopeful read to help us identify where we really want to be and how to get us there. So often we feel powerless to create positive change in our lives. Maybe what's missing is the manual of how to get from here to there. This book is it."
—Donna Thomases, Organizer, Million Mom March
and author of *Looking for a Few Good Moms*

"If you are serious about changing your life, *Unstoppable Women* is a must. It will guide and encourage you every step of the way and you are not alone. The women profiled in this book are remarkable in every way and remind you that your life is packed with unlimited possibilities no matter what your circumstances."
—Frances Jones, co-founder, Feed the Children

"*Unstoppable Women* is a powerful book for helping the reader identify their heart's desire, then develop a plan to make it happen."
—Maureen Beal, CEO, National Van Lines

"*Unstoppable Women* offers readers a virtual "road map" to make a real, positive change in their lives in just 30 days. Cynthia dramatically captures the inspiring stories of courageous and 'unstoppable' women and then provides practical steps that can be followed by anyone wanting to make a positive difference in his or her life." —Robert S. Apatoff, President & CEO, Rand McNally & Company

"'One thing at a time.' 'Take small steps.' We've heard the expressions before, but in *Unstoppable Women*, Cynthia Kersey brings them to life by teaching us exactly how to develop our plans for change in small, achievable, daily steps. She encourages us to strive for 'progress, not perfection,' and to help other women along our way. This book is an invaluable tool for anyone preparing to make changes in her life."   —Karen Baar, author of *For My Next Act . . . Scripting Life After Fifty*

"Cynthia Kersey offers women the perfect strategy to make the changes in their life they now only dream about."
                              —Jane Velez-Mitchell, television news journalist
                                     and correspondent for *Celebrity Justice*

"Finally—a book for and about women that is informational, instructional, inspirational, and most of all, moves you to create a compelling new life of your dreams!"
            —Robin MacGillivray, president of Business Communications Services,
                                              SBC Communications West

"*Unstoppable Women* is as relevant for my teenage granddaughters as it is for me. Any woman can succeed at overcoming challenging circumstances and have unlimited possibilities with this 30-day program that really works. Inspiring and a must-read."
            —Diane V. Cirincione, Ph.D., nationally syndicated columnist of "Your Attitude
                     Is Everything" and co-author of *Change Your Mind, Change Your Life*

"*Unstoppable Women* helps women and men discover pathways to empowerment as we gain insight and inspiration from real life models of courage and transformation."
            —Barnet Bain, producer of *What Dreams May Come* and *The Celestine Prophecy*

"Cynthia Kersey has coached our sales team because she delivers results! *Unstoppable Women* offers a simple yet powerful program that can propel your company to a whole new level! This 30-day program works!"
                                        —Dyan Lucero, U.S. President of Jafra

"No matter where you are in life, *Unstoppable Women* will inspire you with beautifully written stories of courage and provide you with a simple process to change your life, one step at a time."   —Regina R. Testa, vice president, Xerox Corporation

"If you have dreams or aspirations, but are frustrated in making them a reality, this book is a must read. *Unstoppable Women* is motivational and inspirational, but the best news is that it is a practical guide that can help you achieve your goals. The women profiled in this book have remarkable stories and will remind you that you are not alone on your quest."
                     —Monica Luechtefeld, executive vice president, Office Depot

UNSTOPPABLE WOMEN

UNSTOPPABLE WOMEN

ACHIEVE *ANY* BREAKTHROUGH GOAL IN 30 DAYS

CYNTHIA KERSEY

AUTHOR OF THE BEST-SELLING *UNSTOPPABLE*

RODALE

Book design by Joanna Williams

Cartoons on pages 23, 55, 78, 137, and 159 are from Cartoon Resources.

"Autobiography in Five Short Chapters" on page 56 is from *There's a Hole in My Sidewalk: The Romance of Self-Discovery* by Portia Nelson, Hillsboro, OR, Beyond Words Publishing, 1993. Used with permission.

Material on pages 104–106 by Albert Ellis, president of the Albert Ellis Institute, New York City.

Quote on page 110 is from *If You Could See What I Hear* by Kathy Buckley, Dutton Books.

Quotes from J. K. Rowling's story are from her Web site, www.jkrowling.com. The account on pages 118–121 is not endorsed or authorized by J. K. Rowling's representatives.

Quote on page 124 reprinted with the permission of Simon & Schuster Adult Publishing Group from *Awaken the Giant Within* by Anthony Robbins. Copyright © 1991 by Anthony Robbins.

Material on page 161 used courtesy of Martin E. P. Seligman, Ph.D., Fox Leadership Professor of Psychology, The University of Pennsylvania, and director of The Positive Psychology Center.

Quote by Carly Fiorina on page 264 is from *Hard Won Wisdom* by Fawn Germer, The Berkeley Publishing Group.

Library of Congress Cataloging-in-Publication Data

Kersey, Cynthia.
    Unstoppable women : achieve any breakthrough goal in 30 days / Cynthia Kersey.
        p.   cm.
    Includes index.
    ISBN-13 978–1–59486–104–8 paperback
    ISBN-10 1–59486–104–8 paperback
    1. Success in business.   2. Goal (Psychology)   I. Title.
HF5386.K33   2005
650.1'082'0973—dc22   2004027383

Distributed to the trade by Holtzbrinck Publishers

2   4   6   8   10   9   7   5   3   1   paperback

Contents

Acknowledgments

*U*nstoppable Women has taken more than three years to complete including endless hours of research, interviews, writing, editing, and compiling information. It has been a true labor of love and the result of the combined efforts of many people. I especially wish to acknowledge the following:

To Karly Young, my Vice President of Marketing, and the Managing Director of the Unstoppable Foundation, who has invaluably contributed to my life, business, foundation, and to this book and project. Words cannot adequately express my gratitude for your brilliance, vision, input, support, loyalty, enthusiasm, and friendship. You are an immense blessing to me and I am so grateful for your contributions to this project and to my life.

To Sandy Owen, my dear and most unstoppable assistant. Thank you for your love, endless support, devotion, and for helping me manage the details of my life and business. I couldn't do it without you.

To Tim Vandehey, editorial contributor, who provided invaluable editing and expertise to this project. Thanks not only for your editorial contribution to this book, but for being such a pleasure to work with. You're the best!

To Karen Erbach, my research assistant, who once again, enthusiastically embraced this project and helped identify numerous unstoppable individuals. And thanks to Rockne Skyburg for sending me countless potential stories for this book.

To Richard Blank, the best publishing attorney on the planet. Thanks for your friendship, generosity and for the great contribution you bring to my life and business.

To all the people who participated in the Unstoppable 30-day Challenge. This book was born out of your success. You inspire me!

To Amy Kovalski, Mariska van Aalst, and the entire team at Rodale.

Thanks for your hard work and commitment to making *Unstoppable Women* a success.

To Greg Link, Michael Broussard, and Jan Miller for believing in this book and for enthusiastically helping me get this message out to a greater audience.

My deepest appreciation and thanks to the people who read the first or second drafts of the manuscript offering feedback. Your contribution was invaluable. Chrissy Lomax-Primeau, Cynthia Laroche, Denise Koepke, Dr. Ellen Stubenhaus, Elizabeth Estrada, Helen Burton, Jennifer Fender, Joy Armstrong, Judi Paliungas, Karen Erbach, Kathleen Breining, Leslie Buck, Linda Latta, Liora Mendeloff, Liz Edlic, Maureen Slater, Pat Schulz, Patricia Sill, Robert Thiele, Stacey Hopple, Stephanie Blackbird, and Tawni Gomes.

To the people who granted interviews and graciously agreed to participate in the book. Many of you have become special friends and all serve as a constant reminder of what's possible for anyone who is committed to being unstoppable. Thank you for sharing your life stories and for your outstanding examples of passion and commitment.

And finally, of all the gifts that life can give us, friendship is the most profound. I am exceedingly blessed with great friends and mentors who fill my life with love, insight, and laughter. And especially to my dear friends Liz Edlic, Denise Koepke, Elizabeth Estrada, and Mark Victor Hansen who provide unconditional love and encouragement to my life. I am blessed by you!

And to my dear friend, Millard Fuller. You are my role model and mentor and my life is forever changed as a result of knowing you.

Some people come into our lives and quietly go;
others stay for a while and leave footprints on our hearts
and we are never the same.
—Anonymous

My Invitation to You

You've picked up this book for one simple reason: You want to make a change in your life. Maybe it's a little change, maybe a big one. Whatever it is, up until now, something has stopped you from making it happen. Maybe you'd like to develop a healthier lifestyle, go back to school, or pursue your love of painting, but you just can't get yourself to take action. Maybe you've identified a goal, such as starting a business, running a marathon, or creating an investment strategy, but you have no idea where to begin. Or maybe you'd be thrilled to have an extra hour a day to spend quality time with your children, but you're at a loss as to how to find that time.

Whatever your goal, this book will help you achieve it!

In the coming pages, I'm going to introduce you to a *proven* process—called the Unstoppable Women Challenge—that is designed to jumpstart your life into action in just 30 days. And as part of this process, I'll also share with you the real-life inspirational stories of women who are current-day models of possibilities for all of us who dare to dream. No matter what your goal might be, this book will inspire you and give you the foundation and momentum you need to achieve it.

Sound like hype? It's not. In fact, the process is surprisingly simple. Why? Because it *is* a process. I'm going to teach you what I've already taught thousands of others in countless seminars and training programs: how to achieve any goal by creating a *series* of unstoppable moments—single steps forward that will become routine, like signing your name or brushing your teeth, and will ultimately result in personal transformation.

Stop the Cycle of Giving Up

You may be thinking, "I've tried to set goals before, but it didn't work." Or you may believe you're too busy, too overwhelmed, too quick to give up, or

1

too undisciplined to make even the slightest change in your life. Up until now, that may have been true. But the reality is, most people are stopped not because of their inadequacies, but because of their *approaches*.

The biggest problem with most "self-help" programs is that they require people to make drastic changes from day one. Research indicates that when people are asked to make big, sweeping changes in their lives all at once, they get overwhelmed, become discouraged, and commonly give up, reverting to their old patterns of behavior. This undermines their self-confidence and makes it harder for them to make a change in the future.

Instead of blaming ourselves and feeling bad for failing, wouldn't it make more sense to try a new approach? After all, what would you think of a personal trainer who expected her client to run a marathon after only one workout, a weight-loss counselor who expected a client to lose 20 pounds after one day of dieting, or a professor who demanded foreign language fluency after the first day of class? Intellectually, we know that's ridiculous, because any significant change takes time. Yet too often that is the expectation we have for ourselves. We want results today, right now. Since that's not possible, we get discouraged and give up. That's why very few people are able to sustain any real changes in their lives.

It's time to permanently stop the cycle of giving up.

Unstoppable Women is built on the proven fact that the most effective way to create lasting change is to do it one step at a time, letting that initial success lead to others. That's why I'm going to ask you to focus on just one area of your life and to take a single step at a time in reaching your goal in that area. Even the busiest woman can find the time to take a single step, or achieve what I call an unstoppable moment. In doing so, you won't feel overwhelmed by the process, and you'll be able to make the gradual changes that will create lasting results.

What Does It Mean to Be an "Unstoppable Woman"?

Being unstoppable means finding the courage to make a change or achieve a goal in your life that may not remotely resemble your present circumstances. Regardless of your current situation, you don't allow fear, self-doubt, or someone else to stop you, and you consistently take one step forward, refusing to give up, until you achieve your goal.

Being an Unstoppable Woman doesn't require anything super-human. It simply requires that you take one step forward, creating one unstoppable moment at a time. When these moments are strung together, you will have initiated a series of actions that place you closer to your goal.

The good news is that as a woman, you've already created countless unstoppable moments in your life. Think about it: Women are typically the ones to pull it all together when the going gets tough. Despite our jam-packed calendars and numerous responsibilities at home and work, we find the time to help a friend, care for an elderly or sick family member, or volunteer at school or church. We are masters at finding ways to get things done. Now it's time to devote some of that energy to making positive changes in our own lives!

You may already be creating unstoppable moments toward achieving your goals. For example, if your goal is to lose weight, eating a grapefruit when you'd rather have a Twinkie or walking for 30 minutes in the evening instead of sitting down and collapsing in front of the television are unstoppable moments. If you want to take your career to the next level, enrolling in college as an adult despite the fact that you are scared to death of looking foolish is an unstoppable moment. If you're starting a new project at home, getting up earlier to fit it into your day instead of hitting the snooze button for the tenth time is an unstoppable moment. In this book, I'm going to show you how to simply create *more* of these moments so that you can finally make the permanent changes in your life that you really want and deserve.

Why the Unstoppable Women Challenge?

After coaching thousands of individuals over the course of 10 years, I have found that most people get stuck trying to motivate themselves to take action on a particular goal. Typically, they're able to identify a goal that excites them, but they struggle with how to break it down into a simple plan of action and then get themselves to consistently take a single step.

With that in mind, I developed the Unstoppable 30-Day Challenge, a program that I have been coaching with great success to individuals ranging from corporate executives to stay-at-home moms. The Unstoppable 30-Day Challenge helps participants choose a single breakthrough goal, then break it down into a series of simple, achievable steps they can take every day to make their goal happen.

This book has taken the principles from the wildly successful Unstoppable 30-Day Challenge and tailored them just for women. This specially designed program takes into account our busy schedules and responsibilities, yet provides a way to achieve amazing breakthrough changes. By taking just one step at a time, you will create momentum. Each week, you can add another step to your list—or not, depending on your progress. Ultimately, you are in control. You set the pace. Through this process, you'll have the flexibility to identify what works for you and what doesn't and develop the structure and resources to support you in creating lasting change in your life.

A Process That Works for Every Woman

No matter where you are in your life, the Unstoppable Women Challenge can easily be tailored to meet your needs. It will work just as well whether you're 25 or 75, whether you've set and achieved goals for years and now you want to make quantum leaps in your personal or professional life, or you're relatively new at setting goals and want to start small.

You may be at a crossroads, in search of a more rewarding path—a new career, a healthier body, deeper friendships, a more fullfiling family life, or a meaningful mission or project. No matter what your goal, *the time for change is now.*

If you want the next 10, 20, 30 or more years of your life to look different than your life looks today, you've got to make different decisions.

You've got to say, "*Now* is my time!" The women you are about to meet in this book are living testaments to the power of a single decision. They transformed their lives and created extraordinary results—and *so can you*. You, too, can become an unstoppable woman.

I know, because *my* life has been transformed by this material, along with the lives of thousands of others whom I've had the privilege of working with over the past decade. I'm going to show you a process that I've already shared with countless women who accepted the Unstoppable Women Challenge . . . and whose results were nothing short of miraculous!

What if I told you that I would:

- Help you create a breakthrough goal in just 30 days?
- Introduce you to real-life mentors who reveal how they transformed their lives?
- Give you a daily, proven plan that focuses on taking just one step at a time and has produced amazing results for thousands of people from all walks of life—from working mothers to corporate executives?
- Travel this path with you every step of the way, helping you to discover what you really desire in life and how to achieve it?

How could you transform your life with that kind of support, guidance, and inspiration? Could you have better health, greater wealth, deeper love, more lasting relationships, and a more profound sense of joy, happiness, confidence, and freedom? You can have it all, one step at a time, if you'll join me on this journey.

Your Complete Guidebook

This book provides everything you need to succeed on your unstoppable journey. Part One, "Getting Ready for the Unstoppable Women Challenge," takes you through a simple, step-by-step, proven process that enables you to uncover a breakthrough goal for your Unstoppable Women Challenge. You'll then learn how to break that goal down into single steps you can take every day. By completing this section, you will be ready to take on the 30-day process that will make your goal a reality.

In Part Two, you'll begin the Unstoppable Women Challenge. In each of the 30 daily chapters, you'll discover and explore one quality of an Unstoppable Woman that I've gleaned from my own journey, from top researchers, and from interviewing hundreds of amazing women who created extraordinary results in their lives. You'll also read the true-life story of an inspirational role model who embodies this characteristic. Finally, you'll discover how to develop this quality in your own life and find the strength necessary to take your daily step and stay on your path until you have reached your goal.

Each day, you will complete your daily planner, which will help you plan and record your day's activities. You'll also track your daily victories and your unstoppable actions to ensure you are moving closer to achieving your goal. By completing your daily planner, you'll track your success and bring joy into your daily life in the process.

Become Unstoppable!

Are you ready for the journey? Give yourself the gift of investing just 30 days to create something different for your life, one step at a time. No matter what your past has been, you *can* change your future. I don't care if you're 17 or 77. Age doesn't matter. Neither do circumstances.

Will today be the day you finally vote "Yes" to your own future, when you reject the excuses and commit to stepping into your power by saying "This is my time, my life, my moment of truth. I will not stop until I achieve my destiny!"?

If the answer is yes, get ready to take the first step toward realizing the potential in every aspect of your life. I'm thrilled to be on this journey with you. Together, we truly *are* unstoppable!

Part One

GETTING READY
FOR THE
UNSTOPPABLE
WOMEN
CHALLENGE

Are you ready to join the ranks of hundreds of women who have taken the Unstoppable Women Challenge and successfully achieved a breakthrough goal in just 30 days, making their lives richer and more satisfying in the process? If so, let's get started!

Like anything in life that's worthwhile, the successful completion of the Unstoppable Women Challenge requires a bit of preparation, and that's what you'll be doing in the upcoming section, which should take about 90 minutes to complete. The first step is to identify a breakthrough goal that will excite and inspire you. In the next few pages, I'll walk you through an easy and fun process for doing just that. Then I'll help you break down your goal into a series of daily, *manageable* steps that will make change seem natural and energizing.

Consider the payoff: When you accept and complete the Unstoppable Women Challenge, you are building a foundation that will impact virtually every area of your life. Think about it. If you could make one change or create a single result in just *30 days*, do you think you could build on that success and do it again? Absolutely. The Unstoppable Women Challenge helps you create the tools and momentum you need to tackle any new project or dream you have.

Don't be intimidated by this process. Hundreds of women from all walks of life have successfully completed the challenge, and their results were nothing short of miraculous.

UNSTOPPABLE WOMAN SUCCESS STORY

"As a mom with two small children, I didn't think it was possible to be able to juggle my life and my kids and move forward with my career. I thought I'd have to put my career on hold until my kids got older. I had hit a lull until I heard about your program.

"After hearing the stories about other unstoppable women who had accomplished so much, I felt it was possible for me as well. I committed to taking the Unstoppable Women Challenge, and I set a goal to increase my sales revenue by 25 percent in 30 days, the first business goal I had identified since having children. If I achieved it, I would qualify for a trip to Vegas, which I was very excited about.

"The Challenge helped me prioritize every step that needed to be done and how to get into action. I got up 1½ hours earlier every other day to plan out the day. And I discovered that when you have a plan, you're prepared for those unexpected moments of time and can use them to cross a few things off your list. I have a TV and VCR in my car, and if I had to wait to meet a friend and had 15 minutes, I'd pop in a movie for the kids and make sales calls on my cell phone. And finally, to get further insight into achieving my goal while raising a family, I interviewed a woman in my business who was very successful and also had two small children.

"In just 30 days, I exceeded my sales goal and won the trip to Vegas. Never in my life have I felt this incredible about myself as a business person. I've shared so much of what I have learned from the Challenge with family, friends, and team members—all of them are thoroughly convinced this has had a true impact on me and my business and are certain that things will never be the same. I'm sure they're right!"
—*Barbara Amato*

The Unstoppable Women Challenge can be used for any type of goal—business or personal, big or small. And while not every dream—such as getting your diploma or starting a business—can be achieved in 30 days, in that amount of time you can make significant progress that propels you forward, putting you on the path to success.

For example, even though she didn't have any business experience, Sarah's dream was to start a small catering business. Rather than be overwhelmed by the task, she broke her goal down into a series of smaller goals: research the catering industry, take a business course at the local community college, develop a business plan, and so on. The first 30 days, she researched the catering industry. After six months, she finalized a business plan, raised her capital, developed her menu, identified her base of customers . . . and, for the first time in many years, was excited about her life!

Then there is Janet, whose goal was more personal. Janet spent 20 years pursuing her career, and after retiring, she realized she and her adult son were nearly strangers. Instead of living with regret, she acted: She devised a 30-day plan to renew her relationship with her son. She did it step-by-step, arranging lunches and casual dinners where they could talk. She made a point of listening when he opened up, and she took the time to learn about his job and the things he liked. Over the 30 days, they grew closer as the barriers between them began to come down. Her effort was noticed by her son, and it created a bridge for a closer relationship.

The Unstoppable Women Challenge can be used as a model to achieve any goal or dream—personal or professional—whether it takes one day, one year, or ten years to achieve. It is designed to jumpstart you into action. If your goal is a long-range one, once you've completed your first 30-day challenge, simply redefine your goal for the next 30 days and continue.

To get ready for the Unstoppable Women Challenge, you'll need to complete the following four steps:

1. Identify what you want to achieve—breakthrough goal.
2. Convert your breakthrough goal into a 30-day goal.
3. Learn how to plan your daily "one step."
4. Identify a way to help another woman along the way.

Step One: Identify Your Breakthrough Goal

To create a breakthrough goal, think about what really excites you. It should be something that will literally propel your life, career, or relationships to the next level: running for a school board position, losing those unwanted pounds, pursuing a new career, or spending more time with your family. The size of the goal doesn't matter. It's the passion you have for your goal—and your unstoppable spirit in reaching it—that counts.

The results realized by the women in this book prove that the Unstoppable Women Challenge can transform your life as well.

UNSTOPPABLE WOMAN SUCCESS STORY

"I am 53 years old and was not confident about my understanding of money or my ability to be in control of my finances. I've always wanted to do something about it, but I didn't know how to take the first step.

"The impetus came when I decided I wanted to take singing lessons. I had pushed aside a childhood dream to sing and dance, and now I suddenly wanted to be true to myself. I've always found time for everyone else but me. I decided now was my time. I knew I'd have to get my finances in order before I could justify spending money on lessons.

"I thought the Unstoppable Women Challenge would be a great program to help me gain control of my finances. My 30-day goal was to write down my expenses every day to get a handle on how I was spending money. A secondary goal was to educate myself about finances and investing.

"The results have been amazing. I established a budget and follow it daily. I no longer spend money without thought, and I record every expense. And as important, my spending habits have changed. Before each purchase, I ask myself, 'Is this going to take me closer to my goal or away from it?'

"I have saved enough money to take weekly singing lessons and am auditioning for the Sweet Adelines, an international group that incorporates singing and dancing into their performances. I am reinvigorated about my life and feel more in control of my finances and my future. I'm not just working, but developing my creative side as well. And I'm having a lot of fun!"
—Beverley Blair

✎ A. Do a reality check.

To help identify what you really want, first assess your life as it is today. What's working? What's not working? What areas do you want to improve? The exercise below will help you assess eight key areas of your life. On a scale of 1 to 5, with a 1 meaning that you need a lot of improvement and a 5 meaning that you need no improvement, rate yourself in all of the following areas that apply to you:

PHYSICAL
___Appearance—I look my best
___Overall health
___Fitness level
___Healthy diet
___Regular exercise
___Optimal weight
___Flexibility
___Strength training
___Enough energy to do what I need
    to do each day

FINANCIAL
___Current income level
___Good credit
___Balanced budget
___Current savings
___Current net worth
___Level of debt
___Clear investment strategy
___Financial security
___Enough money to do what I
    want, provide for my family,
    travel, decorate my home,
    support causes I care about, etc.

PROFESSIONAL
___Passionate about my career
___Advancing in my industry
___Growing professionally
___Challenged by my work
___Doing what I want to do
___Expert in my field
___Performing at a level of
    excellence

PERSONAL
___Have fun in my life
___Take great vacations
___Travel to places I want to go
___Take time for myself
___Live in a nurturing environment
___Love where I live

RELATIONSHIPS
___With my family
___With my spouse
___With my children
___With my parents
___With my siblings
___Romance—involved in healthy, growing relationship
___Great friendships
___Mentors to learn from
___Spend my time with people I love and care about

SPIRITUAL
___Actively growing spiritually
___Regularly pray/meditate
___Involved in a spiritual community
___Expanding faith
___Regularly express love to others
___Live in peace

MENTAL/EMOTIONAL
___Personally growing and learning
___Not easily angered
___Happy, whole, and complete
___Fear does not control my life
___No unhealthy addictions—smoking, alcohol, drugs, etc.
___Live with gratitude
___Feel loved and supported
___Practice forgiveness

GIVING BACK/LEGACY
___Contributing time to others
___Donating money to causes I care about
___Feel like my life matters
___Making a difference
___Clarity on my life's purpose and passion
___Actively support a cause I care about

B. Identify three areas of your life you want to improve.
The next step is to review the ratings to determine which of the eight areas need the most improvement. Choose the three most important areas that you'd like to work on. When choosing your top three areas, consider what change or improvement would make the most significant difference in your life, providing you with satisfaction, energy, and momentum. Maybe you're at a point in your life where your health or giving back is more of a concern than finances or your career. Or perhaps you're in the prime earning time of your life and taking your career to the next level would make a huge difference in your and your family's financial prosperity. List the top three areas you'd most like to improve:

1. _____
2. _____
3. _____

C. What do you *really* want, and what are you no longer willing to settle for?

Now it's time to really start dreaming. For each of the three areas you've identified, let's explore further what you'd like to change, improve, or achieve. Put yourself in a mindset of complete faith and optimism. Ask yourself the question, "If I knew I could not fail and had no limitations, what would I want for my life in these top areas?" Don't judge if it's possible or worry about how you'll make it happen. Just dream.

If, after going through the list, you're still struggling to identify what you really want, ask yourself the question, "What am I no longer willing to settle for in my life?" Be completely honest. Think about all the areas in your life that you've settled for less than you deserve. What do you believe would make your life better?

In a moment, I'll ask you to write down your answers to these questions. But first, read through the sample chart completed below. The examples listed are responses from various people when they asked themselves the same questions you're now asking. (To give you ideas in each area, the entire chart has been filled in, though you will want to focus on your specific top three areas when completing your own chart.)

After you've done some brainstorming and considered any ideas sparked by reading through the responses of other people who have gone through the Unstoppable Women Challenge, photocopy the blank "What Do I Want?" chart on page 302 or copy the column heads in your planner or notebook. (For a complete set of Unstoppable Women Challenge forms, go to **UnstoppableWomen.com.**) Then write down your hopes and dreams in each of the top three areas you'd like to improve. To provide further insight, answer the question, "What am I no longer willing to tolerate or settle for in my life?"

What Do I Want?

8 KEY AREAS	WHAT DO I *REALLY* WANT?
1. PHYSICAL Appearance Overall health Fitness level Eating patterns Exercise routine Optimal strength and energy	Lose weight Build a strong, lean body Create vitality through exercise and nutrition Look great in a bathing suit Lower cholesterol Join a gym and consistently work out Walk consistently every day
2. FINANCIAL Earnings, savings and investments Net worth goals Money management goals Financial security	Save $5,000 this year Start an investment program Get a financial advisor/coach Save money for children's education Retire at age 50 Increase credit rating/FICO score to over 700 Become debt-free
3. PROFESSIONAL Job satisfaction Passionate about career Advancement potential Education and skills to develop	Start a new business Find a career that I love Get promoted to the next level in my company Become known as an expert in my field Get Master's/Doctorate degree Improve my public speaking skills Improve performance evaluation this year
4. PERSONAL Fun/adventure Vacations Rejuvenating activities Enough time for myself Environment and home	Get pilot's license Visit the great spas of the world Spend time each week doing what I love to do Create a nurturing environment at home Organize my office, files, closet, etc. Find adoptive parents Go to Scotland and visit my roots

WHAT AM I NOT WILLING TO SETTLE FOR?

Feeling fat and unattractive
Poor health and doing nothing about it
Not having the stamina to walk around the block
Setting a poor example for my kids
Not feeling my best
Lack of vitality and energy

Struggling financially year after year
Lack of knowledge in financial matters
Waiting for someone else to save me financially
Being in debt without the funds to retire
Going without things that I want
Not sticking to a budget and overspending on things I don't really need

Lack of career fulfillment
Being stuck at my job
Feeling like I'm not improving
Settling for a job where I am not appreciated or compensated adequately
Not having the education to move forward in my career
Not performing to my capabilities

Not investing time in myself personally, professionally, and spiritually
Not growing into the person I know I can become
Not taking the time to nurture and recharge myself
Not being able to find things easily around the house
A lack of fun and adventure in my life
Embarrassed to invite company over because of all the clutter

What Do I Want? (cont.)

8 KEY AREAS	WHAT DO I *REALLY* WANT?
5. RELATIONSHIPS Family, spouse, children parents, siblings Romance Friendships Finding a mentor Expanding my network	Improve relationship with spouse Improve relationship with my children Raise self-confident children Start a family Find the love of my life Find an amazing mentor Create my unstoppable dream team
6. MENTAL/ EMOTIONAL Personal growth Emotional stability Skills to develop Happy and whole Clarity on life's purpose	Learn a new language Forgive someone who hurt me Constructively deal with my anger Quit smoking, drinking, or any addictive behavior Overcome my fear of flying Develop greater self-confidence Sing at Carnegie Hall or on Broadway

7. SPIRITUAL
Actively growing
   spiritually
Regularly pray/meditate
Spiritual community
Regularly express love to
   others
	Deeper connection to a Higher Power
	Feel a part of a spiritual community
	Expand my capacity to love
	Expand my capacity to forgive
	Consistent with my spiritual practice

**8. GIVING BACK—
LEGACY**
Contribute to others
Donate money to causes
   I care about
Make a difference
	Volunteer my time at a shelter for battered women
	Donate time to work on a Habitat for Humanity
	   House
	Raise and/or give money to my favorite charity
	Adopt a child
	Mentor a child or someone in my field

WHAT AM I NOT WILLING TO SETTLE FOR?

No passion with my spouse
Not having a wonderful relationship with my kids
No social life
Staying in a relationship that is unhealthy
Limited number of true friends
A relationship where I am secondary

Wanting to speak French, but always putting it off
Being angry all the time
Acting out of control and not setting a good example for my children
Engaging in activities that do not support my higher good
Limiting my activities and experience in life because of fear
Not feeling connected to a Higher Power

Not having a spiritual community that I love
Feeling empty and incomplete
Living with bitterness and a lack of forgiveness towards others
Not feeling loved

Feeling like my life doesn't count
Not having the money to share with those less fortunate
Living a life that is all about me
Lack of meaning in my life
Wanting to give back but not taking the steps to do it

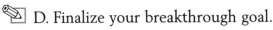 D. Finalize your breakthrough goal.

Now that you've got your creative juices flowing and have identified what you want in three important areas of your life, the final step is to narrow this information down into a single goal you want to work on for the Unstoppable Women Challenge. If you're like me, you have several areas you'd like to improve. By choosing one goal, you're not eliminating all of the other possibilities from your life forever. You're simply focusing on one goal for now. After all, there's always next month!

Keep in mind, your breakthrough goal might take more than 30 days to complete. That's okay. Later, we'll break this goal down into small, incremental steps that you can achieve in 30 days or in a series of 30-day challenges. But first, you'll want to identify an overall goal that totally excites you. In your planner or notebook, write down a goal for each of the three areas you'd like to improve and answer the following questions for each one.

- Why must I achieve this goal?
- What will it cost me if I don't achieve this goal?
- Am I willing to do what is necessary to make this happen?
- Do I really want this or does someone want this for me?

The answers to these questions will determine which goal you'll choose for the Unstoppable Women Challenge. To successfully achieve your 30-day goal, you must truly want to take the action necessary to make it happen. If you have trouble coming up with compelling answers to any of the above questions for a particular goal, it's possible that the goal is not the right one to focus on at this time. Move on to the next goal.

Choose the single most important goal to focus on right now, the one that will generate momentum in your life and provide wonderful feelings of satisfaction and accomplishment. Once you choose the right goal for you at this time, and combine it with the motivation and mindset that you'll create in this program, nothing can stop you.

Once you've decided on your breakthrough goal, write it down. Congratulations! You're now well on your way!

MY BREAKTHROUGH GOAL:

_____

_____

_____

_____

Step Two: Convert Your Breakthrough Goal into a 30-Day Goal

You've identified a breakthrough goal that excites you and that you're committed to make happen. That's the good news. The bad news? You may have no clue *how* to make it happen. Or perhaps you have an idea of what it will take, but the process feels overwhelming or downright impossible. Perhaps you're working full-time, raising your children, or going to school and fear that you don't have the time, energy, or discipline necessary to complete your goal.

Nonsense. The answer lies in the wisdom of this Chinese proverb:

> *"A journey of 1,000 miles begins with a single step."*
> —Lao Tzu

The answer to 30 days of life-transforming action lies in taking one small step at a time. Anyone can find the time and energy to take a single step. Let's say you wanted to read the great classics of English literature, from Dickens to Shakespeare. If you read for just 15 minutes every day, in 7 years, you would have read 100 of the greatest books ever written, and become one of the most well-read people around.

So how do you convert your breakthrough goal into a 30-day measurable goal?

A. Identify the key categories of activities necessary to achieve your breakthrough goal.

It's okay at the outset to be unclear about all the categories of activities necessary to make your goal happen. Do your best to identify the components key to achieving your goal. For example, if you want to start a business, you might first need to research the industry, then identify your target market, then write a business plan, raise capital, and so on.

Here are some more examples to get you started. (For additional examples of breakthrough goals, go to **UnstoppableWomen.com**.)

BREAKTHROUGH GOAL: Lose 40 pounds

- Implement a healthy eating plan
- Exercise
- Drink eight glasses of water daily
- Take vitamins

BREAKTHROUGH GOAL: Increase sales

- Make 10 phone calls a day
- Set 4 appointments per day
- Attend 2 networking functions per week
- Make 2 sales per day

Now it's time to write down your breakthrough goal and fill in your key categories of activities:

BREAKTHROUGH GOAL: _____

- _____
- _____
- _____
- _____
- _____

If you're having a hard time identifying your key categories, consider the following tips:

Seek out the advice of others. Talk to at least three people who are *successfully* doing what you want to accomplish. Ask them, either by phone, e-mail, in person, or in writing, what they would do differently to prepare themselves for this task if they were to start over from scratch. If you don't know them personally, don't let that stop you. Other unstoppable people are your greatest resource, and are usually more than happy to talk about what they've learned along the way. Just seek them out and ask for help. Welcome input from multiple perspectives. Value experience above everything else, and do not take advice from someone who hasn't created the results you want to achieve.

"How are we supposed to get there?"

Focus on one habit at a time. Changing habits is a process. For example, one woman who wanted better health looked at the habits in her life that impeded optimal health. She determined the first thing she needed to do was to stop drinking. When she drank, she overate and also felt an increased urge to smoke. After she quit drinking, her next logical step was to quit smoking. To try to initiate an exercise program while smoking cigarettes just didn't make sense. Once she quit smoking, she joined a weight-loss program, and they encouraged her to engage in daily exercise. Within one year, she lost 40 pounds. Altogether, it took 3 years to achieve her breakthrough goal of a healthier lifestyle, and she did it by focusing on one thing at a time. If she had tried to do everything at once, there's a good chance she would have been overwhelmed and quit.

B. Prioritize your categories of activities

After identifying your categories, it's important to prioritize which category to focus on first. You can do this by designating each as an "A," "B," or "C" priority. "A" priorities are first, "B" priorities second, and "C" priorities third. Here are some examples:

BREAKTHROUGH GOAL: Lose 40 pounds

A-B-C	CATEGORIES
A	Implement a healthy eating plan
B	Exercise
C	Drink 8 glasses of water per day
C	Take vitamins

BREAKTHROUGH GOAL: Increase sales

A-B-C	CATEGORIES
A	Make 50 phone calls a day
B	Set 2 appointments per day
C	Attend 2 networking functions per week
C	Make 2 sales per week

Now it's your turn: Rewrite your list of categories below. Then prioritize them by putting an "A," "B," or "C" in the left column next to each category. You can list as many A, B, and C priorities as necessary.

WRITE YOUR BREAKTHROUGH GOAL:

_____

_____

A-B-C   CATEGORIES

         |

         |

         |

         |

✎ C. Choose a category, or one *specific* result, as your 30-day goal.

After you've identified the categories of activities necessary to achieve your goal and prioritized them accordingly, it's time to convert your breakthrough goal into a 30-day goal. Again, you may feel uncertain about which activities you have to do or what to do first. Don't let that intimidate you! This is about getting you into action. You can modify your activities later if necessary.

To convert your breakthrough goal into a 30-day goal for the challenge, you will focus on achieving one result. This may include completing the category you listed as an "A" priority on your list. Depending on your progress, you'll determine whether to add an additional step/category each week to complete your goal.

Three Characteristics of 30-Day Goals

To be effective, a 30-day goal must be measurable, achievable, and have a timetable for its completion. Let's take a closer look at each of these criteria:

1. Make it MEASURABLE. It's hard to stay motivated and to track your progress if your goal is vague. That's why it's important to have a measurable goal that leaves no doubt when it's achieved. For example, instead of working toward the vague goal of "increase sales," you might decide that, based on your past successes, your breakthrough goal will be to increase sales by 10 percent.

Suppose your breakthrough goal is to be a better mom. How could you measure "better"? You can't. Instead, I suggest you clarify "better" to make the goal more specific. For example, becoming a "better" mom might entail such 30-day goals as "help my child raise his grade point average in school" or "spend at least 30 minutes reading to or playing with my child each day."

2. Make it ACHIEVABLE. It's important to set a goal that's achievable so that when you reach it, you'll be energized and eager to take the next step. Don't set goals so high that you set yourself up for failure, or so low that the goal offers no challenge. Neither approach works. Remember, this program is about creating forward momentum for the rest of your life.

How do you know if your goal is achievable? One way is to find others who have reached your goal. What activities did they engage in to make it happen, and, as important, can you commit a similar investment of time and energy? If so, great. If not, you might need to modify the goal.

For example, suppose your breakthrough goal is to expand your financial consulting business from 10 clients to 50. Clearly, a 500 percent growth in 30 days is not a realistic goal. Perhaps 25 percent is a better start. So, you talk to other professionals who have consistently grown their practices 25 percent per month and learn the things they did. You decide to focus on one particular area, such as learning new selling skills, devising a sound marketing plan, networking in your community, developing new customer service programs, or launching a new Web site. In 30 days, you've started the foundation to grow your business 500 percent, your long-term objective, one step at a time.

3. Have a TIMETABLE. The final way to measure a goal is to attach a timetable to it. By establishing a firm deadline, you'll be able to break the goal down into 30-day increments that gradually achieve your breakthrough goal. For example, if you ultimately want to lose 30 pounds, a short-term reasonable goal might be "I will lose one pound a week for 30 weeks." At that rate, seven months from now, you'll be 28 pounds lighter!

D. Fine-tune your 30-day goal, if necessary.

If you're having a hard time making your goal meet the above criteria, take a look at how the following goals were clarified:

30-DAY GOAL THAT NEEDS FINE-TUNING	NEW SPECIFIC AND MEASURABLE 30-DAY GOAL
Learn a language	Enroll in a Spanish class by September 1st
Find the right contractor for home remodeling project	Identify a contractor and sign agreement for project in 30 days
Start exercising	Walk 30 minutes each day for 30 days
Buy a new house	Find a house that I can purchase for 20 percent under market value in my preferred area
Prepare to take the Real Estate Exam	Finalize review course and be prepared to take the Real Estate Exam with 90 percent accuracy
Increase social circle	Attend at least one networking event each week
Organize my office	Purchase a filing cabinet and file every loose document in my office

Once you've clarified your 30-day goal, write it below:

MY 30-DAY GOAL:

_____

_____

E. Break your goal into bite-sized weekly steps.

Now that you've identified your 30-day goal, next break it down into specific weekly steps. You will then prioritize the steps and focus on one step each week. Depending on the scope of your goal, you may be able to complete a category in less than 30 days and then move on to the next. By breaking your goal up into smaller, one-week steps, you can tackle anything . . . one day at a time.

Some steps may require taking action every day, while others might require action only three to five days a week. For example, if you want to lose weight, it will probably be necessary to follow an eating plan seven days a week. If your goal is to increase your sales by 10 percent, you might determine that you will make five calls per day, five days a week. Or if your goal is to write an article, you might decide that you can accomplish that by writing three days a week.

In some cases, your category may take the entire Unstoppable Women Challenge to complete. For example, if your breakthrough goal is to start a business, the first step or category could be to do market research. This could very well take 30 days or more to complete. But after 30 days of research, your dream is no longer just a dream . . . you're in action. And imagine how much closer you will be to starting your business with the research behind you. This Unstoppable Women Challenge is a model that can be used month after month until you achieve your ultimate goal. You simply redefine your goal and tasks for the next 30 days and go from there.

Note: If a goal is new to you, make your best guess at how many times a week you'll need to take your one step. At the end of the week, you can re-evaluate your pace.

Here's an example:

30-DAY GOAL: Lose 10 pounds

A-B-C	CATEGORIES	# DAYS PER WEEK
A	Implement and follow a healthy eating plan	7
B	Exercise	5
C	Drink 8 glasses of water daily	7
C	Take vitamins	7

Note: There may be steps to take before you can complete each category. For example, "Category A" requires some pre-planning.

1. Identify an eating plan to follow (i.e. 1,200 calories per day, low carbohydrate eating plan, etc.)
2. Plan your daily meals according to eating plan
3. Go to grocery store and ensure you have appropriate foods to eat to follow the plan

You can either complete the pre-planning steps before you begin your Unstoppable Women Challenge or integrate the pre-planning into week one.

30-DAY GOAL: Lose 10 pounds

	Week One	
	CATEGORY	# DAYS/WEEK
Step	Eat 1,200 calories a day	7

	Week Two	
	CATEGORIES	# DAYS/WEEK
Step 1	Eat 1,200 calories a day	7
ADD Step 2	Walk 30 minutes a day	5

Week Three		
	CATEGORIES	# DAYS/WEEK
Step 1	Eat 1,200 calories a day	7
Step 2	Walk 30 minutes a day	5
ADD Step 3	Drink 8 glasses of water a day	7

Week Four		
	CATEGORIES	# DAYS/WEEK
Step 1	Eat 1,200 calories a day	7
Step 2	Walk 30 minutes a day	5
Step 3	Drink 8 glasses of water a day	7
ADD Step 4	Take vitamin supplements daily	7

Now that you've read through an example, it's time to try your hand at breaking down your goal into weekly steps.

Choose one step from the "A" priority categories on your worksheet that will lay the foundation to help you achieve your 30-day goal. Focus on completing that step for week one. You then have the option of adding an additional step. This clear, methodical approach will help you move steadily forward, without danger of being overwhelmed by the ultimate goal. Some tasks may require several steps before they're completed. In this case, make sure each task is broken down into single steps so that you can add one step each day or week, depending on your goal.

WRITE YOUR 30-DAY GOAL :

_____

_____

_____

Week One		
	CATEGORY	# DAYS/WEEK
Step 1		

Week Two		
	CATEGORIES	# DAYS/WEEK
Step 1		
ADD Step 2		

Week Three		
	CATEGORIES	# DAYS/WEEK
Step 1		
Step 2		
ADD Step 3		

Week Four		
	CATEGORIES	# DAYS/WEEK
Step 1		
Step 2		
Step 3		
ADD Step 4		

How do you determine if you're ready to add the next step each week? At the end of each week, you'll complete a "Week in Review" form, which will help you assess your progress. If you struggled to consistently take one step the first week, you'll want to identify what specifically stopped you. Perhaps you should modify your one step by breaking it down even further. For example, if your one step is to make 25 phone calls a day to prospects and you consistently never made over 10, you'll need to allocate more time to your "one step" or perhaps modify your action if 25 calls is an unrealistic objective. When you are successful at completing the first step with at least 70 to 80 percent consistency, it's time to add the next step. By building on your success, you'll gain confidence. Soon, reaching your goals won't be overwhelming, but part of a natural process.

Step Three: Plan Your Day

You have now created your 30-day goal and identified the steps you'll need to take each week to achieve it. But we're not quite finished yet. To make your goal truly achievable, we need to break it down into *single, daily steps*. Each day, you'll decide what your one step will be for that day. For now, I'm going to show you the process you'll use to make that decision.

During the Unstoppable Women Challenge, you'll follow a daily routine that will ensure you have the mindset and strategies in place to identify and complete your single daily step. This routine is critical not only to setting the intention for the day, but immediately getting you into action and creating the momentum that will ensure you successfully complete your 30-day goal.

To incorporate this routine into your life, I suggest that you give yourself the gift of *at least* 15 minutes or so each morning or evening. If that means getting up 15 to 30 minutes earlier than normal, so be it. Nothing is more important than giving yourself this time each day to plan and reflect. You'll reap enormous benefits in focus, energy, and direction that will enable you to complete the steps necessary to stay in action on your 30-day goal.

While I recommend that you schedule this time for the morning, it can be modified depending on whether your energy level is greater in the morning or the evening. Morning people wake up, get out of bed, and are immediately alert. They're eager to start their day. However, by around 9:00 P.M., they're ready for bed and the *last* thing they want to do is put a plan together for tomorrow. If you're a morning person, plan your day first thing in the morning.

If your energy is greater in the evening, leverage that energy. Before finishing your day, plan your next day's activities. Even though it might take a little longer for you to get fully into gear in the morning, your daily plan will be ready to go. Upon getting out of bed, you'll know exactly what you need to do first, and that clarity will move you into action.

Tips for Planning Your Day

- Make your daily planning a special ritual. This is *your* time. Make it as enjoyable as possible: Brew a cup of your favorite tea, light a candle, pray or meditate, and center yourself for a great day.
- Read one chapter from Part Two sequentially each day.
- Before beginning the daily lesson, take a deep breath and use your imagination to put yourself in a relaxed and peaceful state of mind.
- Spend a few minutes in this relaxed state repeating the lesson title, which is the day's insight, and affirmation several times.
- Put the lesson title on a 3 × 5 card and review it several times throughout the day and before going to bed.
- Using what you have learned from the day's insight, plan your day by filling out your Create Your Day Planner.

The Create Your Day Planner

Each Monday through Friday, you'll fill out a Create Your Day Planner form. (As described on page 45, on weekends, you'll take some time for reflection and review your weekly progress.) The blank Create Your Day Planner form is found on pages 308–309. So that you know what to expect, please refer to it as you read through the following line-by-line explanation of the form:

Write your 30-day goal as if it has already happened. Each day, rewrite your goal in the first block of the planner form. This will help you stay focused on your objective for the Unstoppable Women Challenge.

Read one chapter a day. Each morning, you'll read one chapter from Part Two, the Unstoppable Women Challenge, and write down the key learning insight you gained on the planner form. This is a powerful way to start your day: You'll be reading the true story of a real-life unstoppable role model who proves that your goals and dreams are possible. Each person is a living, breathing role model for what can be accomplished by consistently taking action. Because they prevailed, so can you! We'll then explore the key learning insight of the day and how you can apply it immediately to your life.

Write down the one step you must complete for that day. Later in the day, when you've completed this action, write the word *unstoppable* in the "completed" column. If you don't complete the task, leave the column blank. At the end of the week, you'll review what stopped you and why.

Consider adding additional steps. (Optional.) If you chose a goal that you're already having some success with and want to take it up a notch, you might consider adding one or more steps to what you're already doing. Add an additional step *only* if you have already integrated your first step consistently into your routine. The power of this program is that by adding one step at a time, you firmly develop new habits that will create the long-term results you desire.

Hold yourself accountable by working with a buddy. Part of the Unstoppable Women Challenge is working with a buddy who will not only offer support, but also hold you accountable for completing your daily step (see Step Four, opposite). In this part of the form, you'll write down the time you will speak with your buddy. It's important that you speak with your buddy *every day* to review your actions, what's working, and what area needs improvement in order to stay in action on your 30-day goal. Write *unstoppable* in the "completed" column after you speak with your buddy.

Celebrate your victories! The final part of the form is meant to be completed at the end of the day. I'd like you to list the unstoppable moments or "wins"—big or small—that you achieved for the day. Revel in the great feelings that come when you have honored yourself by sticking with your commitments.

The single greatest reward you'll gain is the person you will become in the process. By the end of the challenge, you will have redefined what's possible for your life. And the self-awareness you gain will propel you to even greater heights of unstoppability!

Record the ways you've given back. The final segment of the Unstoppable Women Challenge is to give back to someone else. We'll explore this idea in a moment, but for now, just remember that the last piece of information you'll record each day is the one thing you did to encourage or support someone else on the journey.

Step Four: Identify a Way to Help Another Woman Along the Way

A big part of your Unstoppable Women Challenge is to help another woman create an unstoppable result in her life. And you can do this in two ways. The first, which I mentioned earlier, is to use the buddy system. Find a friend with whom you can go through this challenge, and agree to hold each other accountable. Having a "buddy" is one of the most important components in successfully achieving your 30-day goal. Making a commitment to someone else creates accountability, compelling you to show up and continue to take action, even when you don't feel like it. Having a buddy was a crucial part of Teresa's success:

Teresa decided she was ready to take on the Unstoppable Women Challenge to reach her goal of losing 15 pounds. Because she had failed to lose weight in the past, she recruited her friend Stacy to do the Challenge with her. They kept each other accountable, picked each other up for trips to the gym, talked every night about how good they felt and what they would do tomorrow, and basically kept each other focused and motivated. Teresa and Stacy kept each other from giving up more than once, and as the Challenge went on, they found they were challenging each other to do better and work harder. The result: Teresa lost 12 pounds and Stacy lost 13!

Don't underestimate the power of the buddy system. People who fully committed themselves to a buddy created significantly greater results than those who undertook the 30-day challenge alone. Plus, they had a lot more fun completing the challenge with a partner. Give yourself the edge and choose a buddy to complete this 30-day program.

Note: If you don't have a buddy, go to **UnstoppableWomen.com** and we'll help you find one.

Of course, while working with a buddy will give you an edge, it's also important that you turn that strength around and help your buddy in the same way, so that both of you can achieve your goals and dreams.

Become a Great Buddy

Studies show that encouragement and recognition are vital to the achievement of a goal. So as a buddy, it's your job to shower your buddy with words of encouragement and acknowledgment. It's important to be your buddy's greatest cheerleader. When she takes a daily step and creates a victory, be ready to celebrate with her. Be with her in each moment of triumph. Be supportive and positive. If she fails to take her one step for the day, or she's not making the progress she had hoped for, continue to be supportive. Don't blame or judge.

Want proof that positive support and encouraging feedback produce better results than a drill sergeant attitude? Consider the case of two literary groups and their approach to their members' work.

The first group, which called itself the "Stranglers," was a cohort of young men at the University of Wisconsin whose amazing gifts at crafting the written word were surpassed only by their joy at ripping each other's work to shreds. These would-be novelists, poets, and essayists would meet to read their work to each other—then revel in relentless, brutal butchery of each member's literary output. Their attitude was that a gladiatorial style of "support" would toughen them to future critics.

Another group of writers at the University of Wisconsin, all women, saw the popularity of the Stranglers and decided to start their own group. But if you stepped into a meeting of this writing workshop, you would have seen a completely different dynamic taking place. These literary women were of no less talent than their male counterparts, but in their meetings they encouraged each other, gave positive feedback, and were unfailingly supportive of each other. With a nod to the men who had inspired their group, they called themselves the "Wranglers."

What difference does positive feedback and encouragement make? Well, 20 years later, a detailed look at the accomplishments of University of Wisconsin alumni revealed a fascinating pattern. The Wranglers had produced at least six successful professional writers, including Marjorie Kinnan Rawlings, author of *The Yearling*. And the rough-and-tumble Stranglers? Not a single member of the group had ever been heard from in literary circles.

Both groups were unquestionably talented, and both clearly had a passion for writing, as well as a strong work ethic. So why did the Wranglers thrive and the Stranglers vanish into literary obscurity? By giving each other the gift of mutual support, belief, and faith in their abilities, the Wranglers set the stage for their members to continue to write and create, in spite of the rejection and challenges that every writer faces. The Stranglers strangled on their own negativity.

As you go through the Unstoppable Women Challenge, be a Wrangler, not a Strangler, to your buddy. Your positive words of support and encouragement will motivate her to continue to work toward her goal. And when she returns the favor, you will *both* become unstoppable!

> *"Treat a man as he appears to be and you make him worse. But treat a man as if he already were what he potentially could be, and you make him what he should be."*
> —*Johann Wolfgang von Goethe*

Give Back to the Community

The second way to help another woman create an unstoppable result is to find a way you can be of service to others every day. It doesn't have to be big. There are simple ways to give, whether it's a smile to a stranger, a donation of money to a cause, volunteering your time at a community shelter, or mentoring a child. You'll find countless ways you can give every day if you open your eyes and your heart. By giving to others, you will be invigorated about your goal *and your life* because you will know you are making a difference in the lives of others.

My foundation has created several vehicles for the Unstoppable community to give back and help others. If you're interested in taking part in this way, go to **UnstoppableFoundation.org** and see which best applies to you. Giving to others creates great feelings of satisfaction that will serve you well beyond your 30-day commitment.

> *"We can do no great things; only small things with great love."*
> —Mother Teresa

⚜ **Develop your personal fan club.** Your fan club can range from your co-worker who runs with you in the morning to your sister who is your buddy going through the Unstoppable Women Challenge with you. Find family members, co-workers, and friends who can be supportive of your 30-day goal. It's much easier to stick to a plan if you have others rooting for you and helping you stay focused and accountable. Carefully select those who will be a source of encouragement and share your goal with them.

⚜ **Consider online support.** Now that you've read and completed Part 1 of this book, you're ready to take on your own Unstoppable Women Challenge. If you're looking for a buddy or want additional support, register online for the Challenge. We provide Internet support and individual coaching depending on your needs. You'll also meet a community of other

Unstoppable Women Challenge participants from whom you can gain strength and support. You can share stories, get encouragement, and learn new ways to get past barriers and create positive support. Go to **UnstoppableWomen.com** to find out more and see if joining our community is right for you!

It's time to start the Unstoppable Women Challenge. Taking one simple step every day will transform your life in just 30 days! You are ready to be unstoppable!

Part Two

THE
UNSTOPPABLE
WOMEN
CHALLENGE
30-DAY
PROGRAM

Congratulations! By completing Part One of this book, you've already proven to yourself and to me that you are serious about creating new results in your life. You've done the hard part. Now, let's have some fun!

You are now prepared to begin and complete the Unstoppable Women Challenge, a 30-day process that will turn your goal into reality and transform your life in the process. All you'll need for this challenge are the forms in this book, a journal, a pen, and an open heart.

I will take this journey with you, coaching you every step of the way as you create one unstoppable moment after another. In each of the 30 daily chapters, you'll gain insights into what it means to be unstoppable, meet inspirational role models, and develop the skills needed to achieve your 30-day goal.

The women whose stories you are about to read will become your mentors, your teachers, your friends. They are real and current role models for what you can accomplish if you follow their examples. Wherever you are now, they have been there too. They faced similar challenges—and perhaps even greater ones—yet they continued to take action. Their lives powerfully demonstrate that if we commit to taking a single step, every day, and absolutely refuse to quit, we cannot fail. Every obstacle we encounter is a natural part of the process on the path to creating new results in our lives.

Take heart from their successes. Learn from their experiences. Their lives will open new possibilities in your life and shift your thinking from problems to solutions, from discouragement to an unstoppable conviction that you can overcome and achieve anything.

> *"It's not that some people have willpower and some don't.*
> *It's that some people are ready to change and others are not."*
> —James Gordon, M.D.

Your Journey, Day by Day

So that you know what to expect as you begin, below is a brief overview of what you'll be doing each week. The Unstoppable Women Challenge is designed to start on a Monday and includes weekends, which is when you'll take some time to review your weekly progress.

MONDAY THROUGH FRIDAY (WEEKS 1 THROUGH 4)

Each day includes the following:

• **Unstoppable Insight:** Each day we'll explore one insight into what it means to be unstoppable. I've gleaned these insights from my own journey, from top researchers, and from interviewing hundreds of unstoppable women. Each day, I'll reveal how to practically apply this insight, or characteristic, to your life.

• **Unstoppable Woman Story:** You'll read the true story of an unstoppable woman who powerfully demonstrates the characteristic being explored that day and is a role model, real and current, for what can be accomplished by taking consistent action.

• **Unstoppable Action:** Each chapter closes with one single action you can take to develop the qualities and strength required to stay on your path until you have reached your 30-day goal.

• **Create Your Day Planner:** Each night, you will plan your next day's activities by completing your Create Your Day Planner (see Appendix). You'll also track your daily victories and your unstoppable actions to ensure you are moving closer to achieving your goal. So that you have everything you'll need before you begin, I recommend that you make 21 copies of the blank Planner and keep them together in a binder. Alternately, you may opt to write your responses to the form in a notebook.

SATURDAYS (WEEKS 1 THROUGH 4)

• **Girlfriend To Girlfriend:** *Intimate Conversations with Cynthia:* Like you and the women highlighted in this book, I too encounter difficulties that could threaten to stop me. Each Saturday, you'll read about the personal challenges that I've experienced and ultimately moved through on my unstoppable journey, including transitioning from a 20-year marriage to becoming single, my road to healing and wholeness, and the daily courage required for all of us to fully live an unstoppable life.

SUNDAYS (WEEKS 1 THROUGH 4)

• **Weekly Review:** Each Sunday, you'll review your progress and prepare for the next week. Referring to the information you've recorded in your Create Your Day Planner forms, you'll complete the "Week in Review" questionnaire (see Appendix). You'll celebrate your victories, identify beliefs or behaviors that stopped you, and create a plan of action to move past any obstacles to successfully complete your Unstoppable Women Challenge. I recommend that you make four copies of this form and keep them in your binder.

DAY 30

• **Your Unstoppable Woman Story:** This is where you'll write your own "unstoppable woman" story by completing a post-Challenge questionnaire. This questionnaire is designed to encourage you to acknowledge and celebrate the progress you've made and identify the new beliefs and behaviors you've developed in just 30 days that will support ongoing changes in your life. It also provides the perfect format for you to submit your success story online and share your victories with other Unstoppable Women Challenge participants.

Day 1:
Unstoppable Begins with "U"

Today's Affirmation: This is my time, my life, my moment of truth. I am committed to taking a single step every day for 30 days to create a new result in my life. I release any fear, limiting belief, or situation that could prevent me from making this happen. I am firmly focused on my goal and take full responsibility for my daily actions. I am unstoppable!

The foundation for creating unstoppable results in our lives is to realize that ultimately we alone are responsible for the quality of our lives. Period. No matter what hand life may have dealt us, if we want to improve any area of our lives, whether it's to have more money, more success, more friends, more happiness, more love, it is up to *us* to make the changes necessary to make that happen. Personal responsibility is the key to change, growth, and freedom.

While this sounds like a reasonable approach on paper, it is not a concept that is easily embraced in life. Early in my former marriage, I can't tell you how many times I wanted to change any number of areas in my life, but I waited for my husband to get on board before I actually did something. Whether it was to lose weight, start a physical fitness program, learn about investments—you name it! When he didn't want to sign up for "my" program, I used his lack of interest as an excuse for not doing the things I really wanted to do. After getting fed up with myself, I finally realized that these were *my* goals and not his, and that if I really wanted them to happen, I had to do something about it. It was in that moment that my life was transformed!

Have you ever felt that if only your circumstances were different or the people in your life would change *their* behavior, then you'd be happy or more successful? The moment you realize that *you* hold the solution to your problems is the moment your life changes. That realization moves you out of victim mode and puts you in control of your life. No more blaming others, no more waiting for somebody else to do it. You are free to move forward, to overcome any obstacle in your path, and to create the life you really want.

Our background and circumstances may have influenced who we are, but we are responsible for who we become.

No one would have blamed Marion Luna Brem for staying home, feeling sorry for herself, and living on disability payments. But Marion wasn't interested in making excuses. She chose to do more than endure her misfortune. She chose instead to dream of greater possibilities. And once she dreamed, *she acted*. And because she dared, so can you!

Unstoppable Woman:
Marion Luna Brem's Story

In 1984, Marion Luna Brem was 30 years old—and she was dying. Marion had cancer of the breast and cervix and had undergone two surgeries in 11 weeks—a mastectomy and hysterectomy. Now she was suffering the horrifying effects of chemotherapy. Adding to her pain, the disease had robbed her of her hair, her savings, and now her marriage. The pressure had taken its toll. Marion was left with her two boys and no means to support them. Worse, her prognosis was a death sentence: Doctors told her she had 2 years to live, 5 if she was really lucky.

So, on a hot Texas morning in May, Marion laid with her cheek on the cold bathroom floor trying not to throw up—again. And despite her gut-wrenching pain and paralyzing fear, she knew she could not afford to lie there feeling sorry for herself. Instead, Marion had to focus on taking care of her kids. And that meant finding a job. But she had almost no experience outside the home—not exactly a powerful résumé to launch a budding career. Plus, she was a woman—a Hispanic woman—which in many people's eyes meant she had two strikes against her. Marion thought only of survival. The words "rich" and "successful" didn't even enter her mind.

Deciding to Be Courageous
Where to begin? Susan, Marion's best friend, suggested she look for a job in sales, but Marion worried about her lack of experience. Susan reminded her that there was a lot of value in the job market for the skills she possessed as a housewife: time management, budgeting, not to mention the people skills she developed while being a room mother and a member of the PTA. So with all the resolve she could muster, Marion thought, "Why not?"

Of all the industries to pursue, Marion chose the male-dominated field of selling automobiles. One of Marion's past part-time jobs was a switchboard operator at a Dallas car dealership, so she knew there was good money in car sales. She had also seen firsthand how salesmen talked only to the male half of the couple, virtually ignoring the woman. Intuitively, she knew women were an important part of the decision-making process and believed this was an opportunity. Statistics now reveal that Marion was right. When couples purchase a car, the woman influences the decision 80 percent of the time. Marion recognized the need for car saleswomen, and she was determined to fill that need.

Armed only with her gut instinct and a funky brunette wig, Marion approached the first dealership. "Have you ever thought about hiring a woman?" she asked. "No!" was the curt reply. She heard the same response from 15 other sales managers around town. Yet Marion Brem didn't give up. She couldn't! "I think courage is something you decide upon," she says. "You wake up in the morning and have a meeting with the mirror and say, 'Today I'm going to be courageous.'"

But her approach clearly wasn't working. So on her 16th try, she modified her pitch and said, "Here's what *I* can do for *you*. . . . " After telling the manager her angle on women car buyers, she was hired on the spot! Marion Luna Brem's career in car sales had begun.

From Rookie Saleswoman to Manager

At first, her all-male colleagues embraced the rookie saleswoman. "It really wasn't until I began competing with them, beating them, that I noticed a change of heart," Marion recalls. "But when they see that you're not going away, and not going to personalize their derogatory remarks, then a kind of respect is born."

Brem's first year out, she was named salesperson of the year. Of course, the plaque read "Sales*man* of the Year," and the award included a trip to the Super Bowl and a man's Rolex watch. Still, it was a great honor and a wonderful achievement. Meanwhile, her cancer went into remission and Marion was going strong.

For the next 2 years, Marion was a top producer, but she wanted more. It was then that she approached her boss about a management position. Her proposal was flatly rejected. He said that he'd be "nuts" to take her out of sales with all the money she was making both of them. As difficult as it was for her to leave the security of the established clientele of repeat and referral business she had worked so hard to create, she moved on, believing she would find what she was looking for. That meant, once again, knocking on doors.

After several frustrating weeks of pounding the pavement, Marion was finally hired as an entry-level manager at a new dealership. She quickly climbed the management ladder. Two and a half years later, she was ready to start her own dealership. She envisioned an operation run by women for women. All she needed was a "measly" $800,000 and she was off to the races. To Marion, it might as well have been $800 million.

A Labor of Love

Once again, Marion rolled up her sleeves. "I put together a portfolio on myself. I literally went to the drugstore and got 50 of those school folders," she recalls. Inside, she put her certificates, press clippings, and a biography. Marion called it her "brag folder." On the advice of a trusted friend, she sent the package to 50 CPAs all over Texas—money managers who represented doctors looking for investment opportunities.

Two weeks later, Marion received a call from one of her contacts. It would change her life. The CPA had a client, a cardiologist, who had agreed to become her silent partner. The doctor helped arrange $800,000 in working capital, as well as millions more in loans needed to lease, stock, and market her first dealership. Marion approached Chrysler Corporation—and quickly struck a deal.

Now all she needed was a name for her brand-new dealership. Marion wanted something distinctive—and it had to be feminine. She tried several "feel-good" names, but nothing stuck. Finally, it hit her: Love. "It's the most positive word in the dictionary," she thought. "And it's the way I feel about this project, the way I'm going to treat my customers and employees."

In 1989, less than 5 years after selling her first car, "Love Chrysler" was born, complete with a heart logo on every car. Marion's motto: "It's not just the hearts on our cars, it's the hearts inside our people. We're spreading Love all over Texas!"

Marion's labor of love paid off handsomely. Today, she is cancer-free and the owner of two car dealerships. She recently celebrated the 15th anniversary of Love Chrysler. Her company is 89th on the Hispanic Business 500 with revenues of more than $45 million. And she has authored a book offering unconventional wisdom for winning at work and life, *Women Make the Best Salesmen*.

At the age of 30, Marion Luna Brem had lost her breast, her womb, her marriage . . . and soon, the doctors said, she would lose her life. But Marion literally dragged herself off a cold tile floor, put on a cheap wig, and took on a world dominated by good ole boys. In the process, she raised two kids, beat a devastating illness, and turned steel into love.

> *"Sometimes it's not enough to simply knock on doors.*
> *You've gotta knock them down!"*
> —*Marion Luna Brem*

⟶ Unstoppable Action ⟵
Accept Personal Responsibility

Marion Luna Brem and the other women you're going to meet in this book were given honors, awards, and ovations for their success. But long before they accepted all the congratulations, they accepted something else, something far more important. They accepted personal responsibility.

Each and every one of these women took responsibility for their lives and their own futures. They refused to allow any circumstance, no matter how formidable, to be an excuse for failure. Nothing from poverty and oppression, physical handicaps, early pregnancies, or unsupportive spouses could stop them from achieving their goals. Although life could have offered each one the role of "victim," not one would accept it. Each of these women's lives represents the truth behind creating an unstoppable life: *The only real obstacle that can stop you from attaining your dreams is YOU.*

That is the good news; in fact, it's news well worth celebrating. It means no one and nothing else has power over you. Your success or failure is not up to fate; it's not up to luck; it's not up to bosses and officials, or the devil that made you do it. It all begins and ends with you.

Taking responsibility doesn't mean that we can't enlist the support of others or draw on our Higher Power for guidance, support, and wisdom. To the contrary, both are critical and will be discussed in later chapters. What it does mean is that we must consciously decide that we will not settle! We must choose not to allow anyone or any circumstance—personal, social, or political—to limit our lives and our dreams. Once we acknowledge and accept responsibility, no external barriers can stop us.

✎ Make a commitment to take a single step for 30 days.

With any new goal or project, the biggest challenge we face is not with our ability or intelligence. It's with our commitment. Remaining focused on a goal and continuing to put forth the effort to reach it—one step at a time—is what separates life's great achievers from those who merely dream but never do. Committing to the actions that will get you to your goal and sticking to that commitment through daily distractions and even discouraging setbacks will mean the difference between victory and defeat.

Life happens. During this Unstoppable Women Challenge, it will happen again and again—the routine demands of life will overload you, or unexpected events will blow in from nowhere and threaten to drive you off course. You might run into a crisis at work and feel overextended, your kids might get sick, your computer might burn itself to smoldering microchips (as mine did during the writing of this book), your babysitter could announce she's moving to Des Moines . . . and let's not even talk about PMS. Life has infinite possibilities—and infinite ways to complicate your plans.

When such things occur, we all must confront the urge to give up. Don't do it! When you're tempted to rationalize—"Well, I'll quit for now, but I'll get back on track tomorrow or next week"—*seize the day!* Take one immediate action to get yourself moving toward your task before the temptation to once again throw in the towel gets too strong.

Quitting is a habit. Every time you quit, you damage your self-esteem and send your psyche the message that you're incompetent. You are competent! And each time you take action and stick to your commitment when you felt like quitting, you'll gain a newfound confidence that makes the next step increasingly easier.

By participating in this Unstoppable Women Challenge, you have chosen to *once and for all* get past all of the former excuses that stopped you and step into your power by saying: *"This is my time, my life, my moment of truth. I will not stop until I achieve my 30-day goal!"*

Realizing that being unstoppable is simply a decision that you make every day, every hour, or sometimes every minute gives you the awareness that it is a choice. And every time you choose to honor your commitment and take a single step, you are honoring yourself and exercising your self-discipline muscle. With each step you take, that muscle will grow stronger and stronger, making it easier to bring about change in your life.

Your time is now. Make a pledge to yourself that you are fully committed to reaching your 30-day goal by writing your goal below and signing and dating the commitment form.

MY 30-DAY GOAL:

_____

_____

_____

    I am committed to creating this unstoppable result over the next 30 days. I refuse to allow my fears, limiting beliefs, circumstances, or anything else in my life stop me from making this happen. I will remain firmly focused on this goal and take full responsibility for my results.

Signature _____

Today's Date _____

Create Your Day Planner

PLAN TO BE UNSTOPPABLE! Tonight or first thing tomorrow morning, plan your next day's activities by filling out your Create Your Day Planner (see Appendix). As you go through your day, notice areas where you're tempted not to accept personal responsibility for your life—areas where you're relinquishing control to someone else or to your circumstances. Celebrate this awareness and decide that you're not going to use this as an excuse to settle. Tomorrow, we'll discuss how to find the motivation you need to stay in action and make this change once and for all. In doing so, nothing can stop you!

"I'm not ready to improve my life. I'm still in the complaining stage."

AUTOBIOGRAPHY IN FIVE SHORT CHAPTERS

I

I walk down the street.
There is a deep hole in the sidewalk.
I fall in.
I am lost . . . I am helpless.
It isn't my fault.
It takes forever to find a way out.

II

I walk down the same street.
There is a deep hole in the sidewalk.
I pretend I don't see it.
I fall in again.
I can't believe I am in the same place.
But it isn't my fault.
It still takes a long time to get out.

III

I walk down the same street.
There is a deep hole in the sidewalk.
I see it there.
I still fall in . . . it's a habit.
My eyes are open.
I know where I am.
It is my fault.
I get out immediately.

IV

I walk down the same street.
There is a deep hole in the sidewalk.
I walk around it.

V

I WALK DOWN ANOTHER STREET.

What chapter are you on in your life?

Day 2:
"Why" Beats "How" Every Time

Today's Affirmation: I start each day connecting fully with why I have set this goal and vividly imagine the great benefits and feelings I will experience when I achieve it. Every time I take a single step, I am closer to making this important change in my life and I will not stop until it is fully realized. I will not settle. I am unstoppable!

The number one reason people don't get what they want is because they don't know *what* they want. They haven't taken the time to identify what really excites them. By completing part 1 of this book and identifying a breakthrough goal that excites you and will push you to the next level, you have already come further than most. Now that you're clear on your goal, however, the next step, and perhaps the most important, is to identify the purpose *behind* the goal. The purpose, or the "why," is more important than the goal itself.

Your purpose is your motivation—the driving force behind your efforts to make a change in your life. It will keep you going when obstacles raise their ugly heads. Knowing our "why" intensifies our desire and commitment; if we can create enough reasons *why* we want to make a change, there's nothing that can stop us.

For example, while a goal to organize your office may not seem very compelling, keeping in mind the purpose behind the goal—creating peace of mind, working in a clutter-free environment, and being able to focus on a new project with greater clarity—will motivate you when your energy lags. The more compelling the purpose you can identify behind any change or goal you'd like to achieve, the stronger the motivation to get you through any obstacles you might experience.

Julia "Butterfly" Hill was very clear on her purpose, and she had a lot of opportunities to test its power. Over a 2-year period, she desperately tried to save a 1,000-year-old redwood tree, enduring icy cold weather, loneliness, and even death threats.

Despite the obstacles she faced, her commitment to her purpose wouldn't allow her to quit. Today, she's a powerful example of how one person with a compelling purpose can do the "impossible."

Unstoppable Woman:
Julia Butterfly Hill's Story

You've heard of David versus Goliath, the biblical story of the little guy who took down the seemingly unbeatable giant. It's the perfect description of the uphill challenges Julia Butterfly Hill faced with Pacific Lumber from December 1997 to December 1999.

For 738 days during her 2-year act of civil disobedience, Hill nestled in the branches of a 200-foot redwood tree nicknamed "Luna," fervently trying to save the life of the ancient giant—without losing her own. By embracing her purpose when it presented itself and staying the course, she transformed herself into a powerful role model and demonstrated how one person with conviction can change the world.

An Unlikely Environmentalist
Julia was not the type of young woman one would expect to find living in a redwood tree, despised by logging interests, revered by environmental groups, a figure of controversy. She was born into a poor, religious family, the daughter of an itinerant preacher. Though she had very few material possessions, she was raised with a deep, constant emphasis on faith and the conviction that everyone is put here with a purpose.

How did this attractive young woman of 24 wind up the arch-enemy of the powerful Pacific Lumber/Maxxam Corporation, a company that would have done nearly *anything* to get rid of her? Nothing in her past would have suggested it. By high school, she was an average teenager. In her words, she was a bit "aimless." Then one August night in 1996, circumstances conspired to change her life: The Honda hatchback she was driving was rear-ended by a Ford Bronco.

Julia was badly hurt, suffering some brain damage. Months of intensive therapy followed as she re-trained the neural pathways in her brain to work the way they had before the accident. In the process, she developed patience, courage, and determination that would serve her well later. By the time her body healed, something had changed in her soul. Having faced death, she resolved to really live and follow a more spiritual path.

Discovering Luna

Ten months after the accident, Julia was released from her doctor's care. She journeyed to the West Coast with friends to visit Grizzly Creek State Park and see the giant California redwoods. She found the majestic trees "spectacular," but was horrified to discover that, thanks to uncontrolled logging and clear-cutting, fewer than 3 percent of them remained. The rest had become lumber and patio furniture.

The image of the endangered redwoods struck a powerful chord within Hill. "Learning about the clear-cut made me sick," she says. "I walked out of the forest a different woman. I had no clue what I could do, but I *knew* I was meant to do *something!*"

Hill found out that there was a need for people to "sit" in the trees that were under threat from the chainsaw, preventing loggers from cutting them down. When people move into the trees, it means that every effort to save them had failed.

Julia learned about a 1,000-year-old redwood nicknamed "Luna" that was tagged to be cut down soon. To prevent this, someone would need to be in the tree 24 hours a day, 7 days a week. Julia knew she *had* to be the one. Of course, she had no idea that this would mean her feet would not touch the ground for 2 years!

The High Life

Up Julia went—180 feet, just 20 feet from the top. She lived on two 4-by-8-foot platforms, eating vegan meals cooked on a single-burner propane stove. Twice a week, a support crew brought her food and other necessities, which she hoisted up by a pulley system. Her only supplies were walkie-talkies, a solar-powered radiophone, an emergency cell phone, a crank-powered radio, a tape recorder, a camera, and a pager that functioned as an answering machine. The latter, she says, "controlled her life." The coverage from newspaper reporters and radio stations was as constant as the onslaught of threats from Pacific Lumber.

Neither the continual media attention nor the increasing threats impacted Hill's resolve. Luna gave her a sense of purpose. Doing her small part to help save the ancient redwood forest seemed like the answer to an urgent call. By sitting high in the tree's branches, she could protect the tree and those around it, while the people within the legal system did their work to bring about broad-based public awareness.

Dirty Tactics
Unfortunately, Pacific Lumber's determination to cut down the tree was nearly as strong as Julia's resolve to save it. Workers blew air horns all night to disrupt her sleep or aimed blinding floodlights at her platform. Loggers stood at the base of the tree, cursing at her, threatening to "beat her to a pulp" when she *did* come down.

Sometimes, the measures got extreme. The company brought in a huge twin propeller helicopter to fly within a few feet of her, presumably to blow her off her perch. Hill hung on and took video, unaware that FAA regulations prohibit flying within 200 feet of humans. When the pictures were sent to the FAA, the chopper disappeared.

Even worse, though, in one extraordinary act of brutality, the company shot *napalm* near Luna to burn the clear cut area. Her only protection was a wet bandana she used as a mask. For days, Julia toughed it out, choking on every breath of smoke; her nose bled nonstop, and her eyes were swollen almost completely shut.

Surviving human attacks wasn't her only concern. The weather wasn't cooperating, either. During the winter storms, she was covered with snow. Her primary concern was not only to keep from getting blown out of the tree, but to not get frostbite. While she wore warm clothing, she was constantly freezing. Her sleep was minimal due to the storm's relentless howling and the cold temperatures. There were many nights when she felt she would not survive another night without sleep.

Doubt, Then Affirmation

As the cold, miserable days dragged on, Hill began to doubt her motives and her commitment. She was keenly aware that she was admired by some for what she was doing and despised by others. But as one of the worst storms battered her, she hung on . . . and came out even more committed than before. "When I almost died in that mother of all storms, and embraced death, I learned how to live for the first time in my life. I no longer feared death. This freed me like the butterfly frees itself from its cocoon."

Then Hill received confirmation that others appreciated what she was doing. The group Veterans for Peace gave her their Wage Peace Recognition of Valor award for staying in the tree 100 days. Julia cried as hundreds of people filed up the steep hill to honor her for her unprecedented act of courage.

Victory

One of Hill's goals in sitting in Luna had been to create public awareness of the plight of the old-growth redwoods. And she was succeeding. Press coverage was ever-present, and she was becoming a reluctant public spokesperson and an environmental heroine. "I have always been fiercely private, and being thrown into the spotlight has been an awkward situation."

Resigned to the scrutiny because she knew it would help her cause, Hill realized she would have to arm herself with knowledge. She studied every book she could find on forestry and the effects of clear-cutting and became a self-taught expert. The work paid off, as on April 5, 1999, she did a dual interview on CNN with Pacific Lumber's president, John Campbell, and her expertise on the redwoods made him look foolish.

Faced with the indomitable Hill and her allies on the ground, Pacific Lumber finally gave in. On December 18, 1999, the company signed a formal preservation agreement and deed of covenant to protect Luna and create a 200-foot buffer zone around the tree. Hill rappelled down from the heights of the ancient redwood, moving slowly and stopping occasionally to cling affectionately to its bark. When she reached the ground, she collapsed in the mud, wracked with sobs. "We did it," she cried over and over, tears streaming down her face. "We did it!"

The "Wacko" Turned Hero

Good Housekeeping Magazine nominated Hill as the most admired woman in America. She and her cohorts were delighted by the irony that the same person, just months earlier, had been labeled as a wacko and an extremist.

Julia Butterfly Hill, the unlikely environmentalist, holds the world record for the longest, highest tree-sit. Today she speaks to groups around the world about environmental issues and works with several organizations to preserve old-growth trees and the environment as a whole.

The preacher's daughter has come a long way. Indeed, with great pain and astonishing courage, she changed her life. She discovered her purpose and made her life matter, protecting some of nature's most precious creations, splendid silent giants that, ironically, could not protect themselves from a corporate Goliath. Luckily, they had a David to look after them.

> *"I had asked for guidance on what to do with my life. I had asked for purpose. I had asked to be of service. If you would've asked me if I could have done this when I climbed that tree, I could not have believed it. When a situation demands it, it's our opportunity to rise above our status quos and challenge ourselves."*
> —Julia Butterfly Hill

Unstoppable Action
Identify Your Purpose

"A person who has a strong enough 'why' can bear almost any 'how.'"
—*Anonymous*

Sitting 180 feet up in a tree to protect the environment might not be a cause that moves you, but whatever your goal, you can emulate Hill's passion and purpose. Her story vividly demonstrates how a clear purpose can fuel the courage and resolve needed to make great things happen. Without the purpose she felt in her heart and soul, Julia Butterfly Hill wouldn't have been able to live in a tree for 2 years and endure great discomfort and constant threats to her life. When obstacles came her way, sometimes on a moment-by-moment basis, Hill stayed firm because her purpose was too important to allow anything to stop her.

Identify your "why."

When you want to make any change in your life, 20 percent of the result is knowing *how* to do something, but 80 percent is knowing *why* you're doing it. If you can create enough reasons why you must make a change in your life, nothing can stop you.

Now that you've identified your breakthrough goal, think about all the reasons why you *must* achieve it. Make a list of all the reasons that will excite and motivate you to stay in action every day. What are the specific benefits you will experience? How will you feel about yourself? How will this victory impact your self-image and confidence? How will it benefit your loved ones? For example:

BREAKTHROUGH GOAL: Earn an additional $1,000 a month
- I'll pay off a debt.
- I'll feel like I'm in control of my life.
- I'll have the confidence that I can do it again and even more.
- I can support my favorite charity.

- I'll be proud of myself.
- My spouse will be proud of me.
- I can join a gym.
- A portion will go toward my child's tuition.
- I'll be developing the discipline and willpower to achieve other goals in my life.
- I can take that course I've been wanting to take.

WRITE YOUR BREAKTHROUGH GOAL:

_____

Reasons WHY you must achieve this goal over the next 30 days:

- _____
- _____
- _____
- _____
- _____
- _____

Determine what it will cost you *not* to achieve your goal.

Just as important as identifying the benefits you will receive as a result of achieving your goal is identifying the consequences of *not* achieving your goal. Think hard about the consequences you'll experience personally, professionally, and spiritually if you *don't* take the daily actions necessary to make your goal happen. What will it cost you if you don't start working out consistently? If you don't make the prospecting calls you need to make each day? If you don't stop smoking? If you don't forgive your loved one? And as important, how will that make you feel? Our emotions drive our behavior, so fully connect with how it will *feel* if you don't achieve your goal. You'll be a lot more likely to take action and keep taking it if you regularly consider the cost of not following through.

Below, list the consequences of not achieving your breakthrough goal. For instance, the person in the previous example might list the consequences of not earning an additional $1,000 a month as follows:

CONSEQUENCES
What is it going to cost me if I don't achieve this goal?

Personal costs:	Diminished self-esteem, disappointment in self, perpetuating the belief that I can't do it, look like a failure, feel demoralized
Professional costs:	Not be seen as a leader, loss of income, missed opportunities, stuck in a career with limited potential
Spiritual costs:	Lack of peace of mind, not living up to true potential

What are the consequences if you don't reach your goal? Fill them in below.

CONSEQUENCES
What is it going to cost me if I don't achieve this goal?

Personal costs:	
Professional costs:	
Spiritual costs:	

✎ Start every day by focusing on why you want to achieve your 30-day goal and the cost not to follow through.

Each day, spend a few minutes connecting fully with *why* you set your breakthrough goal and the deep satisfaction you will experience in just 30 days when you have achieved it. Think about how achieving this goal will positively impact other areas of your life. Feel the joy and excitement you'll experience by honoring your commitments to yourself today to make that goal a reality.

Just as important, review what it will cost you if you don't achieve your goal. What if you don't start eating a healthier diet, lower your cholesterol, or save money for the future? And how will those consequences make you feel? Our emotions drive our behavior, so fully connect with the pain of failure to motivate you to take action.

Remember, you have the power to condition your mind, body, and emotions to motivate and drive you to change your behavior in ways you may not have thought possible.

Create Your Day Planner

PLAN TO BE UNSTOPPABLE! Tonight or first thing tomorrow morning, plan your next day's activities by filling out your Create Your Day Planner (see Appendix). You've just spent some time thinking about why you must reach your 30-day breakthrough goal and the wonderful benefits you will reap when you achieve it. You've also thought about the consequences that will result if you don't stay committed. With this single focus in mind, now is a good time to tackle a task you might be dreading. Keeping the "why" of your goal in the forefront of your mind will motivate you to take on even the most tedious, difficult, or frightening steps in your Unstoppable Women Challenge.

Something to Think About

In 1995, 13-year-old Kentuckian Deanna Durrett was dining with her family when she noticed how easy it was for teenagers to purchase cigarettes from a vending machine. As an experiment, she went to 20 other restaurants and was successful in purchasing cigarettes every time.

Appalled, she returned the cigarettes to the restaurant managers and demanded that they get rid of the machines. Surprisingly, four did so. The experience turned Durrett into an anti-smoking crusader. Since that time, she's met with President Clinton, appeared on "Larry King Live", and lobbied before Congress for anti-smoking laws. She also received the National Youth Advocate of the Year Award in 1999 from the Campaign for Tobacco-Free Kids. Additionally, she is the first teenager to serve on Kentucky's chapter of the executive board of the American Lung Association.

"Advocating for change is not always easy, but if you are passionate about the issue, you *will* find the strength and resolve to continue fighting. If I have kept one child from smoking, then it has all been worth it."

Day 3:
Tap Into Your "Internal Caller ID"

Today's Affirmation: *My beliefs about myself shape my every action, thought, and feeling. By using my "Internal Caller ID," I can consciously choose beliefs that support my goals and eliminate those that stop me. When I listen to my voice of faith—my internal optimistic and hopeful voice—I initiate a positive force that enables me to create one unstoppable moment after another. Step by step, I am achieving my 30-day goal. I am unstoppable!*

You can be passionate about your Unstoppable Women Challenge breakthrough goal and have a list a mile long of reasons why you want to achieve it, but if you don't believe it's possible, you'll quit before you even begin.

The best way to identify your level of belief behind any goal is to notice your "self-talk"—the thoughts and beliefs you silently say to yourself when you think about the goal you want to achieve. I like to think of this recognition of your self-talk as your "Internal Caller ID."

Our self-talk is comprised of two internal voices. The first is the voice of faith, which reflects our higher self. It's that hopeful and optimistic internal voice that believes in the possibilities of our lives. The other internal voice—the voice of fear—comes from a place of worry, doubt, and hopelessness. It tells us we're not enough—not good enough, smart enough, disciplined enough. If we follow it, this voice will rob us of our dreams. By tuning in to our "Internal Caller ID," we can become aware of the voice of fear and cut it off as soon as possible.

How do you identify which voice is speaking? Think of your breakthrough goal and then listen. Are your immediate thoughts "I'm so excited" or "I can't wait to get started" or "I know I can do it"? Thoughts reflecting the possibilities of your life are your voice of faith.

On the other hand, if your thoughts are, "Yeah, I'd love to do that *but* . . . "

- I don't have the time.
- It's too late.
- I'm too old.
- I'm too young.
- I have no knowledge in that area.
- I am a single parent and don't have the resources.
- People will think I'm crazy.
- My spouse/family won't support me.
- Why even try, I'll just be disappointed?

. . . you're recognizing your voice of *fear*.

The voice we choose to believe will determine who we become and what we accomplish. For example, Margaret, 63, had told herself for 20 years that she was too old to learn how to play the piano. "It's too late," she'd say, as she buried her burning desire to play down deep inside herself. Then, one day, she went to a local symphony concert and noticed that the pianist was an elderly gentleman. She approached him after the performance and learned that not only was he 84, but he had learned to play at 70! This completely changed Margaret's belief about herself; she realized she wasn't too old to learn. She signed up for piano lessons the next day and was finally on her way to realizing a lifelong dream.

The next story, about Lynn Donohue, is a perfect illustration of the power of listening to your voice of faith. Her goal—to become a bricklayer—led her to confront not just the obstacles of her own self-doubt, but also old-fashioned chauvinism. Her perseverance in the face of continual pressure to quit is the stuff unstoppable women are made of.

Unstoppable Woman:
Lynn Donohue's Story

When Lynn Donohue's supervisor on a construction job sneered at her, "Next thing you know, they'll have *monkeys* doing this job!" she dug in her heels and made a promise to herself: "Someday *you'll* be working for *me!*"

For years, Lynn had been a young woman with no direction, a dropout at 15. Then, while working in her father's bar, she read an ad about women getting into non-traditional female jobs. Her heart leapt when she saw the pay scale for bricklayers—$17 an hour! It would take her 6 hours in her father's bar to make as much!

Lynn eagerly began a 3-month course in masonry. "It was love at first sight," she says. "I fell in love with bricks, and I wanted more than anything to become a bricklayer. I had never had a sense of direction, much less a dream. But now I had a goal *and* a dream. And, yeah, I hoped to make lots of money. And to be proud of myself."

Fighting Old Prejudices

Not so fast. The first of the obstacles that would test Lynn's commitment was about to appear. Before someone can become a recognized bricklayer, or "journeyman," he or she must first serve time as an apprentice. Well, given the testosterone-soaked culture of construction, do you think folks were beating down the door to hire a woman apprentice? The local union hall didn't even have a ladies' room.

In the true unstoppable spirit, Lynn didn't back down, even though the union wanted no part of her. She called every masonry contractor in the phone book, but she was rejected by all of them. She made the rounds at their offices, but the more often she came around, the more irritated they became. She frequented the union hall, trying to meet someone, anyone, who would give her a chance. And there, too, she was treated as a pest.

Lynn felt her resolve only grow stronger. "I wasn't going to give up," she says. This was the most important dream she had ever had. So she got smart: Rather than try to bulldoze her way into a group that was determined to exclude her, she changed tactics.

Be Careful What You Wish For

Lynn and her mother investigated New Bedford's Equal Opportunity Employment laws and found out she had some legal muscle behind her. So, after much negotiating with the union (which didn't want her), MF Construction (which didn't want her either), and the city's Equal Opportunity Employment officer (who sympathized with her), she was taken on as an apprentice for MF Construction.

Lynn had no idea what she was really getting into. What did bricklayers wear on the job? What tools did they need? She didn't have the first clue. One thing was for sure; she wanted to blend in as much as possible, so she bought some boy's size plastic boots and one-sized men's gloves and showed up for her first day on a construction site. She spent the rest of that day, and many days that followed, with her ears burning from the laughter, disdain, and insults of her male co-workers. Some told her she needed to go back to her kitchen, while others treated her as though she were taking away a friend's or relative's job. But she had sacrificed to put herself in this position, and she knew she had no choice but to endure. "I had failed at just about everything in my life," she says. "Dropping out of school, never finishing anything, never winning anything, never getting compliments. I was determined to show everyone I could make it as a bricklayer."

That meant continuing to punch the clock—showing up for each new job and each union meeting and enduring the same torrent of jokes, indifference, and open hostility. If she were lucky, she'd earn the grudging respect of a few of the men who appreciated her solid work. But Lynn really didn't mind any of it. By hanging tough, enduring the taunts and the obscene jokes, and doing her job as best she could, she was developing an inner strength that surprised even her.

The Best Female Bricklayer in the Country

Lynn knew that unless she could make the establishment admit she was as skilled as any man, she would never get far. So she continued to grow as a bricklayer and found a masonry course to take. "The thought of taking a college course with my eighth-grade education was intimidating, but I had fallen in love with the trade and longed to learn more," she says.

For the next year, Lynn spent every night in her basement, training to win the apprentice bricklaying contest—building a 4-foot-wide brick wall, then tearing it down. She had become *obsessed* with taking first place as an antidote to all the ridicule she'd endured for being a woman in a "man's" industry. "I wanted to win for the time I was locked in the porta-potty," she says, "wanted to win for all the women who struggled to make it in a man's world." The work paid off: She won the next competition, becoming the first woman in the country to take first place.

Then one day on a job site, she saw Ted Murphy, who is renowned for his ability to lay more than 1,200 bricks a day. She introduced herself, saying she hoped someday she would be as accomplished as he. Murphy replied, "Kid, you've got three strikes against you—you're not strong enough, you're not tall enough, and you're a woman!" The devastated Lynn quickly vowed, in another example of her unstoppable spirit, to prove him wrong.

Injury, Then Opportunity

In March 1983, Lynn became a full journeyman, completing 6,000 hours of on-the-job training. She was finally a bricklayer and would receive full pay (apprentices got only half). Her dream was finally going in the right direction . . . and gaining momentum.

Then she fell from a 23-foot scaffolding. She could have sued, but didn't. As sore and bruised as she was, she was determined to show up for work the next day, aware this would be a turning point in her relationship with her co-workers. And she was right. In spite of themselves, the men couldn't help but respect her moxie.

Slowly, with study, expert mentoring, hard work, and dedication, Lynn mastered the skills to merit a foreman job. As a foreman, she could work more side jobs that helped her hone her skills, and she could save some extra money. But when her union business agent tried to land her such a position, every contractor turned him down. It was that maddening chauvinism at work again: The contractors were afraid that the men they hired wouldn't take orders from a woman.

Lynn was told to forget about becoming a foreman. "My life as a tradeswoman passed before my eyes," she says. "I was sick to death of being in a man's world that wouldn't let women in."

But anyone who thought she would lay down her tools and "return to her kitchen" would be sorely mistaken. If the only way she could get a foreman job was to hire herself, that's what she'd do. She decided to start her own business. To make her goals concrete (no pun intended), she wrote them down: "Five years from now, I will have $100,000 in the bank and be the best masonry contractor in southeastern Massachusetts." She placed her written goal in her top dresser drawer, where she saw it every morning and ritualistically read it aloud as she got ready for work.

As her confidence grew, she began taking on more side jobs, hiring her old cohorts who apparently had no problems taking orders from a woman, and saving every penny. She devoured books on construction, contracting, and anything associated with the building trade. The more she repeated her goal aloud, the more real it became, motivating her to stick with her plan. Finally, she saved $10,000 to buy a new truck, and with two employees, opened Argus Masonry.

Setting—And Reaching—Goals

By November 14, 1984, Lynn had put away $103,268 in profit—not only surpassing her $100,000 goal, but doing it in half the time.

Now for goal number two. She said to herself, "I will establish a $100,000 retirement account by December 1991." She followed the same ritual: reading her goal aloud every morning. Just 3 years later, she had her retirement nest egg—all before age 30.

And if that's not enough, Lynn went for and reached one more major financial goal: paying off all three mortgages on her properties (a total of $385,000) in 5 years. And, of course, she did it in only 3 years.

In addition, she turned Argus Masonry into a multi-million-dollar business with more than 50 employees. The woman in a man's world, whose skills were unwanted, had gained not only the respect of her peers, but much of their business as well.

Much More Than a New Career

Lynn Donohue has used her experience to become a published author: Her memoir, *Brick by Brick*, was published in 2000. She has even established the Brick by Brick Community Organization in Greater New Bedford to help high-school dropouts and others struggling in their careers.

But her journey from barmaid to bricklayer to entrepreneur is about so much more than money in the bank or the respect of others. It's about forgiving yourself and others and retaining your self-worth in the face of defeat and criticism. In the past, Lynn admitted to failing at just about everything in her life. Poised on the critical fine line between a life of lost opportunities and "might have been" regrets, and the fear and exhilaration that come with believing in a dream, she chose the dream. When confronted by obstacles, she dug in her heels and, for the first time in her life, didn't quit. Refusing to listen to self-doubt, she changed her life through sheer will.

Lynn succeeded because of a commitment of unbelievable depth and strength; she simply *would not let herself fail*. And she won in the most inspirational way imaginable. She's proof that the best way to make sure an Unstoppable Woman does something is to tell her she can't do it!

Unstoppable Action
Develop Empowering Beliefs

How do we change our limiting beliefs and turn our voice of fear into our voice of faith? Awareness of our inner voices is the first step. Let's start by identifying your "yeah, buts"—the negative beliefs that enter your mind when you think about your breakthrough goal. It's important to identify all of the reasons why you believe you can't achieve your goal and the beliefs that have stopped you in the past from accomplishing a goal or dream.

Below are some of the disempowering beliefs from participants in the Unstoppable Women Challenge:

- I can't lose weight, so why bother making such an effort?
- I don't have the willpower.
- It's selfish to want more. I should be happy with what I have.
- I'm not smart enough.
- I'm lazy.
- I am not good enough to be financially free.
- You have to be lucky or in the right place at the right time to become rich.
- You have to work so hard just to make it through each month.
- I'm silly to think I can change or that circumstances will change in my favor.
- I am just ordinary, so who would want to listen to me?
- I have to do it all myself. Nobody will help me.
- I need other people's approval.
- I don't follow through on commitments.
- Everything must be perfect and in place in order for it to work.
- If I really was good enough, I would be financially free already. What's wrong with me?
- I am a poor money manager and don't like to deal with money. Can't someone do it for me?
- There's something wrong with me that keeps me from realizing my dreams.

The Burden of Disempowering Beliefs

After reading the list above, it's easy to see why a person with such disempowering beliefs would be stopped. Who wouldn't be? Our limiting beliefs create an enormous burden on us emotionally, psychologically, and spiritually.

Tap into your "Internal Caller ID."

Now it's your turn. Fill in your breakthrough goal, and then stop and listen. Write down the beliefs that come from your internal voice of fear— the beliefs that have either stopped you in the past or could stop you now from moving forward to achieve your breakthrough goal.

FILL IN YOUR BREAKTHROUGH GOAL:

_____

Disempowering Beliefs

- _____
- _____
- _____
- _____

Now think about this: None of the beliefs you wrote down are true. *Not one.* They do not reflect the truth of who you are or what's possible for your life. Unfortunately, too often we believe these lies and use them as excuses for not moving forward. We can stop that vicious cycle. Once we acknowledge the "story" or limiting belief that has stopped us in the past, we can change it.

Developing New, Empowering Beliefs

Our beliefs about ourselves shape every action, every thought, and every feeling that we have. So to change our lives, we must change our belief systems. By using our "Internal Caller ID," we can consciously choose beliefs that support our goals and eliminate those that stop us. When choosing the voice of faith, we initiate a positive force that enables us to create one unstoppable moment, or win, after another.

The first step to creating a new empowering belief is simply to turn around a limiting belief. For example, let's examine a common disempowering belief:

"I am too undisciplined to _____." (Fill in the blank based on your goal, such as lose 10 pounds, save money, live within a budget, or be a patient mom.)

Now let's turn that belief around:

"I have the discipline to _____" (write in the same goal).

How is this belief true, or perhaps even more true than your original statement? If you're having a hard time finding the evidence in your life to support this new belief, don't worry. On Day 4, you'll develop more than enough evidence to support this belief. For now, simply turn the statement around so that it is an empowering belief.

Here are a few more examples of how to change a limiting belief into an empowering one:

LIMITING BELIEF	NEW EMPOWERING BELIEF
Voice of Fear	**Voice of Faith**
I don't have the time.	I have plenty of time to do the things that are truly important.
I want to wait until the timing is right.	If I wait until the "perfect" time, it will never happen. Things will fall into place as I go.
I'm lazy.	I'm not lazy, I just need to come up with more internal motivators to get me to take action.
I can't lose weight anyway, so why bother making such an effort?	I can lose weight, and my health and vitality are worth the effort.
I'm not good enough to be financially free.	I am good enough to be financially free and can learn the strategies to make that happen.
I'm silly to think I can change at this point in my life.	I can change anything one step at a time.
It is selfish to want more. I should be happy with what I have.	It is not selfish to want more. As I expand as an individual, I can offer more to others.
I can't depend on others.	I can depend on myself.
I need other people's approval.	I need my approval.
I don't follow through on commitments.	I do follow through on my commitments when they're important to me.
It's too late to start.	It's never too late to start.
I don't deserve success.	I'm a good person and I deserve to succeed.
I cannot control my bad habits.	I am in control—not my habit.
I need to create the perfect action plan with *every* single detail thought out.	I don't need to create the perfect action plan. I simply need to know my next steps and take them one at a time.

✎ List your old beliefs and then turn them around by listening to your voice of faith.

LIMITING BELIEF	NEW EMPOWERING BELIEF
Voice of Fear	Voice of Faith

Would you like reminders of common limiting beliefs and new, empowering beliefs? Go to **UnstoppableWomen.com** and download the chart today.

 Create Your Day Planner

PLAN TO BE UNSTOPPABLE! Tonight or first thing tomorrow morning, plan your next day's activities by filling out your Create Your Day planner (see Appendix). As you're taking daily steps to achieve your 30-day goal, reflect on your inner voice. Is it empowering you or telling you lies that make you feel small and inadequate? With a little practice, you can train yourself to listen only to your voice of faith. Tomorrow, I'm going to give you additional tools to turn up the volume on your voice of faith so that you can become a master at making the changes you want to make.

Day 4:
What I Am Seeking Is Seeking Me!

Today's Affirmation: Any true desire of my heart is there for a reason. What I desire wants me as much as I want it, and I possess everything I need to achieve my 30-day goal. My faith expands each time I take action. By taking a single daily step, I am communicating to myself—and to the world—that I believe in myself and in my dream. Regardless of my present circumstances, I know I will achieve my goal. With God, all things are possible. I will not settle. I will not stop. I am unstoppable!

Althea Gibson, the great black Wimbledon champion, said, "You must first be a believer before you can be an achiever." Less than a century ago, who would have believed that Dr. Mae Jemison, a black woman, would travel into space? Or that Condoleezza Rice would become the first woman, the first African-American, and the youngest National Security Advisor to the President, a role traditionally dominated by white men, before being nominated as Secretary of State?

These women's accomplishments began with faith in themselves. How does one cultivate faith? It doesn't happen *to* you, it happens *through* you. Your faith expands each time you take action. Unfortunately, many people wait to have faith before they make the big leap, but it doesn't work that way. You must leap before the net appears. When you prove to yourself that you're committed to creating real change in your life, the faith will come!

I'm not asking you to have blind faith. You have reason to have faith, based on your own past successes and the successes of the women you're meeting through this book. These women *are no different from you.* Each of them created extraordinary results in her life. Each had an unshakable belief in her desires, even when no one else did.

Belief is a prerequisite for becoming unstoppable. When you believe in yourself, you can transform your desire and goals into physical realities. In the beginning, you may not *feel* very brave or confident, much less unstoppable. Doubts will arise whenever you do something new. That's natural. But by taking one step at a time, you will begin to feel your confidence grow. Every action you take raises your self-esteem and your belief in yourself. You're no longer sitting around waiting for something magical to happen. You're the creator of that "magic."

With the Unstoppable Women Challenge, you're focusing on one change, one step at a time—a pace that will produce permanent results. By taking even the smallest steps, you are communicating to yourself—and to the world—that you believe in yourself and your dream.

In Latin, desire means "of the father." A desire is something that arises from deep within us. Any true desire of your heart is there for a reason. If you have a genuine hunger to make this change in your life, you also have the means inside you to make it a reality. Affirm to yourself daily that "With God, all things are possible!" Deepak Chopra said, "Within every desire is the mechanics of its fulfillment." In other words, if you aspire to do something, it's because you also possess the potential to do it.

The part that stops most people before they even get started is working through their fears—the limiting beliefs that they're not good enough, worthy enough, smart enough . . . and the list goes on.

In the story of Grandmaster Dr. Tae Yun Kim, you will see a woman who had the cards stacked against her from birth, by something as fundamental as her gender. But because she discovered in herself a passion and desire to learn the martial arts, she broke down a 5,000-year-old barrier and changed her culture and her future.

Unstoppable Woman:
Grandmaster Dr. Tae Yun Kim's Story

When Tae Yun Kim was born in Korea in 1946, her grandfather asked the ancestors what he had done to deserve such a curse. Since Kim was the firstborn, the household would have been blessed had she been a male. Now her family believed that they were cursed forever. "When a woman has a baby, she is supposed to eat seaweed soup, a healing food for the new mother," recalls Kim. "When my grandfather found out I was a girl, he dumped the seaweed soup."

Growing up, Kim always felt anger and humiliation from her father. And though her mother didn't completely reject her, she came to resent her daughter more as time went by. The fact that Kim's father turned to another woman over the "shame" brought on by Kim's birth only made things worse.

A Message from War

Unwelcomed and unwanted by everyone, Kim made friends with nature—the flowers, birds, and the trees. Her life was very harsh, with chores from morning till night. She also endured brutal beatings from her parents, who blamed her for any ill fortune that befell the family.

Then, when Kim was 5, the Korean War invaded her little town. The family escaped—but left Kim behind, not wanting to "waste" food on their cursed daughter. All alone, the little girl screamed in terror as blasts of artillery fire came closer. A young girl ran by Kim, yelling for her to run with her or be killed. Relieved that someone actually showed her some kindness, Kim ran as quickly as her little feet would carry her, trying desperately to keep up with her new friend. Then without warning, there was a hellish explosion—and her friend was blown to bits.

Lying stunned, seeing the broken body of her friend and so many others dead on the ground, Kim had an epiphany. "I thought, 'Here are all these men lying around and they're dead. If I'm such bad luck, why am I still living and they're not?'" she remembers. "At that moment, I realized I must have incredible luck, no matter what others thought." With this new sense of self-worth inside her, nothing would ever again be the same for Kim.

Taking On 5,000 Years of Tradition

The next year, Kim went to live with her grandparents. Her uncles were all martial artists, and she'd wake up to them doing their exercises in tae kwon do, the graceful, high-kicking Korean martial art. She was fascinated. "In our culture, a girl grows up, cooks and sews, and when the matchmaker finds her a husband, she produces sons," Kim says. "I didn't want to end up like my mother, beaten and shown no respect. I became determined to learn tae kwon do."

Kim asked her uncles to teach her the difficult martial art. They laughed. No woman had ever learned tae kwon do for 5,000 years! Tradition could not be changed. They told her to forget such foolishness and focus on learning the only skills a woman would need: cooking, sewing, and taking care of children.

But Kim would not be discouraged. The desire to learn tae kwon do was like a fever in her, something she *had* to do. Somehow, she knew *this* was the path she was meant to follow. "To me, the martial arts are not just a sport," she said years later. "They are a way of living one's life to its fullest potential. They are a way of bringing harmony to your life, regardless of the circumstances around you." She continued to beg her uncles to teach her. Finally, the youngest humored her and agreed. He hoped that when she felt the bruises, she would give up.

Meeting Her Master

Desperate to stop her from bringing more shame upon the family, Kim's grandfather sought out the village Buddhist monk for help. The monk spoke to Kim, but instead of advising her to know her place, he asked her a question no one had ever cared enough to ask: "What do you want to do with your life?" Kim answered, "I want to be a teacher and make people happy." The monk replied, "Then that shall be your destiny." He turned to

Kim's grandfather. "You have always trusted me," he said. "Do you trust me still?" "I do," replied the old man. "Then you must close your eyes to the past," said the monk, "and trust that it is destined that I teach her."

Kim was just 8 years old the day she met her master. "He saw in me what no one else had ever seen: that I would be the *one*, someday," she says. "I didn't know what he meant at the time, but he believed in me." At that moment, 5,000 years of tradition were shattered, even though it would be 31 years before she fully achieved her dream.

Every day after school, Kim met with the monk, and they trained until late at night. He taught her the skills of tae kwon do and mentored her in the ways of life, Buddhism, and self-discipline. But at home, Kim suffered terribly for the dishonor her family believed she was bringing to them.

She was frequently locked up so she couldn't go out and train with the monk, and she was regularly beaten. To shame her, her family cut her hair freakishly short. When she was able to get out and meet her master, the village boys threw snakes at her. Life became more miserable each day. Still Kim continued her training. She also fed and cared for her master, who would have starved without her help. He was the only person in her life who had ever cared for her, and she adored and respected him.

The monk brought her to the market to teach her about human nature, to the sacred temple to teach her what mattered in life, and to the forests to teach her about *ki*, or life energy. The Chinese call it "chi," and it is the energy inside and around us. They were inseparable: the wise old man and the wide-eyed child. At age 13, Kim was awarded a black belt, representing the highest degree of skill in her art. To Kim, this was an enormous triumph. Knowing that she had made her master proud filled her with joy. Sadly, no one in her family shared her victory.

Stranger in a Strange Land

In 1968, when she was 23, Kim's master encouraged her to leave Korea. He knew she would never achieve her full potential in her homeland. Reluctantly, she took the advice of the only person she truly loved and respected, and left him to go to the United States.

Hopes high, Kim settled in Vermont. She found the countryside beautiful, but sadly, she also found something unexpected: prejudice simply because she was Asian. She was refused service in restaurants, and for a while no one would rent her a place to live. To make ends meet, she pumped gas on weekends and did janitorial work at local hotels. She didn't take the mistreatment personally and was thankful to be working and learning the American culture and language. Slowly, she was sure she was moving toward her dream.

The key, Kim believed, was to start teaching. The local high school seemed like a good place to start, so every day for 4 weeks, she waited outside the principal's office. Finally, he asked what she wanted. When she explained in broken English her desire to teach martial arts, he said there was no budget. Undeterred, she offered to teach for free. Money didn't matter, she told him. What mattered was opening the spirits of as many children as possible to her knowledge.

The principal agreed, assigning Kim the toughest, most unruly kids in the school. And when these troubled students' grades shot up to straight A's by the end of the semester, Kim began seeing admiration and trust from the parents of the town. Kim was a survivor, and she taught her students to take charge of their lives through martial arts training.

Backed by this new support, Kim finally opened her own tae kwon do school in her garage. Over time, the school began to flourish, and Kim's recognition as a teacher grew. She was asked to train the U.S. women's martial arts team and led it to the 1978 Pre-World Games in Seoul, South Korea, where they won many medals. To her joy, she returned to her homeland as a "Master," where she had once been little more than a slave.

Kim the Entrepreneur

Despite her international success , Kim still needed to make a decent living. In 1982, a picture of a computer appeared in Kim's mind as she was meditating. She had never used a computer before, but she felt this image was significant. Along with some friends, she invested everything she owned into a start-up computer company called Lighthouse Worldwide Solutions.

In true Grandmaster style, Kim successfully weathered countless business obstacles along the way. Lighthouse Worldwide Solutions is now an international, multi-million-dollar business. She also launched "The Tae Yun Kim Show," a national talk show focusing on people who have overcome great odds. She has become the world's most renowned authority on ki, or vital energy. Kim has also received many honors, including the Susan B. Anthony Award for "lifting the hearts of so many people born to so very little," and for advancing women's rights with encouragement and inspiration. Grandmaster Kim continues to write, lecture, and teach.

Desire Becomes Healing

Everything has changed for Kim because of her unwavering commitment to follow her true desire and not be a victim of circumstance. Even Korea has changed, and in 1995, she was named a Korean "Cultural Living Treasure," for preserving the purity of the martial arts and ki training.

Recently, she followed one more desire: She visited her home village, where the people had so despised her. Everyone was living the same way they had decades before, while *she* had risen like a lotus flower from murky waters. But resentment was not her mission, so she extended tears of forgiveness to everyone. And as she met her mother's eyes, Kim knew she had finally made her proud. They have since developed a wonderful relationship.

How far can you go? What are your limits? No one knows but you. Desire, if it's trusted and followed, is a powerful force. As Grandmaster Kim shows, if we trust what is in our hearts and minds, they will lead us to the fulfillment of our dreams. The power always lies within us.

> *"When somebody tells me something can be done, I am not*
> *even interested. When they say it can't be done, I'm interested.*
> *Columbus, Thomas Edison—they are my mentors. My motto:*
> *He can do it, she can do it . . . why not ME!"*
> *—Grandmaster Dr. Tae Yun Kim*

⤳ Unstoppable Action ⤳
Adopt New Empowering Beliefs

It's easy to look at our present circumstances and let them dictate whether we think we can or cannot do something in the future. For example, perhaps you've attempted to lose some weight for years, yet when you look in the mirror, those unrelenting pounds are *still* staring you in the face. Or maybe you've made efforts to earn extra money, but your checking account remains consistently overdrawn. Or perhaps you've tried to lower your blood pressure, but your doctor tells you it's still too high. It requires enormous faith in yourself to stay focused on your goal when your current situation reflects something quite different. To have faith regardless of your present circumstances requires great discipline—yet that is *exactly* what must happen if you want to make real changes in your life.

How Can I Adopt New Empowering Beliefs as My Truth?

After completing the "disputing your beliefs" exercise on Day 3, you may be thinking, "Turning around a belief on paper is one thing, but how do I actually believe it's true?" Fair question. And the answer lies in two simple steps:

1. Build evidence to support your new belief through *success imprinting*.
2. Take inspiration from *role models*.

Success Imprinting

One proven way to develop empowering evidence to support your new belief is through a technique known as success imprinting. Belief, or self-confidence, is developed from past successes, or, as psychologists call them, success imprints. Success imprints are created anytime you have successfully achieved something that was thought to be difficult. Finishing a 5K run for the first time imprints a positive message on your subconscious, which makes the next race appear easier.

The same is true at work. Every time you accomplish something difficult, such as closing a complex sale, dealing with a challenging customer,
or completing a project on time, you've created a success imprint that not
only strengthens your self-esteem, but builds the belief that you can do it
again in the future.

Failures also create an imprint on our psyche and have the opposite
effect on our self-esteem. That's why it's critical that we focus on each
positive result, even if it seems like a baby step, so that we continue to create more of them in the future. Once you believe your goal is possible, the
difficult will become routine. For example, for years it was assumed that
no one could break the 4-minute-mile barrier. Physiologists of the time
considered it dangerous for anyone to even attempt to run a mile in less
than 4 minutes. But on May 6, 1954, Roger Bannister broke that "unreachable" barrier. And once he did, the next 3 years saw 16 runners around the
world also record sub-4-minute miles.

Success necessitates that we overcome obstacles. It is a natural part
of the process. Each time we do so, we create a success imprint that
strengthens our belief system and leads to greater and greater successes.
When we consciously choose to rewrite our negative beliefs into positive
ones, self-esteem and self-confidence will develop exponentially.

Restate your new belief:

"I have the discipline to _____
_____."

(insert your goal)

Now sit with your new belief. Think back to a time when you
were disciplined in *any* area of your life. Perhaps you have lost weight
in the past or engaged in a walking program. Or maybe you got your
CPA license, learned a foreign language, co-chaired a committee in your
local non-profit, or managed to get your kids to and from school every
day on time.

Isn't it true that everyone's life provides plenty of evidence to support any belief—positive or negative? It's all in how you look at it—your

frame of reference. You can look at past marital problems as evidence that you're hard to live with, or you can look at the fact that you got through them as evidence that you can grow and learn to communicate. Which is true? Whichever you choose to believe. What's important is to choose the belief that will move you forward in a positive direction. When you adopt the belief that fuels your energy and empowers you to stay in action, you have learned a very powerful strategy that you can use at will.

Here are some examples of past successes from other Unstoppable Women Challenge participants:

- Got Bachelor of Arts degree, making me the first in my family to get a degree
- Became a mother
- Became a manager at my work
- Had the highest sales achievement in the branch for the month of May
- Obtained real estate license
- Toured Europe on my own
- Became head stylist in salon
- After staying home with my kids for 10 years, I got the job I wanted
- Delivered my son without anesthesia
- Lost 20 pounds
- Completed flight instructor training
- Went to school as a single mom without welfare assistance
- Obtained master's degree in 2 years, while working full time
- Earned top dancer award in age group at convention
- Obtained RN degree
- Quit smoking and never went back
- Finished a quilt

Carol Biondi, who took the Unstoppable Women Challenge, couldn't even think of one success she had experienced, so she asked her daughter for input. Here is her daughter's list:

- Mom prepared great dinners—no matter how small or large—for the family
- Created amazing house decorations for Halloween. People came from all over to see mom's decorations, and she was even featured in the paper.
- Raised two great children

Like this woman, many of us tend to overlook or undervalue the accomplishments we've already achieved in our lives. Do any of the following apply to you?

- Are your children loved and well cared for?
- Do you have meaningful work?
- Do you contribute to your community?
- Are you working in a field that you care about?
- Have you created wonderful friendships and strong relationships?
- Are you healthy and able to do the activities you enjoy?
- Have you survived a financial setback, an illness, divorce, or death of a loved one without bitterness and are moving forward?
- Do you have a good relationship with your in-laws?

These are all great accomplishments; don't ignore or forget about them. They are important success imprints that can help you build your self-confidence and achieve your 30-day goal.

List *at least* three past successes that you're proud of (they need not relate to your breakthrough goal).
As you write your list, think of victories both big and small, such as a time when you achieved a goal that you didn't think was possible, fulfilled a commitment when it wasn't convenient, provided service to a customer that was above and beyond what was required, or honored your commitment to work out when it was the last thing you felt like doing.

SUCCESS IMPRINTS

List past successes that you're proud of:

1. _____

   _____

2. _____

   _____

3. _____

   _____

Role Models

The second way to adopt new, empowering beliefs as truth is to identify and learn from others who have achieved what we want to achieve. If they were successful, success is possible for us as well. The proof is in the people—people who have persevered, believed in themselves, and created systems that made it possible for them to succeed.

For example, if you want to take your business to the next level, but you have two small children at home, find someone in a similar circumstance who has created success while having young children. If you want to lose weight and get your body in better physical condition, find someone who was similarly out of shape and became incredibly fit. Find out exactly how he or she did it. Learn from their experience and adapt what worked to your situation. Virtually any goal can be achieved by finding models of possibility and following their strategies.

There is no reason to believe that you cannot achieve the same results of those whom you admire. How much we eventually achieve in life may well boil down to one simple ingredient: the quality of the models we choose to emulate. Who inspires you? Who has created a result that you want to create?

Role models are everywhere, in many forms, and they demonstrate what's possible, providing an invaluable source for motivation, strength, and hope. Draw strength from those who most inspire you. These people are inarguable proof of what's possible if you refuse to be stopped.

List three role models who prove that your goal is possible.

ROLE MODELS
List people who have achieved what you want to achieve and who demonstrate it's possible.

1. _____

2. _____

3. _____

What you are seeking is seeking you! There is a *reason* you have this longing in your heart. Having the courage to move forward to pursue your goal in the absence of knowing exactly how it will all happen takes a great deal of faith. Don't worry about how everything will fall into place.

Draw on your own past successes and the role models you have identified, as well as the women you're meeting in this book, as inarguable proof of what's possible for your life. All you have to do each day is focus on the single step you need to take. The rest will be revealed as you continue the process. Don't settle. Believe in yourself, and there will come a day when others will have no choice but to believe with you.

> *"Therefore I say unto you, What things whatsoever you desire, when ye pray, believe that ye receive them, and ye shall have them."*
> —Mark 11:24

 Create Your Day Planner

PLAN TO BE UNSTOPPABLE! Tonight or first thing tomorrow morning, plan your next day's activities by filling out your Create Your Day Planner (see Appendix). As you reflect on your progress, congratulate yourself for every step you've taken forward. Share your success, big and small, with a friend or your buddy. Be grateful for your progress, and know that you are continuing to tap into a Source that is driving you to live a life that has greater possibilities than you've known up until this point. Tomorrow, you'll continue your journey by learning a powerful tool that will enable you to permanently end the "giving up" cycle.

Something to Think About

Cathy Hughes, founder and chairperson of Radio One, the largest black-owned media company in the country, was turned down 32 times in her efforts to raise $1.5 million to fund her company. Her thirty-third presentation was to another woman. Before Cathy could finish her appeal, the banker had agreed to lend her the money. Radio One now has more than 50 radio stations around the country.

> *"Believe in yourself and there will come a day when others will have no choice but to believe with you."*
> —Cynthia Kersey

Day 5:
Facts Are the Enemy of Truth

Today's Affirmation: I have complete control over the meaning I attach to any situation and how I respond to it. Whenever I feel discouraged or am tempted to quit, I immediately stop and look at my disempowering interpretation of my situation. I recognize this as my voice of fear and acknowledge that it does not represent the truth of what's possible. I turn the belief around and create a new belief that moves me forward in a positive direction. I am unstoppable!

Life brings many challenges. Some challenges we expect; others blindside us. Some are hurdles, others skyscrapers. The "story," or meaning, we attach to these challenges will determine whether we stay in the game or throw in the towel—whether we make the changes we desire or settle and say to ourselves, "I didn't really want that anyway."

How you deal with challenges—during these 30 days and beyond—will determine whether you achieve your goal or give up and settle for less than you deserve. If we really want to create different results in our lives, we must become aware of how we interpret the "facts" or "events" of our lives and understand that our explanations often do not represent the "truth" of what's possible for us. In a very real sense, facts are an objective account of the event that occurred. No interpretation or meaning is attached. (For example: "I was rejected by a potential investor for my project;" "My husband left me;" "I lost my job;" "I was diagnosed with an illness;" "I can't get pregnant.") Truth represents what's possible in any situation. ("Each rejection brings me one step closer to an investor for my project;" "I will find a new, better relationship;" "I can find a better and more fulfilling career;" "My health will improve;" "I can adopt," and so on.)

Many people believe that events control their lives and that their circumstances have shaped who they are today. It's not true. It's not the events of our lives that shape us, but how we respond to those events, what we think they mean, and whether challenges trigger the "giving up" reflex in us or motivate us to hang tough and keep fighting.

Thousands of people have used the process outlined at the end of this chapter to effectively dispute their pessimistic beliefs and permanently change their internal language. It's crucial to develop and use this invaluable skill on a daily basis—sort of a daily unstoppability workout—because it helps us to look at the challenges we inevitably face in a new, productive light.

For example, a colleague told me about a man who had been diagnosed with a degenerative disease that would cause him to go blind in 6 months. After hearing the news, the man went into a great depression, believing that his blindness meant the end of his life. Even before he lost his eyesight, he killed himself. The fact of his coming blindness was so unbearable, it literally blinded him to the truth that his life could have even greater meaning. His *interpretation* of his condition was unrelentingly negative, and ultimately fatal.

On the other hand, there are people who react to events that would seem to cast a permanent black cloud over anyone's life by growing stronger and living more fully than ever before. In the next story, the catastrophic twist of fate that came into Sharon D'Eusanio's life wasn't nearly as strong as her ability to *interpret* it in a way that created amazing new possibilities for her.

Unstoppable Woman:
Sharon D'Eusanio's Story

Bad things happen to good people; that's an undeniable part of life. But when horror strikes good people from out of nowhere, the temptation is to ask "Why?" or to surrender to the weight of the disaster. Sharon knows all about sudden horror. But rather than surrender to the devastating power of a personal disaster, she responded with a fresh sense of optimism and a fierce will not to dwell on the bare facts of what she had lost, but to see the possibilities of a future redefined by a life-changing experience. Robbed of her sight, she learned to see with her heart.

A Shot in the Dark

As Sharon drove home one evening in May 1980, she was so exhausted from a long day that she didn't bother to look at the car that pulled up beside her. Her home and family were on her mind. So she never saw the man in the car—or the gun he pointed at her head. All she saw was a flash of light. Then . . . *nothing.* Sharon would never see anything again.

With blood streaming down her face, she managed to maneuver her car safely to the side of the road. In pitch darkness and raw panic, she screamed for help. It came in the form of a "good Samaritan" shouting, "My God! What happened to you?"

Sharon's supposed savior picked her up in his arms and carried her to the back seat of his car, and as they sped off, she assumed they were headed for the hospital. Instead, the man took Sharon to an apartment and threw her on a mattress. *He was the man who had shot her!* He stripped her, stabbed her repeatedly, and raped her broken and bloody body.

Ten hours later, Sharon lay mutilated and battered on the mattress. Assuming she was dead, her attacker left. She was alive, but barely.

When she heard his car drive away, she painfully dragged herself up and managed to make her way out of the apartment, screaming like crazy. A man heard her cries and said, "My God! What happened to you?" . . . the very same words her attacker had uttered just hours before. Sharon was terrified, but she had to make a choice. She decided to trust.

Thankfully, the Samaritan was real this time. He drove her straight to the hospital, where she began the fight of her life. But something had changed: She had looked death in the face and survived. And while a neurologist, an ophthalmologist, an internist, a cardiovascular surgeon, and a gynecologist worked to repair her battered body, she vowed that if she *did* live through this, she would have a full life, nothing less.

"I believed that *eventually* I would adjust to the loss of sight, and that I could live a happy and fulfilling life. As for the man who attacked me, he took 11 hours of my life. I was determined not to give him any more of my time. My time was precious and it belonged to me and my children."

Already, she was putting the "facts" of her situation—she was permanently blind—behind her, and embracing the "truth" that she could remake her life in any way she wanted from this point on.

Refusing to be a victim, Sharon played a key part in helping the police catch her assailant, a man who had already served a prison term for raping and stabbing a woman. There would be no repeat offense: Her attacker was convicted and sentenced to 104 years, with no parole for at least 30 years.

As Sharon's body grew stronger, she struggled to make a new life for herself and her three children. Regrets about her children were her most difficult obstacles and her only real indulgence in self-pity. "The most difficult aspect of my blindness to deal with was the loss of never seeing my children grow and change," she says. "I could no longer see my children's artwork. I would never have the opportunity to see my daughter grow into a woman and my boys into men. But I reminded them about how close they came to not having a mother at all. And that's been the focus—what is really important is that I'm still here."

Rough Waters

Ironically, adjusting to her loss of eyesight was only the first challenge Sharon would confront. Before she even came home from the hospital, she was fired from her job as an insurance adjuster. "They cleared out my desk while I was still in the hospital," she says. "All my years of experience and study was now rendered useless. I hd no career to go back to."

Then the other shoe dropped, hard. Tensions between Sharon and her husband of 10 years had been increasing ever since the attack. One of the first things he said to her when she arrived home from the hospital was, "I never knew how much I needed you." Not loved. *Needed*. He had relied on her to take care of him as well as the children—do the laundry, clean the house, and so on. Now he would have to share the burden.

He started complaining about his chores and about how difficult things were for *him*. Tensions continued to mount and finally a decision had to be made. She told him to leave.

Sharon said, "I was living alone with three small children (ages 10, 9, and 4), and I couldn't see." To make matters worse, her soon-to-be ex-husband decided that because Sharon was blind, she couldn't adequately care for the kids, so he took her to court to get custody. Oh, yes . . . he wanted the house, too.

On top of everything that had happened, this betrayal was just too much. For the first time, Sharon lost it and began to sob uncontrollably. *No one* was going to take her children away from her! After all she'd been through, there was no way she was going to back down. She met her ex-husband in court, beat him in a fair fight, and kept custody of her kids, the house, the mortgage, and all of the bills.

Relearning Everyday Living

Sharon assured her children that though things were not going to be easy, together they would make it. And make it they did, often through tears and laughter—one step at a time. Sharon realized she would have to relearn the everyday acts and tasks she had taken for granted when she was sighted. Simply walking around the house required careful memorization of the locations of all the furnishings, and every footstep demanded complete focus. Getting from room to room left her exhausted at day's end.

Brushing her teeth, she assumed, would be easy—until she grabbed a tube of ointment one day instead of toothpaste. Slowly, she taught herself to perform the most basic acts—showering, making the bed—without vision. She even learned her way around the kitchen again by feel, though the children would laugh when she left her fingerprints in the butter or the cream cheese.

With the kids' help, Sharon handled it all. Her boys read the daily mail to her and she enlisted the help of a friend each month to pay the bills. She relied on neighbors and a local taxicab service for transportation. For more challenging tasks, she found a friend or neighbor to provide assistance.

No Time for Rage and Fear

Then there was the question of income. Sharon was not going to be earning money as an insurance adjuster any time soon. But she took some comfort in knowing that the state of Florida had a Crimes Compensation Act to provide financial assistance to crime victims. Better yet, the victim advocate in Ft. Lauderdale had told her not to worry; in view of the heinousness of the crime, there would be no difficulty in securing the maximum amount of financial help.

Unfortunately, it wasn't that easy. The director of the bureau of the Crime Victim's Compensation in the Department of Labor ruled that she had not suffered "serious financial hardship" according to their definition, so she didn't conform to the section of the code that would have provided financial assistance. "How could they possibly say I didn't suffer serious financial hardship?" she questioned with amazement.

Despite the obstacles she faced, Sharon *knew* this hard time would pass and that she was building incredible reserves of strength, character, and resilience. She was certain that eventually new doors would open for her. Remarkably, she never interpreted all the horrors and hardships as anything more than temporary setbacks that would drive her to greater things. She decided that rage and fear were wastes of her time and energy. She was determined to do and be the best she could with what she had. Giving up was simply never an option.

The Door Opens Wide

Moment by moment, Sharon began to make it all work—*her* way. She stubbornly continued with her life as independently as possible, refusing to conform to anyone else's notion of what a woman who was blind or a crime victim should do. She attended school functions, took the children to the movies, baked cookies, sewed on buttons, and hemmed her kids' pants. And if the tissue box ended up in the freezer once in a while, so what?

Then, in 1981, author Dr. Wayne Dyer called her and told her he not only wanted to write a story about her for *Family Circle Magazine*, but he wanted her to speak at a woman's organization about her experience. She agreed, but, ironically, this woman, who had survived so much, was petrified about making a speech. After all, she couldn't exactly use note cards!

The day of the speech, she started with, "I'm the mother of three children and was a professional woman with a career. On May 23rd, 1980, everything changed." That was all she needed. The audience was captivated by her incredible story of violence and rejection, survival and triumph. Sharon told them that if *she* could survive and live life fully, so could other victims of terrible crimes. She challenged them to live their lives fully and not to give in to accepting less for themselves. After she finished, a crowd of women shared their stories of tragedy and told her that hearing her story made them feel less alone.

As a result of that speech, the door not only opened, it *flew* open. The next week, Sharon had three more talks scheduled. Before she knew it, a new career had begun. She became a strong advocate for victims' rights and in 1985 was honored by President Reagan for outstanding service on behalf of victims of crimes.

Along the way, Sharon found love again. On a blind date, she was introduced to Ray D'Eusanio, a man she vaguely remembered from her school days. They were married in 1995. "What happened to me gave me a broader perspective on life," she says. "It connected me with what's important. I became a better mother, a better person, and discovered a real connection with a partner who showed me true love and friendship. We would never have met if this hadn't happened."

A Future Filled with Possibilities

Today, Sharon works as Deputy Director for the Division for Victims' Services and Criminal Justice Programs for the Florida Attorney General. She has written a book, *Feel the Laughter*, and still travels around the country to more than 100 speaking engagements a year. She considers it her *responsibility* to help as many people as possible through her own experiences.

"After I was shot, I could have turned to drugs, alcohol, or suicide," she says. "But to me, life is precious. It was important for me to be here for my children and to experience what life has to offer." Sharon could have dwelt on her misfortunes and what she would miss in life, but she made a choice to instead focus on the possibilities that her present and her future offered.

One fateful night in May 1980, a young woman spent 10 hours in a darkness most of us cannot even imagine. But she lived to tell her story. And she continues to tell it. People may be horrified by the *facts* of what happened to Sharon D'Eusanio. But those who hear Sharon speak cannot help but be inspired by the *truth* of her life, which is that life is a precious gift to be treasured, and where there is life, there is *always* hope.

She would know.

*"I focus only on the things I can control. I can't change the past
and I can't predict the future. From the day you're born until the day
that you die, you will experience anything and everything that life has
to offer. It is up to you to decide what you are going to do with it.
You have the power to make the choice."*
—*Sharon D'Eusanio*

Unstoppable Action
Turn New Beliefs into Positive Results

Through all the punches life threw at her, Sharon D'Eusanio never gave up, even when it would have been perfectly understandable to do so. Instead, she created a new life of meaning and dignity for herself and her children. How? She didn't allow the "facts" about her life—she was blind, she had no job, and no husband—to define her life. Instead, she made the truth of her potential for finding new strength and helping others to change their lives become her defining force. Here's the difference:

Fact: Sharon's eyesight was gone. This changed how she maneuvered around the house, transported her children, paid her bills . . . virtually everything.

Truth: What is lost to adversity is based only on our *interpretation* of the event. For example, Sharon lost her ability to drive a car. But there are countless other ways to get around. With this interpretation, her world didn't end because she lost the ability to drive. Sharon decided that *she*, not her blindness, would determine her limits.

The lesson: How we *think* about adversity may defeat us before we ever act. With a disempowering interpretation of adversity, you may permit a "fact" to overwhelm you mentally before you even start to deal with it physically.

There is a way to fight disempowering beliefs. A great model to follow was developed by pioneeering psychologist Albert Ellis, one of the most influential psychologists of the 20th century. Mastering this technique can immediately change your life for the better and he suggests starting with your ABCs.

Learning Your ABCs

To discover your ABCs, you're going to again tap into your "Internal Caller ID." To start, you'll want to become aware of your "self-talk"—the thoughts and beliefs you silently say to yourself when faced with adversity.

Instead of immediately reacting to your situation, you'll learn to stop and identify—and change, if necessary—the belief you attach to the adversity. Your belief about your situation will determine your response—and the consequences that result.

Albert Ellis defined three parts to the ABC evaluation:

Adversity. Adversity is the actual event that transpired. Adversity can include events such as failing a test, rejection by a prospect, or a poor performance review at work. Adversity can also include events that didn't happen that caused you disappointment. For example, perhaps you didn't get a promotion, failed to follow through on a commitment, or fell short of achieving a specific result you anticipated. Some people regard these events as a dead end—game over. They were thwarted in their efforts or they made a mistake and that's it; the goal is unreachable. Others see barriers, reversals, or errors as the chance to meet a challenge, improve their skills, and get stronger.

During the remaining days of the challenge, when adversity strikes and you are temporarily stopped from taking your one step or you simply feel discouraged or frustrated, I want you to get out your notebook and write down the triggering event that happened—just the facts, *not* your evaluation of what happened. If the fifth prospect in a row hung up on you before you could state your sales pitch, that's what you write: "Fifth prospect in a row hung up on me." Don't write, "People are rude. I hate this job and will never make another sale." That's the meaning (belief) you attached to the event. A tip to help you objectively describe adversity is ask yourself, "How would a video camera capture this event?" A video camera would simply record the facts of the event without any emotion or judgment.

Belief. Your evaluation of this event triggers a belief. A belief is the interpretation, positive or negative, of the adversity. It's how we explain and interpret things that go wrong. When adversity finds us, our first reaction is to analyze it. It's our inner dialogue that asks, "Why did this happen?" "What did I do?" "What does this mean to me?" The answers to those questions affect *every* aspect of our decision-making. When you find yourself struggling with your interpretation of an event, get out your notebook and record your immediate feelings and interpretations about what happened. You might write, "I'm upset because they were so rude. I must not be a very good salesperson. I'll never make quota." Do you see how this type of interpretation creates no hope and the propensity to just quit?

Consequences. When we explain adversity with beliefs that are self-defeating and negative ("I am incompetent" or "I'll never change"), we give up. We stop striving, and paralysis sets in. But when our explanations and interpretations of adversity are thoughts like, "Well, I'll learn from that mistake and do better next time," we're empowered. Feelings lead to actions, and with empowering feelings come decisive, productive actions.

When you've encountered adversity during the challenge, I'd like you to use your journal to record the consequences you experienced. Write down not just your emotions, but the resulting behavior or action you took. Often, you'll have more than one feeling or action. That's fine. Write them all down. You might end up with, "I was discouraged, so I stopped making calls and turned on the television."

Disputing Your Beliefs

How do we replace limiting beliefs with empowering ones? We must dispute and question them and *not accept them as truth*. What would you do if a stranger suddenly appeared at your door and started shouting things like, "You're incompetent! You're a loser!" Would you sink to your knees and start sobbing in shame, crying, "You're right! You're right!"? Of course not. That's ridiculous. You'd assume the person was crazy and you'd slam the door. End of story.

But what happens when we say equally damning things to ourselves? We believe them, unequivocally. We don't question them. After all, if we say it, it must be true, right? Don't we know ourselves better than anyone else? Not necessarily. Limiting beliefs are nothing but our voice of fear. The saying, "We have met the enemy and the enemy is us" couldn't be more accurate. Our disempowering beliefs are not based on truth but originate from past experiences ranging from parental disapproval, a teacher's critique, or a friend's judgment. Yet we treat them like they're truth, written in stone.

When you tune in to your reactions to adversity, you'll be able to recognize when your explanations are leading you toward self-defeating behaviors. With this powerful new self-awareness, you can stop yourself, *dispute* your initial reaction, *analyze* it, and *discover* a new explanation that leads you toward positive action and greater motivation.

Consider the following example:

GOAL: I'll make five new sales this month.

ADVERSITY (Triggering Event): Ms. Prospect won't return my calls.	
BELIEF: (Disempowering Interpretation) I must have done something wrong to blow the sale or offend her.	NEW BELIEF: (Empowering Inerpretation) Maybe she's busy and doesn't have time to return my call. I can't control what she does, all I can do is the best I can and hope she's open to doing business. If not, NEXT. It's her loss.
CONSEQUENCES: I feel annoyed with the prospect and discouraged. I want to quit for the day and go have a Haagen-Dazs.	NEW CONSEQUENCES: I'm ready for the next call. I know it's a numbers game and my hard work will pay off.

Do you see the difference in the outcome when you change your story? Maintaining a self-defeating belief always results in unproductive outcomes. Once we realize that disempowering and self-defeating evaluations are never in our best interest, we can quickly dispute them and create a new outcome that moves us forward.

GOAL: I will lose 10 pounds this month.

ADVERSITY (Triggering Event): I followed my eating plan but didn't lose one pound this week.	
BELIEF: (Disempowering Interpretation) This is not working. I'm not geting any results. I *never* lose weight no matter what I do.	**NEW BELIEF: (Empowering Inerpretation)** I have already lost five pounds, so just because I didn't lose any more weight this week doesn't mean my plan isn't working. There is nothing wrong with me. My body is adjusting to my new eating plan, and I'll lose weight if I stick with it.
CONSEQUENCES: I'm discouraged and frustrated and feel like quitting. What's the use?	**NEW CONSEQUENCES:** I am excited about how I will look when I achieve my 30-day goal. I will stay with my plan because I know it will pay off. I am unstoppable!

The next time you're faced with a disempowering belief, try the following tips:

1. Turn around your disempowering belief and take the opposite position. How is this belief true or even more true than your original statement?
2. Question your beliefs:
   - Does this belief move me forward in the pursuit of my goal, or cause me to give up?
   - Does this belief improve my self-esteem or diminish me?
   - Is this belief helping me perform better, or stopping me?

With some practice, you'll learn to fight these negative habits of explanation and see your challenges in a new way—as temporary bumps in the road.

Complete your ABCs.

Now it's your turn. The next time you get stopped taking your "one step," think about what happened and fill in your ABC evaluation. Get out your notebook and copy the chart below or make a photocopy of the blank form on page 307. Then fill in the adversity, beliefs, and consequences you're experiencing. When you have recorded your ABCs, look over your beliefs carefully. You'll see that your own internal dialogue and pessimistic explanations caused you to feel helpless, dejected, and tempted to quit. Now dispute those beliefs. Come up with new explanations that will empower you to move forward. These new optimistic explanations will make the difference between staying in action and giving up.

My ABCs

ADVERSITY (Triggering Event):	
BELIEF: (Disempowering Interpretation)	NEW BELIEF: (Empowering Inerpretation)
CONSEQUENCES:	NEW CONSEQUENCES:

Use this tool whenever you get stopped or discouraged. There's always a story behind your feelings and actions. When you take the time to become aware of the meaning you give to adversity, you will be on the road to creating more and more unstoppable moments.

More important, you'll be well on the way to taking control of your mindset and changing the behaviors that have stopped you in the past. With these obstacles out of the way, you are clearing the path to even great success!"

"No matter how bad something is, it has a limit. It all depends on how long you're going to drag it out. No matter how good something is, that has a limit too, so you'd better get in the moment and enjoy it."
—*Kathy Buckley,* If You Could See What I Hear

Create Your Day Planner

PLAN TO BE UNSTOPPABLE! Tonight or first thing tomorrow morning, plan your next day's activities by filling out your Create Your Day Planner (see Appendix). Use the ABC tool with your buddy and talk about a time this week when you were stopped or discouraged. Help each other to identify the story and interpretation behind your feelings and actions. As you become more aware of the stories that stop you and develop the habit of disputing your self-blaming, defeatist reactions to adversity, you'll find your outcome changing from depression and passive helplessness to activity, energy, and empowerment.

Day 6:
"Girlfriend to Girlfriend:" Courage Is Its Own Reward

Today's Affirmation: I gain courage, strength, and confidence every time I take one step forward and do the thing I think I cannot do. I am unstoppable!

It takes courage to believe we can change, to take the first step, to try things that scare us and put ourselves into uncomfortable and uncharted territory, where we're faced with the possibility of looking foolish or failing.

Our actions may not appear to others to be courageous at all. But no one can measure courage at a glance. Others may not know where we've come from, or realize the internal fortitude required just to put ourselves out there. And what's easy for one person might take enormous courage for another. What's important is that we are courageous in our own eyes. Other people's opinions are none of our business.

Case in point: I was speaking at a conference in Cancun, Mexico, and brought my girlfriend, Denise, along for an extended vacation. We took a day trip to Chichén Itzá, the ancient city that was the pinnacle of Mayan civilization. One of the structures believed to be built before 800 A.D. is El Castillo, the tallest standing pyramid. People were making their way to the top of this 82-foot structure, and they said the view from the top was magnificent. From the ground, the climb didn't look *that* imposing. Besides, other people were doing it, so how hard could it be? Despite our reservations and fear of heights, we agreed to give it a go.

On the way up, it was a breeze. I ran ahead up the 91 steps on the face of the structure and wasn't even winded. The view was incredible, and you could see for miles. Getting down was another story. Clearly they didn't have building codes in 800 A.D., and consequently the steps were deep and very narrow. Worse yet, there were no ropes or rails to hold onto.

As I looked down seven stories, I became paralyzed. My sense of balance was completely off kilter, and I questioned the wisdom of our decision. My girlfriend was equally shaken, and we both realized that the only way we were going to make it down those seven stories was to sit on our butts and go down one step at a time. Despite the fact that we felt like idiots, we were more interested in getting down without injury.

On the way down, we saw a couple who coincidentally had seen me speak at a conference and had purchased a copy of my book. The man joked, "Look at Ms. Unstoppable now!" Focused on the situation at hand, I was too busy to respond. Later, I reflected on his comment and realized that to the undiscerning eye, I didn't look too unstoppable in that moment. But the truth of my circumstances revealed something different. It embodied *exactly* what it means to be unstoppable. Despite my fear of heights, I went to the top. It wasn't a pretty sight coming down, but I did it. I pushed myself beyond my comfort zone and didn't let my fear stop me.

Courage isn't limited to Herculean acts such as climbing the tallest mountain, running into a burning building to save a child, or being willing to take a bullet for the President. Most of us will never experience such feats.

Courage is in the everyday. It's found in the girl who's afraid of the water, yet gets in the pool to learn how to swim, or in the middle-aged person who returns to high school to learn how to read and write.

It takes courage to try things that scare us, to follow our hearts, and to stand for what we believe to be right. Sometimes courage requires sitting on our butts just to make it down the hill one step at a time. But rather than letting fear hold us back, we look it squarely in the eye and say we are bigger than our difficulties! And we move forward. It may not be pretty, but that's not what's most important. It's taking the first step that counts!

El Castillo

Congratulate yourself on the completion of this week. The first step is always the hardest and requires the most courage. Reflect on why you are participating in the Unstoppable Women Challenge and why you must continue taking the steps necessary to change your life. Each time we muster the courage to take a single step and follow the truth of who we are, we set our spirits free. And when that happens, nothing can stop us!

Day 7:
Week 1 in Review

Welcome to the end of Week 1. Congratulate yourself for taking action! If you are struggling *in any way*, don't be disheartened. You're not alone. In the beginning, it can feel daunting to make a change in life, even when we really want it. Many Unstoppable Women Challenge participants had struggles and were tempted to quit. After all, it's easier to move back into our old patterns of behavior, even when those behaviors ultimately create great pain in our lives.

But take heart. Those who hung in there and stayed with the process became aware of the behaviors that supported their efforts and those that didn't. Awareness is the first step toward change. As they modified their approach from week to week, they were able to identify better structures or resources to support their efforts. You can, too.

It's like learning to ride a bike. It can be a little rough initially, but once you develop the skill, it becomes automatic.

The Week in Review Form

Complete the Week in Review form (see Appendix). Be honest with yourself about your activity. Notice what types of things stopped you or threatened to stop you. Don't beat yourself up if you didn't do everything perfectly. Remember, this is about progress, *not* perfection! What is most important is that you're becoming aware of the things that stop you so that you can eliminate them and build momentum. In doing so, you will have developed a foundation over these 30 days that will serve you in making any change you desire.

Day 8:
Following Your Bliss Isn't Always Blissful

Today's Affirmation: I am in control of my actions and choose productive behaviors that move me forward. I continue to take action every day, even when results aren't immediately visible. I know that taking consistent action is one of the most important things I can do to change my life, and I will not stop until I achieve my goal. I deserve it! I am unstoppable.

You can have the drive of Madonna, the heart of Mother Teresa, or the charisma of Oprah Winfrey, but if you can't get yourself to do what is necessary every single day to accomplish the Unstoppable Women Challenge, your dreams will remain only dreams. Fortunately, you don't need the drive, heart, or charisma of those unstoppable women to achieve your 30-day goal. You do need to be willing to *consistently* take a single step.

Thousands of people have successfully completed my programs and not one has ever said to me, "Cynthia, I loved getting out of bed an hour earlier to plan my day," or "I couldn't wait to get on the phone and make those prospecting calls," or "The highlight of my day was going to the gym and working my butt off." Many times, that was the *last* thing they wanted to do. But it was the very thing they *had* to do to successfully meet their challenge and ultimately achieve the result they desired.

Too often, people express the desire to change, but they can't discipline themselves to follow through. They get discouraged and disappointed with themselves because they know what they need to do, but they can't seem to get themselves to do it.

We all have long-ingrained habits that are hard to break. But once we become aware of them, we can eliminate them. Recognizing them is critical, because if they go unidentified, they can become the saboteurs of our success.

For example, a woman who has unsuccessfully tried to lose 20 pounds might look at past behaviors that have impeded her success, such as mindlessly eating junk food while watching television, sleeping in and missing her workouts, or falling prey to the old "I'll start again on Monday" syndrome. These behaviors consistently stopped her from achieving her goal. The great news is that once she recognizes her disempowering behaviors, she can develop a structure to help her eliminate them once and for all and replace them with productive behaviors that will help her achieve her goal.

The following story about J. K. Rowling, author of the enormously popular *Harry Potter* books, illustrates this point beautifully. Though J. K. led a hard life of poverty before getting published, the pure pleasure she took in writing enabled her to consistently take action and keep writing, even when things looked bleak. Eventually, her passion led to her success.

Unstoppable Woman:
J. K. Rowling's Story

"You'll never make any money out of children's books, Jo." As inaccurate predictions about popular culture go, this one rivals the infamous "guitar groups are out" line a record executive laid on the then-unknown Beatles. Because "Jo" was the English writer Joanne Kathleen Rowling—J. K. Rowling to millions of devoted readers, author of the mega-best-selling *Harry Potter* books.

The story sums up the mountains she had to climb—poverty, broken relationships, and the persistent doubts of others—to follow her passion and make a living in the only career she'd ever wanted: writing.

Of course, no one could have known the degree of unwavering belief and absolute determination J. K. would need to follow her bliss through rejection and depression. Those qualities enabled her to persevere through the tough times, even though circumstances conspired to drag her down. In fact, J. K.'s passion became her unquenchable hope for a better future.

A Love of Writing Since Day One

J. K. recalls writing down stories as early as age five or six. Her first one was about a rabbit that came down with the measles. "Ever since, I wanted to be a writer, although I rarely told anyone so. I was afraid they'd tell me I didn't have a hope," she says.

At 26, J. K. moved to Portugal, where she taught English. She loved it, in part because her schedule finally gave her time to write a story she couldn't get out of her head. During a rail trip in England, she had a vision of a train transporting a boy to a boarding school for wizards. "I had been writing almost continuously since the age of six but I had never been so excited about an idea before." To her enormous frustration, she didn't have a working pen and was too shy to borrow one from a fellow passenger, so she had to rely on her vivid imagination for 4 days. When she got home, she started to write *Philosopher's Stone*.

Sadly, on the heels of this revelation, J. K.'s mother, Anne, died suddenly at age 45. Rowling's response shows how embracing pain and grief can infuse one's work with greater richness. She channeled her sadness into the *Harry Potter and the Philosopher's Stone* (its British title) chapter "The Mirror of Erised." The Mirror of Erised reflects what you most wish to see, and Harry sees his dead mother smiling and crying at the same time.

From a Dark Place, a Brilliant Tale

Shortly after her mother's death, J. K. married a journalist named Jorge. A few months after the birth of their daughter, Jessica,the marriage ended. J. K. left with a 4-month-old child tucked under one arm and the ever-growing Harry Potter manuscript tucked under the other.

They lived with friends until she get an apartment and found a one-bedroom flat in the Scottish capital of Edinburgh, living on furniture lent by her sister and some friends. She declined offers to go out at night with friends and stayed home with Jessica, writing in her apartment. Without a typewriter or computer, she wrote and rewrote in longhand. Here she would complete *Harry Potter and the Philosopher's Stone*.

On just $103.50 a week, J. K. could barely make ends meet, and she sank into deep depression. But astonishingly, as she had done with her grief over her mother's death, J. K. directed her despair into her work, easing her own pain and adding new levels of resonance and meaning to her writing. From this personal darkness came a new group of fictional characters: the Dementors, the prison guards of Azkaban, who possess the power to suck the happiness out of people. Despite the odds, J. K. was able to use her despair to fuel new ideas and provide new energy.

What J. K. needed was a warm, friendly place to write. She got it at a neighborhood café called Nicolson's. Waiters left her alone as she wrote while Jessica slept. Eager to finish the book and attempt to get it published, J. K. wrote every available moment. "Sometimes I actually hated the book, even while I loved it."

The Story Works Its Magic

Finally, six years after she first had the inspiration, J. K. finished *Harry Potter and the Philosopher's Stone* and sent the first three chapters to two agents. (With no money for copying, she actually typed the complete book twice!)

The first rejection came quickly in the form of a letter. J. K. forced herself not to be discouraged. She believed in Harry Potter, both as a character and as a symbol for her own unbeatable spirit. So she waited for the second rejection, unaware that forces were working on her behalf. She had sent her second manuscript to Christopher Little. The agent's assistant, about to go home for the day, was drawn to the manuscript lying in the rejection pile because of its unusual black plastic folder. A lover of children's literature, she took it home and fell in love with it. The next day, she gave it to Little and insisted that he read it.

Little quickly sent J. K. a letter asking for the balance of the manuscript on an exclusive basis. When she got the letter, she was overcome by joy. "It was far and away the best letter I had ever received in my life, and it was only two sentences long," she says.

She had an agent. Now she needed a publisher, and Little sent the manuscript to 12 of them. J. K. was forced to develop a thick skin as week after week, the rejections trickled in. Then publisher number 12, Barry Cunningham of Bloomsbury Publishing, made an offer, a relative pittance for which J. K. couldn't have been more grateful.

A Star Is Born from a Writer's Passion

Finally, in June 1997, *Harry Potter and the Sorcerer's Stone* was published. The initial print run was just 500 copies. Still, J. K. was so excited that she spent the whole day walking around Edinburgh with the book tucked under her arm. This was the culmination of her passion for storytelling, a love of writing fueled not by the desire to be rich, but by the drive to tell wonderful stories about unforgettable characters. If she had remained a low-profile author and a part-time teacher, she would have been very happy.

However, within three days of publication, the American rights to the book sold to Scholastic Books. This changed everything. The book was published in September 1998 and reached #16 on the *New York Times* bestseller list by December 1988. To date, it is estimated but unconfirmed that worldwide sales figures of the Harry Potter books is approximately 260 million copies and they have been translated into 62 languages.

Today, J. K. Rowling is said to be wealthier than the Queen of England and the toast of children's literature. I'm sure she can't help but reflect on her publishers' advice—"You'll never make any money out of children's books"—with a smile. Maybe someday she'll have that prediction engraved on a plaque to hang in her home, along with another piece of advice: Never, ever let go of your dream!

Unstoppable Action
Replace Unproductive Behaviors
with Productive and Empowering Behaviors

J. K. Rowling's experience proves the old saying that determination is all-powerful. Aside from talent, she had a burning need to tell a story, a story that would not stay untold. So committed was she to telling that story that she consistently took action, enduring many hardships just so she could write. And the results can hardly be argued with!

Consistent action in the face of hardships and seemingly little progress enabled Rowling to achieve a life-long passion. As you progress with your Unstoppable Women Challenge, it's important to identify the behaviors that stop you from taking consistent action on your goals.

Identify Your Unproductive Behaviors

Spend some time thinking about what has stopped you in the past. The behaviors that come to mind will probably not surprise you. Chances are, you've been dealing with the same patterns over and over again. The great news is that you can develop a structure to help you eliminate them once and for all.

To help you get started thinking about the behaviors that are holding you back, here are some common behaviors that have stopped other Unstoppable Women Challenge participants:

GOAL	BEHAVIOR THAT HAS HELD ME BACK
Exercise 5 days a week	Slept in too late and didn't work out.
Create and stay within a budget	Spent money on insignificant items
Save $100 a week	Spent too much money daily on coffee

Lose 10 pounds	Ate junk food in the evenings
Integrate more "balance" in my life	Worked constantly and took no time off
Write an outline for my book	Didn't schedule the time in my calendar to focus on the outline

Sometimes, our limiting behaviors may seem harmless—perhaps they're simply a form of procrastination, a failure to do something rather than an outright action that works against your goal. Do you procrastinate in any of the following ways?

- Talking too long on the phone
- Spending hours playing computer games or surfing the Web
- Incessantly preparing and not taking action
- Inability to say "no" to the things that don't move you forward
- Not having a clear objective
- Not planning your day
- Failing to ask for help
- Waiting until late to do daily tasks, thus being so tired that you risk not following through
- Disorganized office
- Focusing on unproductive tasks

Write down the three behaviors that have stopped you in the past or that are currently getting in the way of you achieving your breakthrough goal.

What behaviors have stopped me from following through on my goal?

1. _____

2. _____

3. _____

Use Pain as Leverage

The will to continue, to persevere, even when results don't immediately happen, is one of the most important qualities in changing our lives. Fortunately, there are powerful motivators to fortify our commitment: pain and pleasure. The behaviors you link to pain and pleasure in your Unstoppable Women Challenge will determine your results.

In his book *Awaken the Giant Within*, Anthony Robbins states, "We are not random creatures; everything we do, we do for a reason. We may not be aware of the reason consciously, but there is undoubtedly a single driving force behind all human behavior. This force impacts every facet of our lives from our relationships and finances to our bodies and brains. Pain and Pleasure. Everything you and I do, we either do out of our need to avoid pain or our desire to gain pleasure. And what we link pain and pleasure to will shape our destiny."

For example, one of the biggest reasons diets rarely work is that we're pitting our desire to be thin against the pain of giving up our favorite "comfort" foods. Pain always wins. So to make a long-term change and lose weight, we've got to reprogram ourselves to associate pain with *giving in* to those fattening foods, and pleasure with eating healthy foods. Fit people will tell you nothing tastes as good as being thin feels. That is a great example of linking pleasure to feeling thin versus the short term payoff of tasty food.

By changing in our minds what we link pain and pleasure to, we can immediately change our behaviors. In doing so, we are in control of our actions and not the other way around.

✎ Identify the consequences of continuing your unproductive behaviors.

On the lines below, list three consequences of continuing your unproductive habits or behaviors. The more pain you can identify, the stronger the leverage you will create to eliminate these behaviors, which are stopping you from making real change in your life.

CONSEQUENCES: USING PAIN AS LEVERAGE

1. _____

2. _____

3. _____

As humans, we are more motivated to avoid pain than to gain pleasure, so develop a full understanding of the consequences you'll experience if you fail to take the necessary actions each day to make your goal happen. When we change the things that bring us pain and pleasure, we'll change the way we live.

Replace Unproductive Behaviors with Productive and Empowering Behaviors

Once you've identified the behaviors that have stopped you in the past, and the cost of continuing those behaviors, the next step is to identify new behaviors that will support you in achieving your goal. Take some time to brainstorm very specific behaviors you can incorporate into your life that will move you forward, step by step.

You will not be able to incorporate every new behavior at once. And that's okay. This is a process. Start with one behavior and do it consistently. Then add another productive behavior. In no time, you will consistently be engaged in behaviors that support the results you want to create.

WHAT BEHAVIORS STOPPED ME IN THE PAST?	WHAT BEHAVIORS DO I NEED TO ACHIEVE MY GOAL?
GOAL: Exercise 5 days a week	
Sleeping in too late and missing my workout	Go to bed an hour earlier the evenings before my workout

GOAL: Create and stay within a budget	
Spending money on insignificant items	Limit spending to $50 per week

GOAL: Save $100 a week	
Spending too much money on coffee	Reduce to 2 times per week

GOAL: Lose 10 pounds	
Eating junk food in the evenings	Plan a healthful evening snack

GOAL: Integrate more "balance" in my life	
Working constantly and taking no time off	Schedule time off for activities I enjoy

GOAL: Write an outline for my book	
Not scheduling the time in my calendar to focus on the outline	Schedule 1 hour each day to write and don't accept any interruptions during this hour

If procrastination tends to be your problem, consider the following examples of positive behaviors that can move you into action:

- Focus on priorities first thing in the morning
- Tackle the most difficult issues first
- Carry work with you so that you can be productive when free moments occur, such as when you're waiting to pick up your children or sitting at the doctor's office
- Don't take phone calls in the morning until your priorities are complete

- Go to sleep earlier so that you wake up rested and ready to start your day
- Plan your day just like a job

✎ Write down the three new behaviors you will do to support your breakthrough goal.

WHAT BEHAVIORS DO I NEED TO ADOPT TO ACHIEVE MY BREAKTHROUGH GOAL?

1._____

2._____

3._____

📖 Create Your Day Planner

PLAN TO BE UNSTOPPABLE! Tonight or first thing tomorrow morning, plan your next day's activities by filling out your Create Your Day Planner (see Appendix). Spend a few minutes today talking with your buddy about the behaviors you've both identified in yourselves that are holding you back. Then brainstorm productive behaviors you can immediately incorporate into your life. Be sure to compliment your buddy when she follows through in the days ahead!

Day 9:
Focus on Progress, Not Perfection!

Today's Affirmation: I congratulate myself each time I take a single step forward and acknowledge the progress I am making. Perfection is not my goal. It's progress. If I have an off day, I simply become aware of the behaviors or beliefs that got me off track, make adjustments for tomorrow, forgive myself, and move forward. I will not settle. I am my greatest fan! I am unstoppable.

It's an old saying, but absolutely right: Nobody's perfect. The common link among all the women whose stories are in this book is that they made mistakes—they struggled, had setbacks and failures, they tripped and stumbled—but (and this is the key) they pulled themselves up, kept on going, and learned from their mistakes.

A wise person once said that we learn more from our mistakes than we ever can from our successes. That's true. With the Unstoppable Women Challenge, perfection isn't the goal. It's *progress*. Try thinking of the Challenge as a metaphor for your life. The behaviors and beliefs that have stopped you in the past will most certainly reappear during this program. That's a good thing, because awareness is the first step toward change and ultimate freedom.

Through the process of completing each step over 30 days, you'll develop the qualities and strength you need to break old habits and create new empowering ones, giving you the strength and focus to stay on your path until you reach your goals. Along the way, you'll make mistakes. And that's okay. Remember, this is a process, one in which the journey is just as important as the destination.

The next unstoppable woman you'll read about is living proof that making progress every day and not worrying about being perfect along the way is a sound strategy for reaching your goals. Millions of people feel like they "have a book inside them," but few ever put a single word to paper. Why? It could be that they're worried about not being the second coming of Hemingway or Anne Rice—worried about not being perfect. So instead, they never take action and their dreams never become a reality.

That description does not apply to Karen Quinones. She had never thought about writing a book, but when a voice inside her (and her daughter) told her to, she listened. It took her life savings and a leap of faith to self-publish her work, but today she has a bestseller and a new mission in life.

Unstoppable Woman:
Karen Quinones Miller's Story

Karen and her 11-year-old daughter, Camille, were watching the movie *Set It Off* starring Jada Pinkett Smith. After the movie ended, Camille said to Karen, "Jada Pinkett is so pretty and she's married to Will Smith. They're the black king and queen of Hollywood. I'm wondering why they don't make a movie together. Someone should write a book and they should make the movie. Mom, why don't you write the book?"

"To quiet her so I could get some rest I said, 'Okay, I'll write the book, now go to bed,'" says Karen.

Role Reversal
In the morning, Camille asked Karen if she had started the book. Karen was shocked. "I had never considered writing a book, and especially not a novel," she says. "But my daughter was so persistent, I thought what the heck. Let me give it a try."

So Karen started the book, and instead of her taking Camille to the skating rink and fulfilling other mom tasks, Camille waited on her mother. "She stayed home at night and cooked for me while I worked on my book and she never once complained," says Karen.

Two months later, the book, *Satin Doll*, was finished. Camille was thrilled, and when Karen read what she'd written, she was completely shocked that it had turned out so well. She decided she needed to get it published.

Some Agents Rejected Her Twice
So Karen read everything about publishing she could get her hands on and learned how to write a query letter to agents. "Instead of sending one letter, I decided to send 35 at the same time so I could pick and choose which one *I* wanted," she says, amused by her own naiveté. "I got 50 rejections—some agents rejected me twice!"

But Karen was not to be deterred. It dawned on her that she should self-publish the book. "Camille loved the idea," she says. "I went to Borders and bought every book on self-publishing."

Karen ordered 3,000 copies of her book from a printer, spending her savings, and even money from her pension plan. "My brother thought I was completely out of my mind, but he ended up loaning me several thousand dollars," she says. "I was a single mother supporting my daughter alone, so my friends were appalled."

Karen's colleagues were equally stunned. She was a reporter for the *Philadelphia Inquirer*, one of the top 10 newspapers in the country, a newspaper where journalists aspire to work. She was a professional writer—she was supposed to find a publisher, not go the do-it-yourself route.

"One of my mentoring editors took me in her office and in a kind, motherly fashion said, 'Karen, why are you doing this? Do you know how hard it is to self-publish a book? I don't think it's a good idea, and I love you and respect you too much to not tell you the truth. And I don't ever want you to feel ashamed if it doesn't work out. I want you to know if there's anything you need, you can count on me.'"

While she was touched by the sentiment, Karen couldn't understand why everyone thought it would be so impossible. "I felt it would be hard work, but it never occurred to me that it wouldn't work."

Ignorance Is Bliss?
Then she started meeting other self-published authors. "The look on their face when I told them I was printing 3,000 copies was sheer horror," she says. "They said 'There's no way you can sell 3,000 books in a year'. I thought, 'In a year? I want to sell 3,000 copies in three months.' In my case, ignorance was bliss. Had I known that the average book only sells 3,000 books in a lifetime, I would have never self-published."

Karen had never sold anything in her entire life, not even lemonade or a Girl Scout cookie, and she started to realize the enormity of the challenge.

Desperate to make her money back, Karen took a leave of absence from her job to start selling her book. She and Camille started making flyers and doing whatever they could to promote the book. "I had one of those really slow printers, so we put it on a timer," she says. "The printer held only 150 pages so Camille would put in the first load at 9:30 P.M. before she went to bed. I'd set my alarm and at 11:30 put in another 150 pages, and then at 1:30 A.M. Camille would get up and put in another 150. At 3:30 in the morning we'd both get up, take the flyers, and hit the streets. She took one side of the street and I'd take the other."

When Camille invited friends to come to the house for a sleepover, Karen would put them to work distributing flyers. As the money ran out and she started borrowing from Camille's college fund, the two of them would dress in identical suits and take their press kit to every bookstore in Philadelphia.

Hot Off the Presses

Karen got orders from every bookstore, 300 in all before the book had been printed. This fired her up even more. But then, as if to prove the self-publishing doomsayers right, disaster struck.

"By December 7, we had our book in hand and had our launch party," Karen relates. "There was only one problem. Before *Satin Doll* went to press, I had it edited and proofed twice. But when I took the first book out of the box, my heart sunk. I had sent the unproofed edition to the printer. I now had 3,000 books filled with typos. The last line of the entire book even had words transposed."

Karen was devastated. "I realized that I could give up or just suck it up. I sold those books anyway and people would say, 'Karen, your book has a lot of typos.' "I said 'I know, and I'm fixing it for the next printing.'"

Karen and Camille laminated flyers and put them everywhere. They put laminated posters everywhere outside the bookstores—utility poles, telephone booths, on each side of the inside of the booth, even inside newspapers. They made bookmarks, went to the bookstores, and while Camille acted as lookout, Karen put a bookmark in every single African American fiction book in the store. "I even moved my book to the *New York Times* bestseller display," she says. "I did everything I could think of."

Finally, the Payoff

Slowly, steadily, all Karen's risk taking and tireless work started to pay off. "Within six weeks, we sold all 3,000 books," she says. "Then we started getting calls from publishers. Random House offered $10,000 for two books. I declined. Then Simon & Schuster called and offered $57,000 for *Satin Doll* and a second book. I told them I had to speak with my business manager. I asked Camille what she thought and she said we should hold out a little bit. So I took her advice and waited."

Two days later, Karen got an e-mail from an agent who had turned her down twice. The agent had heard two editors talking about *Satin Doll* at a party and that they thought they could get it for under $60,000. The agent suggested that Karen hire an agent quick. "I e-mailed her back and said 'You're hired,'" Karen says. "By the time we got our contract straight, there were so many publishers interested that we had to hold an auction."

Ironically, the day of the auction, Karen had her electricity turned off for lack of payment, and was on her way to pay the gas bill so they wouldn't turn that off.

In the end, *Satin Doll* sold to Simon & Schuster for $165,000. "They published my second novel, *I'm Telling*, and *Satin Doll* went on to become a best seller," says Karen. "I just signed a contract for my fifth and sixth books. Camille is 17 years old and wants to go to college next year and major in films so she can produce *Satin Doll*."

Not bad for the author nobody wanted.

*"When someone tells you 'No,' it just means they don't share
your vision. When you hear 'No' (and you will), you can't take it
personally. It's just one more opportunity for you to rise above the obstacles.
Life isn't perfect, and you don't have to be perfect, either. You just have
to be committed, passionate and persistent."*
—*Karen Quinones Miller*

⌦ Unstoppable Action ⌦
Reward Yourself

No one can follow each step of the Unstoppable Women Challenge perfectly. Life happens. So if one day you're not perfect, that's okay. There's always tomorrow. Each day notice what you're doing right and how you can improve, versus beating yourself up for areas where you have fallen short. Instead of being your own harshest critic, make the decision to be your biggest fan. Focus on the daily activities that moved you forward, and give yourself a pat on the back the moment you take a positive action or a step in the right direction. Call your buddy or another friend and share your success. Just be sure that the person you share it with is someone who will show enthusiasm and support you in your victory. Revel in the great feelings that come when you honor yourself by sticking with your commitments.

If you find ways to reward yourself when you reach milestones in your Unstoppable Women Challenge, you'll be more likely to stay in action. I've seen this time and time again with the women I've coached. When you have something to work toward, even if it's a daily reward consisting of a nice cup of coffee while reading something you enjoy, you're more likely to push yourself and stay disciplined. And let's face it—we all deserve a reward!

When I was training for a marathon, each Saturday my training group took our long runs. I always scheduled a massage immediately after the run. When I was running those seemingly endless miles, I knew that relief for my aching muscles was only hours away.

✎ Identify ways to reward yourself for meeting your goals.
Take some time to think about ways you can reward yourself for staying the course and meeting your goals, day by day. Don't overlook this stage—you've earned it! For single victories each day, give yourself small rewards, such as a phone call to a friend, a favorite snack, listening to a CD that you love, or renting a great movie. Rejoice in bigger rewards—dinner with a friend, going to the theater, or getting a massage—to celebrate weekly or bi-weekly milestones.

And remember, the single greatest reward you'll earn is the person you become in the process. Time after time, people have told me that the *process* is what changed their lives. For the first time, they knew what they wanted, developed a plan, and took action to achieve their goals. Who they have *become*—more confident and self-aware individuals—has been their ultimate reward.

To get you started, here are some ideas for immediate, weekly, and long-term rewards, many of which come from Unstoppable Women Challenge participants:

Immediate rewards:
- Place a gold star on my planner when I've completed an action
- Each day, put a dollar in my "play jar"
- Call my buddy for kudos
- Walk along the ocean by myself for an hour
- Curl up with a really good book or novel
- Take myself to a movie
- Have a long soak in the bathtub

Weekly rewards:
- Spend some quality time with my two nieces and appreciate their youth, spirit, and view of the world
- Take a nap on Saturday afternoon
- Go to lunch with one of my amazing friends
- Make a long-distance call to a friend
- Buy myself new nail polish and do my nails, even if I'm house painting the next day
- Sleep in
- Read my favorite magazine
- Rent a movie and make popcorn
- Buy flowers for myself
- Go for a sauna
- Take a dance lesson

End of challenge rewards:
- Get a facial and massage
- Go to a concert, play, or festival
- Buy something to improve my home
- Buy new clothes
- Throw a celebration with my buddy
- Go away for the weekend
- Test drive my favorite car

REWARDS: USING PLEASURE AS LEVERAGE
Daily Reward

- _____
- _____
- _____

Weekly Reward

- _____
- _____
- _____

End of Challenge Reward

- _____
- _____
- _____

Make your reward a surprise. One Unstoppable Women Challenge participant wrote 20 rewards on 3 × 5 cards, placed each in a sealed envelope, and then put them into a decorative "reward" box. When she completed a difficult task, she picked an envelope out of the box, not knowing what the reward would be.

Create Your Day Planner

PLAN TO BE UNSTOPPABLE! Tonight or first thing tomorrow morning, plan your next day's activities by filling out your Create Your Day Planner (see Appendix). Be sure to record your day's Unstoppable Victory—and then reward yourself for it! Remember that the pleasure you'll associate with completing your daily actions will propel you to become even more unstoppable.

Day 10:
Act Your Way into a New Way of Being

Today's Affirmation: Every time I take a single step toward the achievement of my 30-day goal, I build momentum and develop a success imprint in my psyche that strengthens my self-esteem and reinforces the belief that I can do it again in the future. By acknowledging and celebrating my daily victories, I reinforce the Truth that I am worthy and capable of creating the life and the results I deserve. I am confident. I am capable. I am unstoppable.

Self-esteem expert Nathaniel Branden defines self-esteem as the "reputation we acquire with ourselves." He further writes in *The Power of Self-Esteem* that "self-esteem is the confidence in our right to be happy, the feeling of being worthy, deserving, entitled to assert our needs and wants and to enjoy the fruits of our efforts." Self-esteem and self-confidence are clearly the most important characteristics of an unstoppable woman.

Unfortunately, research proves that women of all ages and backgrounds struggle with a lack of self-confidence. A survey performed by *New Woman* magazine revealed that 42 percent of men had high levels of self-esteem, compared with 34 percent of women. A closer look at the survey shows that while many of the women surveyed were successful high achievers, they still had lower self-esteem than men. Low self-esteem is widespread even among women at the top levels of corporations and the entertainment field.

Often, though, a diminished self-confidence impacts women's ability to procure top-paying, sought-after positions. Diedra Landrum worked with hundreds of clients as a career counselor and she observed, "Women often understated or minimized their abilities, training, and accomplishments while men often overstated theirs. I'd have to pump the women up in terms of their image of themselves and former achievements even though they were clearly qualified for a position. In contrast, men overstated their accomplishments, as if confident they could live up to the increased expectations."

Self-confidence is the mental strength that allows us to excel and not give up when we face life's obstacles. If we want to be unstoppable in achieving any result or making significant changes in our lives, we need a healthy dose of self-confidence.

Is it possible to raise our self-esteem in adulthood? Absolutely! And it starts by regularly communicating confidence to ourselves. A good analogy is hammering a long nail. One hit is not enough. To raise our self-confidence, we need to hammer at it over and over, consistently reinforcing any success that we experience. When reinforcing our achievements time after time, we become convinced that anything is possible.

The story of Dorothy White demonstrates the step-by-step growth of a woman's self-confidence—from someone uncertain of her own skills and abilities, to someone who felt she could achieve success in a small home-based business, to someone who became a leader and entrepreneur by building a thriving company with her own two hands. She's proof that our greatest obstacle to unstoppable confidence rests between our own ears and that if we take the bold step to venture into the unknown and reinforce each success, nothing can stop us!

Unstoppable Woman:
Dorothy White's Story

If there's a tougher, more backbreaking job than cleaning houses, it's picking cotton. Dorothy White has done both. As a child in southern Georgia, she spent many of her days just as her mother, father, and siblings did—picking cotton under the hot summer sun. Even then, she was learning to be a perfectionist. "I would come home crying because everybody picked more cotton than me," says Dorothy. "And my daddy said, 'Are you picking your row clean? Don't worry about what the others are doing. Take one row at a time and make sure you clean your row.'" It was advice that would serve her well.

Years later, she and her husband Jim were raising three children and Dorothy was content as a housewife. But when Jim became ill and couldn't work, she worried that they wouldn't be able to feed their family. Dorothy had no college degree, no office skills, no job experience, and perhaps worst of all, no confidence that she could earn a living for her family. But her faith gave her perspective.

"I was happy staying at home and raising my kids," she says. "But God never gives you more than you can handle. I needed to get serious about a profession." This was a turning point in her life, and she knew it. She *had* to find the confidence to make things work for her family.

A Clean Start

Dorothy did have one skill: She could clean like the dickens. It was something she'd done since she was a child, and over the years she had honed her skills. It was a logical next step to try to turn her house-cleaning skills into a business. She got hired by a cleaning service and spent three days in a personal "boot camp," absorbing every detail of how the experienced maids did their jobs. She took note of the products they used and asked endless questions.

Ready to strike out on her own, Dorothy responded to a classified ad for a cleaning lady. When she arrived, she was shocked to find herself in competition with four or five large cleaning companies. Assuming she would lose out to the bigger companies, she gave the homeowner her phone number and said, "I don't have a company, but one thing I know how to do is clean. If these people don't work out the way you want them to, give me a call and I'll come in and clean your house."

A few weeks later, the homeowner called and asked Dorothy if she was still available. The company she had hired had merely done a surface cleaning that was cursory and sloppy. This was Dorothy's chance to prove to her first customer that she had made the right choice.

A Surgeon at Work
Dorothy spent the next 8 hours scouring, scrubbing, and sweeping. It wasn't enough for her to simply *do her job*. She cleaned that house like the Lord Himself was supervising.

Dorothy scoured sinks, scrubbed the grout with a toothbrush, and made every surface gleam until you could see your reflection in it. Dorothy viewed her work as a reflection of her character and she took no shortcuts.

When the homeowner returned, she was stunned. The entire house was immaculate. Dorothy had even found long-lost watches and missing jewelry while cleaning behind stoves or underneath couches.

Impressed, the woman asked Dorothy what she charged. Dorothy told her $20. Shocked, the woman told her $20 wasn't enough, and asked a neighbor's opinion. The neighbor, who was equally impressed, said she paid her cleaning person $45 but didn't get anywhere near the results. Dorothy won over two new clients that day, and eventually all eight homes in the cul-de-sac. What was second nature to Dorothy White was the secret to all successful businesses: Work hard and do a great job, and you'll secure a loyal customer base that will do your marketing for you.

Booming Business
Slowly, the word spread. Dorothy was building a reputation as the cleaning lady who exceeded all expectations, who wouldn't leave a house until

it was spotless. Soon realtors were hiring Dorothy whenever they wanted to showcase a home. Her client list expanded, and after a year, Jim pointed out that she was running a business. She was incredulous. "A business?" she said. "I'm just cleaning. I'm just trying to make ends meet. I don't know anything about a business."

But she *was* running a business, and her reputation was growing faster than she could wash a window. She needed an accountant and a name. The perfect name came when she was cleaning a home while some teenagers were hanging around. One of them called her "the miracle lady," and she decided to name her company Miracle Services, Inc.

Next, she decided it was time to expand her business. She hired a three-person staff and they all cleaned as a unit. She picked them up in a van and they worked together, side-by-side, though Dorothy always took the toughest rooms herself to show the new recruits how it was done.

With her expansion came the need for Dorothy to start officially marketing her business. She could no longer rely just on word of mouth. She got a neighbor with nice handwriting to write the flyers and then organized her kids into "marketing teams" to distribute the flyers.

In 1983, one of her clients asked her to clean his office building. She accepted the challenge and was amazed at how much easier they were to clean than homes. "We could clean an office in a fraction of the amount of time and didn't have to worry about working around the family. No one was around."

Dorothy was hooked and wanted to pursue the lucrative business market, but admits she was shy about selling herself. She overcame her fear by just doing it, with the gentle nudging of her husband. Dorothy made countless phone calls, but kept getting stuck in an endless voice mail loop. So she and Jim decided she should take to the streets, to talk to the managers of the government offices in person.

They got a map of Washington, D.C., marked the likely prospects with red dots, and hit the rainy streets of the capitol in their old Ford station wagon. But Dorothy had her doubts about this strategy. Ever unsure how others would see her, she was convinced she'd look silly walking into some bureaucrat's office, soaking wet from the rain on a day when no sensible person would be outside, asking to clean their building. But Jim, always sensible and confident in his wife's abilities, set her straight. "Honey, I've been a salesman for years. This is the *perfect* time to look for business because no one else will be out there. You'll be great!" Armed with an umbrella and a briefcase, Dorothy began knocking on doors. And the more doors she knocked on, the more confident she became.

Time proved Jim right. When she was approved for government contracts, Dorothy White got work cleaning major buildings all over Washington, D.C.

Confidence from Self-Knowledge

Dorothy is frequently asked, "How did you develop all your confidence?" She answers, "Confidence grows when you do a job well and you do your best. I wasn't concerned about my competition. I knew what I could do and I made a great business by cleaning up after their mess. Every day, I strived to be better." By 1984, she and her crews were cleaning over 150 homes.

With her confidence sky-high, she decided to pursue big commercial contracts full-time. She and Jim soon discovered that it was her personality that got her many of her largest corporate clients. Always conscious of her lack of education, Dorothy learned it didn't matter. "I used to believe that my lack of education was a disadvantage. I now realize that my success has nothing to do with education. It has everything to do with my drive to do my best, to treat others with respect, and to be likeable." This philosophy helped Dorothy get the business of corporations like General Electric and Kraft.

Challenges and Rewards

The business boom came with some growing pains. Dorothy realized how little she knew about running a business—how to submit a bid, deal with liability, get insurance for her employees, and much more. She knew nothing about payroll, taxes, the IRS, worker's comp, and myriad other business matters. "I feared that I had taken on more than I could handle. I was just a simple cleaning woman, not the head of a company."

Faced with these challenges, Dorothy realized how she had developed her confidence in the first place, when she saw that she didn't have to compete with anyone else's education or knowledge. "I focused on working harder and longer than my competition and each day I sought out information that I needed to get better at running my business."

Her business thrived—and others took notice. In 1989, Dorothy won a Governor's Citation from the State of Maryland. Later, she won the Minority Entrepreneur of the Year Award from the U.S. Department of the Interior, two Small Business Administration awards, and Entrepreneur of the Year in 1996 from Ernst & Young.

But no honor touched her more than speaking to business groups and students. Speaking to the graduating classes of Johns Hopkins University and Loyola College, Dorothy said, "I don't have a college education like you . . . What can I tell you? I don't have a college degree." But they responded, 'Mrs. White, you may not know it, but you have a master's degree in how to run a business. And we don't know anything. How can we do something with our lives like you've done?'"

Sharing Wisdom

Today, Dorothy and Jim White have sold the business and retired. Miracle Services, Inc., has more than 600 employees and an annual gross income of more than $10 million. Dorothy spends much of her time speaking to children about how to believe in yourself and make your dreams happen. She also shares her personal keys to success outlined in her autobiography, *The Miracle Lady: The Dorothy White Story*:

1. Have a dream. Know what you want.
2. Acquire the knowledge you need to make your dream a reality.
3. Knowledge is everywhere and it's mostly free.
4. Never, never, never quit on your dream.
5. Once you've got your opportunity, work like a dog. If nothing else, you can work harder and longer than the woman with the Ph.D.

6. Always do your best. Any work well done is God's work.
7. Always make sure your customers are happy.
8. Always make sure your employees are happy.

Practically everyone who comes into contact with Dorothy White sees someone extraordinary. Of course, she's no different from the woman she was when she started cleaning houses . . . except for one thing: the self-confidence she lacked for so long. She has it now, in generous portions. She's developed it by starting with nothing except her will and her work ethic (and one devoted husband) to rely on. She has grown into one unstoppable woman, changing not only herself but the lives of those she's touched. And that's miraculous.

> *"Everyone has a gift. You have to find what you love. And the*
> *most important thing is that when you do something, be good at it.*
> *If you do a good job, someone's going to notice. You might not get*
> *all the business, but you'll get one. And then you'll get two, then three.*
> *And as your success grows, so will your confidence."*
> *—Dorothy White*

Unstoppable Action
Develop Self-Confidence One Step at a Time

It's a long way from the cotton fields to ownership of a multi-million-dollar company. Many people would have said Dorothy White wasn't up to the journey, but their opinions don't matter. White's confidence in herself started small, but the more she accomplished, the more it grew, and the bolder the steps she took. She learned a lesson that all successful individuals have learned: Confidence is a self-fulfilling prophecy. The more you believe you can do, the more you *can* do.

Yet, as we have already established, women struggle with a lack of self-confidence and are traditionally very hard on themselves—focusing on their failures and skills they lack versus their strengths and successes. This attitude is evident in even the most difficult of circumstances. Emergency room doctors tell stories of women who are brought into the ER with injuries from a car accident or some other trauma. Often, the first thing these women will say is, "I'm sorry, I didn't shave my legs." Even in a life-and-death situation, women are apologizing simply for having hair on their legs!

A huge part of growing your self-confidence and achieving victory in your 30-day goal is telling your inner critic to stop and be quiet! And that starts by disputing those negative voices or stories that run through your mind and focusing instead on your daily success. On Day Four, we talked about what psychologists call "success imprints," or past successes, and you were asked to make a list of these imprints. That exercise is valuable because self-confidence is developed from past success. Success imprints are created anytime you have successfully achieved something that was thought to be difficult. In Dorothy White's case, even though she was terribly uncomfortable selling herself to potential customers, each time she left an appointment, it sent a positive message to her subconscious that she not only lived through the experience, but that she could do it again.

The same is true for you in the Unstoppable Women Challenge. Every time you take your one step, you've created a success imprint that not only strengthens your self-esteem, but builds the belief that you can do it again in the future.

Write down your daily victories.

Every time you have a victory, note it in your planner. Notice at least one action every day that you are proud of and that moved you one step closer to the achievement of your 30-day goal. Maybe you're becoming more aware of the inner critic that tells you you're not good enough or deserving enough. Instead of losing the faith and quitting, you stop yourself, dispute your voice of fear, tap into the truth of your possibilities, and move forward. That is a huge victory.

Review your daily victories regularly, particularly at times when you're feeling the most down on yourself or like you're making no progress. By focusing on your victories, you create a success imprint that strengthens your belief system that you can do it again; you are worthy, you are capable, you are unstoppable.

Use each success to build momentum for your next success. After a victory, always do something to leverage your enthusiasm *in the moment*. Make one more phone call, do one more rep in the gym, plan your day for tomorrow. Success breeds success. Nothing is more attractive to others than a person who is "on fire." Leverage the great energy you experience to create even greater results.

 Create Your Day Planner

PLAN TO BE UNSTOPPABLE! Tonight or first thing tomorrow morning, plan your next day's activities by filling out your Create Your Day Planner (see Appendix). Think about actions you've taken in the last few days that are unrelated to your goal but of which you are proud. Did you spend extra time with your child to help her with her homework or to finish a school project? Did you cheer up a friend or take the time to mentor a co-worker? Perhaps you met a tight deadline at work or cooked up a fantastic meal. Whatever you did that you're proud of, take some time to congratulate yourself on your accomplishment. Successes in your 30-day challenge will propel you forward in other areas of your life. Don't forget to acknowledge them.

Something to Think About

When talk turns to cultural trends, Faith Popcorn is the crystal ball. From her company, Faith Popcorn's BrainReserve, to her four books, *The Popcorn Report, Clicking, EVEolution: The Eight Truths of Marketing to Women,* and *Dictionary of the Future,* she's got the market cornered on predicting what trends will take over the American pop cultural landscape. Ad agencies, marketing gurus, and corporate leaders treat her predictions as gospel. She's powerful in the corporate world—but she wasn't always. To reach her goals, Popcorn had to "act her way into a new way of being."

Turning herself into a best-selling author and a million-dollar brand took nothing short of audacity and guts. With a little money her mother had given to her, Popcorn started BrainReserve in her studio apartment. But she had no track record, so she couldn't get work, and without work, the company résumé was bordering on pathetic.

After three years of disappointment, Popcorn knew the only way out of the quagmire was to roll the dice and "think big, act big, and project ourselves into our future." When a senior VP from a large marketing firm asked to tour their offices, they rented the top floor of the upscale Lotos Club and created a virtual office: desks, tables, phones with no dial tone. Friends and freelancers came in to make things look bustling. Faith recalls, "I always thought I was behind where I should have been. So I acted the way I was *going* to be. It came from an impatience and a restlessness with the present."

The VP didn't hire them, but that didn't deter Faith, and the experience gave her a taste of the future. "That was just one more person who didn't hire us. But we forged ahead and eventually our hard work paid off. As our predictions about the culture started to manifest, not only did we come to believe in ourselves but so did the Fortune 500."

Thirty years later, Faith Popcorn's BrainReserve has its own building not far from her original studio as well as a multitude of offices in North America, sixty consultants, and a Global TalentBank of 9,500 experts.

"I think one of the blessings of getting older is that you get more self-confidence. My self-confidence has increased with my birthdays."
—*Supreme Court Justice Sandra Day O'Connor*

Day 11:
Don't Fight a Problem, Solve It!

Today's Affirmation: I begin today in a state of resourcefulness. I focus my energies on solving any problems that I may experience rather than fighting against them. Asking the right questions instantly changes my focus and helps me to identify a solution that enables me to stay in action to achieve my 30-day goal. I am unstoppable!

My dear friend and mentor, Millard Fuller, founder of Habitat for Humanity International, gave me the following advice on more than one occasion: "Don't fight a problem, solve it!" This simple yet profound statement has helped me tremendously to effectively move past challenges, and it can do the same for you. Often, when people experience difficulties in their lives, they spend most of their time fighting the problem, raging over the fact that it exists, asking questions like, "Why me?" or "Why can't I . . . ?" or complaining that "It's not fair!"

When that happens, nothing changes except their perception of the size and magnitude of the problem—it grows! But we can change that dynamic in an instant by shifting our focus from the problem to the solution. One of the quickest ways to do that is to ask better questions.

Instead of asking, "Why me?" try asking yourself, "What can I do to make things better?" or "How can I improve the situation?" These questions instantly change your focus and empower you. Problems happen; it's a part of life. But the problem doesn't have to be the end of the story. If you determine to ask better questions—questions that search for a solution—you'll rewrite your own ending.

Liz Murray had a problem more serious than most of us will ever face. She grew up with drug-addicted parents, in a world where she had absolutely no support and usually no roof over her head. But despite these seemingly insurmountable odds, she succeeded in transforming her life in a way that can only be called miraculous. How did she do it? Rather than feeling sorry for herself and fighting the problem, she focused her energies on solving her problem and, in the process, became self-reliant and created extraordinary opportunities for herself.

Unstoppable Woman:
Liz Murray's Story

You've heard of the part of New York City called Hell's Kitchen? Liz Murray had her own version, without the famous name. But it was just as hellish. As she and her sister were growing up in the roughest part of the Bronx, her parents were hardcore drug addicts, often shooting up in front of the girls. "They were barely able to provide for my sister and me because drugs took all the income," she recalls. By the time Liz was six, her mother was a raging alcoholic and her father's drug habit was out of control.

Liz's parents were too busy getting high to provide for their daughters in any way. The girls never got new clothing, and Liz took to knocking on neighbors' doors at dinnertime to get something to eat. "My sister and I were very dirty and had lice in our hair," she says. "Our teachers at school were suspicious about our situation and called the Bureau of Child Welfare. But my sister and I got very good at preparing for these visits." Coached by their parents, the girls would make up stories about why they weren't in school. Amazingly, the social workers accepted the stories at face value. Year after year, the girls stayed home, watching their parents pass out and scavenging for food, and no one did anything to help.

Becoming Self-Sufficient
Under the circumstances, Liz had no choice but to become self-reliant. When she was nine, she started working, bagging groceries for tips, bringing home $20 to $25 a day, which she would use to buy groceries. She also pumped gas for tips, relishing the feeling of independence this gave her.

One of Liz's methods of coping with her situation would powerfully influence her future. She would hide out in her room and read unreturned library books. So even though she was never at school, she would always get a 90 percent or better on the year-end test that determined if she would jump to the next grade. In spite of everything, she was becoming a scholar.

Bad Times, New Friends
In 1990, when Liz was 10, her mother was diagnosed with AIDS. Liz's sister and mom went to live with Liz's godfather, leaving Liz alone with her father. But the state got wind of the situation and took Liz into custody for her own protection. The people at social services told her that in 24 hours, she could be released to her mother and godfather. She waited. No one came to claim her for 35 days! During the same period, her father was evicted from the old apartment and ended up homeless. To Liz, it began to look like her choices were running out.

She was finally released to her godfather and stayed with him for a few years, but this wasn't much of an improvement. He was abusive, and her mother's health was failing fast as she continued to drink. While Liz cared for her mother, she attended the eighth grade and befriended a girl, Chris, from school.

Like Liz, Chris came from an abusive household, and the girls formed a close bond in sheer self-defense. They would skip school to wander New York, and Chris often secretly spent the night with Liz to avoid going home to her own brutal father. But when Liz's godfather learned of this one night and demanded that Chris get out at 3:00 A.M., the two girls packed up and ran away, never to come back.

"I was 15 and Chris was 14," Liz says. "We became homeless. At first we thought it would be a big party, visiting one friend's house after another. We believed that we would get apartments and jobs and everything would go smoothly."

That vision quickly soured. When they couldn't beg shelter from friends, Liz and Chris would ride the train all night or sleep on rooftops or in stairwells.

From Death, a New Beginning
In 1996, Liz's sister shared the news that their mother had died. They got a Catholic cemetery to donate a funeral, and her mother was buried in a pine box with her name written on it—misspelled and scribbled in magic

marker. At one end of the box was written "Head" to tell the gravediggers which way to place the body in the ground.

The indignity and sadness of her mother's end shook Liz to her core. To make matters worse, Chris went back into the state child welfare system. Liz was now alone and at the lowest point of her life. "I realized that my self-image as an independent woman of the streets was a delusion. I was 16, with an eighth-grade education, and I was homeless," Liz says.

She was clearly at a crossroads. "I had learned to get by and had done well under the circumstances. Who would blame me, right? I had every excuse in the book to give up and become another statistic. But I also knew I was capable of something more." But where to begin? Liz started by asking a simple question: "What if I made the most of every day? What if even a single action was guiding me to a greater goal? What could be possible?" Armed with only her faith in what *could* be, she looked at the problem—her entire life up to this point—and decided to come up with a plan to change it.

First, she had to get a job. She found one, going door-to-door soliciting donations in support of political initiatives. Her survival depended on her success, and her determination paid big dividends. She broke all sales records, and within two months, she made $8,000—even more than her boss!

Next step: education. The public school in her district was enormous and could be dangerous, and Liz feared she couldn't get a good education there. So she tried to get into a small private high school, but her abysmal GPA meant no private school would touch her. She didn't want to tell an admissions officer she was homeless for fear of becoming a ward of the state again. Finally, she used a friend's address and phone number and was accepted to Humanities Preparatory Academy.

For Murray, it was as if she'd been born to study. She tore into her schoolwork, taking Shakespeare, joining student government, and getting at least a 96 in every class. To her teachers and fellow students, she wasn't a homeless daughter of drug addicts. She was a star. School was everything she had hoped it would be.

A Fateful Choice

Completing four years' work in two, Liz graduated at the top of her class. She won a trip to Boston with her school, and the group made a short trip to Harvard. She fell in love with the prestigious university. On the spot, she realized that she wanted to go to an Ivy League university, a dream she wouldn't have even dared allow herself just two years before. Now, though, empowered by her academic success and her soaring belief in herself, she knew this was where she wanted to be.

But how would she pay for a first-rate education costing tens of thousands of dollars a year? Liz applied for every scholarship she could get her hands on. One was a $12,000 scholarship offered to needy students by the *New York Times*. She noticed that while they didn't ask much about GPA or SAT scores, they did ask one question that stood out for her: "Were there any obstacles you had to overcome?" Well, she had certainly earned her Ph.D. in overcoming obstacles. So she poured her heart into that application, telling her entire life's story. She mailed it in, but with 3,000 people competing against her, she didn't hold her breath.

Next, Liz and her sister got an apartment together, but just after they signed the lease, her sister lost her job. Bills mounted; eviction was imminent. At the same time, Liz learned she was a semi-finalist for the *New York Times* scholarship and had to go for an interview . . . on the same day and time she had to go to the welfare office to get the money she and her sister needed to keep their apartment.

At the welfare office, the clock ticked. Liz knew that if she didn't get service soon, she'd miss her *New York Times* appointment. But she needed the money! She tried to explain her predicament to a welfare worker, but her plea got her nowhere.

She had to make a choice. Stay, or go to the interview and lose the month's income? This was it, the ultimate test of her belief in herself and her brighter future. And in an act of immense courage, she turned her back on the past, walked out of the welfare office, and bet her and her sister's futures on her interview at the *Times*. The last thing she said to the scholarship panel at the *New York Times* was, "I hope you realize how important this is to me."

A Choice Rewarded

A few days later, Liz got the news—she had won the scholarship! The five winners were profiled in the newspaper; her life story was no longer a secret. Almost immediately, strangers, moved by this young girl who had come so far against such incredible odds, were coming out of the wood-work to help. They paid her bills and the sisters kept their apartment. People were so moved by her story that they donated more than $200,000 to the *Times* to fund more scholarships.

Then Harvard came calling. When Liz opened the acceptance letter, she screamed. "I felt like I had wings," she says. "I felt like I could do any-thing." She attended for two years, then left to take advantage of oppor-tunities to speak to other young people. After all, she was a living exam-ple of what could be done with a focus on the future, a ton of determina-tion, and a little help from some friends.

To this day, Liz credits her successes to the question she asked her-self after her mother's death. "I attribute every single thing that's hap-pened to me to that moment when I had a little conversation with myself and I made the decision to be active instead of reactive. I decided that I was going to get up every day and make the most of what was put in front of me. Since then, phenomenal results have come in."

In 2003, the Lifetime television network produced a movie about Liz's life, called *Homeless to Harvard*, starring Thora Birch. Her autobiog-raphy, *Breaking Night*, is due out. And she and her father, who has AIDS, have reconnected and are in each other's lives again.

Surprisingly, Liz has never held a grudge against her parents. "I cared for my parents very much, and despite what was happening, I felt they cared for me," she says. "I know that may sound strange. I had lice in my hair and holes in my clothes, and we had animals in the house making a mess. But my parents had a disease. If I hadn't eaten a hot meal in two days, my mother hadn't had one in three, maybe four. They were not being better parents somewhere else and coming back to be malicious to my sister and me."

Liz Murray had every reason to give up, to give in to bitterness or despair and let herself become just another statistic. But she didn't. Instead, she took a hard look at her problems, made no excuses, and told herself she deserved more. More important, she believed that she had the ability to change her present and shape her future. At her mother's funeral, standing on the edge of a pauper's grave, she made a brave decision: The ending of her story would be different. Then step by step, page by page, chapter by chapter, with will, intelligence, and faith in herself, she rewrote her life.

"Anything that is within someone else's reach is also within yours.
Set your goals no matter how impossible they may seem. Then focus
on what is between you and that goal. And then,
simply take out the obstacles as they come."
—Liz Murray

Unstoppable Action
Stop Overthinking and Start Taking Action

Liz Murray's problems could have overwhelmed her. She could have allowed herself to be paralyzed by the enormity of the task of pulling herself up from the streets to a productive, rewarding life. Instead, with the practicality and clear-headed thinking she had developed taking care of herself and her sister as children, she focused on solving her problems one step at a time.

The Difference Is in the Approach

The key to solving any problem begins with our approach. Not surprisingly, women and men approach problems differently: Women tend to think and men tend to act. When a woman experiences a challenge, such as getting fired from her job, she thinks about why it happened. She mulls the situation over and over in her mind, reliving every painful detail of the experience, which ultimately creates feelings of depression and despair. Most men, on the other hand, act. A man might go for a jog, wash the car, or perhaps immediately pick up the paper and start looking for another position without even thinking about why he is now unemployed.

Psychologists call this obsessive thinking and analysis of a situation *rumination* or *overthinking*. Women who overthink dwell on the problem and the feelings brought about by it, and they often have difficulty getting past it so that they can focus on solving their problem. What's worse, they typically attach a negative meaning or interpretation to their situation. And often, this negative interpretation involves blaming *themselves* for some perceived shortcoming or fault. The end result is frequently depression. Simply stated, they're "fighting" the problem . . . and it's winning.

Such thinking often begins with a small incident, perhaps thinking about a rejection while making prospecting phone calls. You ask yourself, "Why wasn't this prospect interested?" Then your mind whispers, "I really didn't handle that call very well." A thought like "I am not good at prospecting and will never make another sale" follows, and you're trapped in that state of overthinking, where each destructive thought leads to another.

The insidious thing about this state of mind is that the negative thoughts grow like weeds. At first the thoughts are confined to a specific event. Then they spread to other areas of your life, perhaps where you feel insecure. Soon you're wondering, "Am I incompetent in every area of my life?" or "If I can't even do well at sales, why do I think I could start my own business?"

Overthinking distorts our lives. Instead of seeing our past and present clearly, we see what our pessimistic mood wants us to see: long-ago failures, the worst things about our current situations, and how we're likely to mess things up in the future. Susan Nolen-Hoeksema, Ph.D., professor of psychology at Yale University, has found through 20 years of scientific studies that overthinking makes stressful situations seem greater, problems more insurmountable, and our reactions to stressful times more intense, lasting, and negative. In short, overthinking makes our lives more difficult.

Fortunately, the kind of overthinking that leads to debilitating self-doubt can be stopped. The key is changing the way you think when you experience a problem. You *will* have setbacks and difficulties. Everyone does. But they're not the end of the world. The secret is to consciously catch the destructive, self-defeating things you say to yourself and stop the internal condemnation.

✎ Notice your internal conversations.

The moment you catch yourself overthinking a situation, *stop*. A simple but wonderfully effective strategy for freeing yourself from overthinking is to distract yourself. Dr. Nolen-Hoeksema's research, as outlined in her book *Women Who Think Too Much*, shows that people who receive positive distractions from overthinking for just eight minutes show a remarkable change in their moods and in breaking the cycle of repetitive thought.

Here are some suggested ways to break the negative cycle of overthinking:

Use the STOP acronym. The next time you catch yourself over-thinking a problem or situation, try this acronym to break the habit:

S—SAY the word "stop" to interrupt your internal destructive thoughts. Tell yourself firmly to stop overthinking.

T—TAKE a deep breath. Then, take a break: Go for a walk or a hike, read a great book, listen to your favorite music. Do something to take your attention away from overthinking and, if possible, to change the environment.

O—Focus on the OUTCOME of your 30-Day Goal. Affirm why you are committed to your goal.

P—PRAISE and acknowledge yourself for the progress you are making. Remember, you're looking for progress, not perfection!

Use your muscles—and your mind. Dr. Nolen-Hoeksema's research found that distractions involving activity and concentration are the most effective at stopping overthinking. If you find yourself ruminating for more

"Never mind a book on how to improve *myself*, I need a book on how to change every-one *else* in my life."

than 15 to 20 minutes, *do something;* if you're sitting down, get up and leave the room, read something for your enjoyment, or work on a hobby. Or try getting some exercise—whether you choose tennis or jogging, getting a workout provides a healthy distraction and a biochemical boost to your brain.

Let go and let God. Give your problem over to a Higher Power through prayer. Or try meditation or yoga.

Developing the skill to stop overthinking is critical because once you stop this destructive thought process, you will be free to focus on solving the problem instead of fighting it—and yourself.

Create Your Day Planner

PLAN TO BE UNSTOPPABLE! Tonight or first thing tomorrow morning, plan your next day's activities by filling out your Create Your Day Planner (see Appendix). Has overthinking been holding you back in your Unstoppable Women Challenge? If so, plan some positive distractions for those times when you find yourself "stuck" in negative thinking or when your energy seems to lag. Take a short walk, have a chat with your buddy, or get up and dance to your favorite music for 10 minutes. These distractions may give you the boost you need to break the cycle of overthinking and to discover some creative ways to meet your challenges head on.

Day 12:
Awaken Your Inner Optimist

Today's Affirmation: I am in control of my thoughts and actions. Any setback or difficult situation I experience is only temporary. My ability is not the cause of any failure, but simply my effort attached to that specific task. I can always improve. I am unstoppable!

Jane and Joan are twin sisters. In many ways they're identical, but in the way they view the world, they couldn't be more different. Jane is a pessimist—whenever her boyfriend glances at another girl, one of her college professors calls on another student, or she goes to a doctor's appointment, she always imagines the worst. In her mind, her boyfriend is always about to leave, her teachers are planning to fail her, and she has some terrible illness. She is frequently depressed and has a hard time being productive.

Her sister Joan, on the other hand, sees things differently. To her, misfortune is fleeting, and tomorrow is always a better day. Problems are part of life, and she approaches even the most frustrating events with a sense of confidence and energy. She's doing well in school and feels great.

For more than a quarter-century, Martin Seligman, Ph.D., professor of psychology at the University of Pennsylvania and past president of the American Psychological Association, has been studying how optimists and pessimists view the world. In his book *Learned Optimism*, Dr. Seligman explains that one of the major reasons optimists and pessimists live such different lives has to do with how they explain the setbacks and challenges they encounter. For example, while pessimists view setbacks as permanent and see themselves as being to blame for the problem, optimists view setbacks as temporary and take into account outside factors that may have contributed to the problem. It's not hard to see which view leads to greater personal power and a higher Unstoppability Quotient.

The way we explain the things that happen in our lives—either with a pessimistic or an optimistic viewpoint—has consequences for our future. Hundreds of psychological studies have shown that pessimists give up easier and experience depression more frequently. Optimists do better in school and work and are generally happier people. Optimists are the ones who excel at tests, run for office, and often get elected.

If you are a pessimist by nature, you can take heart in some recent news from the world of science. One of the most life-changing discoveries of recent psychology is this: *Individuals can choose to change the way they think and react to the world.* The way we view life's events is a habit, no different than what we choose to eat for breakfast. And habits can change.

You've already begun to explore how stopping negative thoughts and breaking the cycle of overthinking can free you to take positive action. Today, we'll take this idea even further by exploring how you can develop an empowering mindset of optimism.

Emmy Award–winning actress Camryn Manheim had every reason to look at the world through pessimist's eyes. Instead, she chose to look at her life as an optimist. When the "experts" in the entertainment business told her she would never be an actress because of her weight, she didn't let their predictions stop her. She believed that her talent would carry the day. And over a cribbage board, she got the chance to prove herself right. Since then, she has never looked back.

Unstoppable Woman:
Camryn Manheim's Story

Camryn grew up in a household where the arts and education were highly valued. Her parents, both Ph.D.s, would spend their summers taking Camryn and her siblings on road trips to museums, monuments, and cultural points of interest across the U.S.

But when Camryn expressed a desire to become an actress, they were concerned. Hollywood was a tough place if you weren't bikini perfect, and her parents were afraid that the creative community wouldn't be supportive of Camryn.

At 15 years old, her parents took her to the Renaissance Fair in Agoura, California. She immediately knew she belonged in this place of merry men and women of all shapes and sizes, dressed in colorful costumes, acting, singing songs, and being happy. The curvy body was not seen as "fat," but as voluptuous and adored.

A Personal Renaissance
Camryn dreamed of joining the Renaissance Fair and at age 16, she got her wish. For four consecutive summers, Camryn transported herself into a world where women with curves were worshipped. It was here that she learned to love her body.

Later, she applied to the University of California at Santa Cruz but was denied admittance because she didn't have enough language credits. Instead, she attended Cabrillo Junior College and studied sign language. You can imagine her parents' reaction. As two very proud educators, they had sent their only son to Harvard, and now their daughter was going to a community college to collect language credits. Camryn often jokes, "Any child who goes to a community college cannot be buried in a Jewish cemetery."

Undeterred, Camryn took beginning and intermediate sign language simultaneously and passed both in one semester. But Camryn found another blessing at Cabrillo College: acting coach Wilma Marcus, who encouraged her to get on the stage. Marcus made such an impression that Camryn promised that when she won her first acting award, Marcus would be the first person she thanked.

A High Achiever

By the time she graduated from the University of California at Santa Cruz, Camryn had run a theater company, taught a class, and bought a home. She was a big fish in a small pond, but it was time to move on to a bigger pond—and for an aspiring thespian that meant only one place.

Fat in New York

So Camryn went to New York City, and after many harrowing auditions, New York University (NYU) accepted her into its master's program: a three-year acting boot camp, twelve hours a day of work sequestered on the fifth floor of the Tisch School of the Arts. The work helped her hone her skills and polish her talent, but she quickly discovered that of the 29 students in her program, some would be cut. She knew that because she didn't fit the slim, blonde stereotype, she was a prime target. She found the fear of failure quite motivating and worked harder than ever before.

However, when instructors confronted her in front of the entire class about her "weight problem," Camryn understandably displayed an attitude. She didn't think the classroom was an appropriate venue for such personal discussions. Yet she lived with the fear of the "cut," so she restrained herself. "I bit my tongue and held my temper all for those three little letters: M. F. A. (Master of Fine Arts)," she says. "In retrospect, it should have been called B. F. D. (You figure it out!)"

Later, when the dean met with her to review her progress, the dreaded "weight problem" was raised again. He suggested that if she were thinner, more opportunities would be available to her. She was truly perplexed. Art was supposed to imitate life, and there were plenty of fat people in the world, right? So why was this such an issue?

Under this scrutiny, Camryn became desperate to drop some weight. She didn't drink, smoke, or use drugs, but under the intense pressure to be thin, she started taking speed. By summer's end, she had lost 35 pounds and looked better than ever, but she was a physical wreck.

The Pain of Rejection

Camryn hung on to her spot in the class, and right before graduation, she participated in the League Presentations, high-powered auditions for New York's top agents, producers, and casting directors. It was intense and nerve-wracking.

Camryn did her auditions, checked the infamous Wall of Lists . . . and found nothing. Not one agent or casting director wanted to meet with her. It was utterly humiliating. "The League Presentations are the equivalent of a university graduation at NYU," she says. "Either the agents or managers like you, or they don't. You're either given the red carpet treatment, or you're disregarded and rejected." For Camryn, there was no fanfare.

Camryn was rejected in the one area she felt she had talent. She was devastated and spent the next eight months as a virtual recluse, feeling embarrassed, untalented, and pathetic.

To make matters worse, she quickly regained the weight she had lost. After fighting, struggling, and sacrificing so much to get her master's degree, she didn't even attend graduation. She felt she couldn't face anybody, let alone her parents, who had spent $45,000 on her education.

Slipping further into self-pity, Camryn slid deeper into drugs and nearly died from an overdose. At that moment, she knew she had hit bottom, and she was determined to give life another chance.

Saving Herself

The first step was to get her life back in order. So she went back to California, hoping for some support from her parents. Throughout Camryn's life, her parents did everything they could to support her weight loss, including trips to psychiatrists and rewards when she'd lose weight. When she got off the plane and they saw that she'd regained the weight she'd lost, they were obviously disappointed. Needless to say, the time Camryn spent at her parents' house was uncomfortable. Her father even went so far as to suggest she start smoking until she could lose the weight, then think about quitting.

Shocked, Camryn packed her bags and left, but that moment was a revelation for her. "My whole life I had wanted my father to forgive me for disappointing him," she says. "But I had it wrong. I needed to forgive *him*." She had learned an essential life lesson: No one else has the power to make your life what you want. Only you have that power. Later, she realized that her father's plea, while harsh, came from a desire to see her happy, and he felt that would be undermined if she didn't lose weight.

Now Camryn set about getting mentally and physically healthy. She jumped back into the theater, helping casting directors as an unpaid reader in the hopes that she'd get the chance to audition. She gained invaluable insight into what a good audition looked like and how the director and actors exchanged feedback and ideas.

Finally, her hard work paid off. Musical theatre legend Stephen Sondheim was coming to town to view auditions for his show *Merrily We Roll Along*. After seeing Camryn read, Sondheim asked her to have her agent call him to set up an audition! This was the theatrical equivalent of an audience with the Pope—except that she had no agent! But Sondheim was so impressed that he told his casting director to *get* her one! Five years after graduating from NYU, she finally had an agent.

One-Woman Show

Camryn was now working, but many of the auditions she was called for were for fat women who were the butt of the joke. She wanted to be seen as a skilled craftswoman, not just a body. She yearned for good roles written for big women, but there just weren't any. So she decided to create her own. "I was an expert in one area and one area only," she says. "I knew all the ins and outs on what it was like to grow up in America fat."

By going through her old journals and photos, culling the memories from her life—the good and the devastating, the silly and the serious—Camryn pieced together a one-woman stage show, *Wake Up, I'm Fat!* She found a director, a producer, and a theater, and held her first live reading in front of a test audience of 75 people. Because most of her show revolved around her issues and experiences with being fat, she wasn't sure that an audience of thin people could relate. But to her surprise and satisfaction, they did. The experience was eye-opening. She realized that while she had been beating herself up for years over her weight, other people had been doing the same because of their height, their job, their skin color, and on and on. Everyone could relate to what she was saying.

By opening night, the show had sold out. Then Camryn was tested again. When she arrived at the theater, she noticed that the marquee wasn't turned on, the concession stand was dark, and the lobby lights were dim. She wondered if the theater had been burglarized. But it was worse than that. The fire marshal had declared the theater unsafe and was closing it down—for a month! It was a crushing blow. All her friends and family who had come to support her were showing up and being told the show was canceled.

Camryn determined that whatever she had to do, her audience was going to see a show! She called every theater she'd ever worked at until she found one that would be available starting the following night.

Next, she called every ticket holder for *Wake Up, I'm Fat!* and told them there would be a show the following night. "Just twelve months earlier, I would have let this defeat get the best of me," she says. "I would have given up. But there was a new power within me and I refused to accept this fate."

The Practice

Her one-woman reflection on life as a plus-size actress was a hit, drawing standing ovations, sold-out houses, and approval from her parents. Then Randy Stone, vice president of casting at Twentieth Century Fox and a friend of one of Camryn's managers, saw the show and loved it.

He mentioned that David E. Kelley, creator of *Ally McBeal*, was writing a new pilot called *The Practice*, and wanted a streetwise, sassy female lawyer. Camryn knew she'd be perfect. But when Kelley saw a tape of her past work, he thought she was too conservative. Too conservative! Conservative is the last word you would use to describe Camryn, and Stone persuaded Kelley to meet with her despite his reservations.

Camryn flew out to Los Angeles, but what followed was a painfully awkward interview that reeked of disaster. Camryn figured the interview was over and as she got up to leave, she noticed that David had a cribbage board in his office. Camryn was a great cribbage player, so good that she often played for money and usually won. She *knew* this was a defining moment. She blurted out, "Hey, do you play cribbage?" Kelley came alive.

"Yeah, but I don't think you want to go there with me." He carried on for a few minutes about why he was such a great player. Then Camryn seized the moment, and that confidence and attitude that infuses so much of her acting reared its head. She looked David Kelley in the eye and said:

"You know, David, I could continue to have this conversation with you, and I could continue to try to impress you, and I could beat you at cribbage at the same time." With that, the dynamic changed. Kelley copped some attitude. The playing field leveled. Next, Camryn offered to play Kelley for the role. "If I win, I walk out with the script. If I lose, you'll never see me again!"

Kelley declined the game, but he sent Camryn the script a few weeks later—where the character description was changed to match her! She knew she had won a very big battle. A short time later, when her agent called to tell her she'd gotten the part, validating 20 years of doubt and fear and hard work, she sat down in the middle of the kitchen floor and wept for joy and relief. Finally, finally, she had made it.

Victory

In 1998, Camryn Manheim won the Emmy Award for her work on *The Practice*, and as promised, Wilma Marcus was indeed the first person she thanked. Raising her Emmy over her head, she declared in her inimitable style, "This is for all the fat girls!" In doing so, she made a bold and important statement to millions of TV viewers and gave hope to thousands of actresses fighting the uphill battle against "the weight problem."

Camryn's one-woman show turned into a best-selling book by the same name. And for the record, as of this writing, there has been only one cribbage match between her and David E. Kelley. You can guess who won that battle.

"Waiting, waiting, waiting, waiting. All my life I was waiting for my life to begin, as if my life were somehow way up ahead of me, and one day I would just arrive there. But a few years ago I finally realized something. My life was not way up ahead of me. I was standing smack dab in the middle of it. In fact, I was standing on the corner of 'Life' and 'You better get going, Camryn,' and the way I saw it, I had two choices: I could either cross that street or just keep waiting for a few more years of green lights to go by."
—*Camryn Manheim*

⟶ Unstoppable Action ⟵

"The event is not important, but the response to the event is everything."
—*I Ching*

At every turn in her fledgling acting career, Camryn Manheim was told she was too fat and that she had to change herself if she ever wanted to work. Even her friends and family didn't believe she could make it. A pessimist would have blamed herself and seen the obstacle as impossible to overcome. She would have quit. But Camryn is an *optimist*. She knew that she was a talented actress who deserved a chance. More important, she knew that the problem was not her, but Hollywood's obsession with waif-thin women. She believed that if she kept fighting, her talent would win the day. And she was right.

During the Unstoppable Women Challenge, setbacks will most likely happen. Unexpected events will threaten to steer you off course: unforeseen project deadlines, rejection, lack of support from friends or family. Given these challenges, there will probably come a day when you aren't able to complete your one step. But this setback doesn't have to be permanent. It was just a "stoppable moment." That's all.

Your ability to "explain" the events that occur in your life will determine your ability to achieve your 30-day goal and realize consistent change in your life. Take some time to consider how you think about the small setbacks that befall you on a daily basis.

Do you blame yourself when small things go wrong? Do you accuse yourself of being incompetent at everything and assume you'll always be that way? Or do you react by saying, "Hey, that's life. Tomorrow will be a great day, and I did so much today that was right"? How you explain life's little setbacks will determine how hopeful or helpless you become.

Psychologists have identified a trait they have dubbed "learned helplessness." In his book *Learned Optimism*, Dr. Seligman defines learned helplessness as the giving-up reaction, the quitting response that follows the belief that whatever you do doesn't matter. It thereby weakens your sense of control. Learned helplessness is considered by the American Psychological Association to be the landmark theory of the century, and with good cause. It explains *why* many people give up when faced with life's challenges. Your way of explaining the events of your life to yourself is described by Dr. Seligman as your "explanatory style" and determines how helpless or how energized you can become when you encounter everyday setbacks as well as momentous defeats.

A pessimistic explanatory style spreads helplessness. Dr. Seligman describes pessimists as those who explain adversity as *permanent* ("It will never change"), *pervasive* ("It will ruin everything"), and *personal* ("It's all my fault"). Optimists are those who respond to adversity as *temporary* ("It's going away quickly"), *external* ("It's just circumstances"), and *limited* ("There's much more in life"). Take a look at the following very different interpretations for the same event: a job interview that didn't go well.

PESSIMISTIC INTERPRETATION	OPTIMISTIC INTERPRETATION
Permanent: "I'm never going to get a job in my field."	**Temporary:** "Hey, I have two more interviews next week."
Pervasive: "I'm incompetent."	**Limited:** "I'd better work on my interview skills."
Personal: "The CEO hated me."	**External:** "It's the company's loss."

How we think about life actually controls how life unfolds. If we think we're helpless or powerless to change things, we will be. We lose control. Pessimism is a self-fulfilling prophecy. But, fortunately, so is optimism.

There's obviously a great benefit to adopting an optimistic explanatory style. But can anyone develop it? After years of exhaustive psychological research, it has been proven that optimism is not an inborn trait; it can absolutely be learned. Optimism is a habit. We can *choose* how we think.

Go Back to Your ABCs

Remember Albert Ellis' ABC model we used on Day 5 to raise your Unstoppability Quotient? Let's use the same strategies to explore the following example:

Your Unstoppable Women Challenge goal is to lose 10 pounds. One night after work, you go out to dinner with some friends and succumb to a big piece of cheesecake. After savoring the last bite, you start to think about your action. You think:

Adversity: "I went off my eating plan."

Belief: "I blew my diet and am so unbelievably weak. I will *never* lose weight." (personal and permanent)

Consequence: "All my effort over the last two weeks is ruined and I'll never make my 30-day goal, so I might as well eat the cake in the freezer." (pervasive)

The difference between ending your diet and staying on course all comes down to your explanation about what happened. As a pessimist, you explain your indulgence as personal and permanent, a part of your overall weakness and lack of willpower, instead of just a stoppable moment. You decide that one indulgence means you blew your diet. But that's not true. It's only true when you explain it as personal, permanent, and pervasive, then you quit.

On the other hand, consider the different reaction that could occur if you choose to take an optimist's view of the event:

Adversity: "I went off my eating plan."

Belief: "Letting my diet slip for just one night and eating a piece of cheesecake does not mean I am weak and will never lose weight. I ate a light dinner, so on balance I probably consumed only a few more calories than my eating plan allows. I've followed my plan diligently for an entire week." (limited and temporary)

Consequence: "An occasional lapse is normal. I'll get back on track tomorrow and resume my healthy eating plan. It makes no sense to break my 30-day goal and set myself back even further." (external)

Seeing a pattern? When you explain adversity by beating yourself up and convincing yourself that you'll never change, you become dejected and paralyzed. But when you chalk adversity up to a temporary setback, believe that success is just around the corner, and remember that you can get right back on track, you re-energize yourself.

Turn pessimistic thoughts into optimistic ones.

The next time you experience a setback, listen to your internal voice. Is your explanation about what happened pessimistic or optimistic? Do you see your setback as permanent, pervasive, and personal? If so, turn it around. Using your voice of faith, change your pessimistic explanations into optimistic ones by making them temporary, limited to one area of your life, and external.

In doing so, you'll see any setback as simply a "stoppable moment," stay in action, and end the habit of giving up once and for all.

Here are some additional tips for awakening your inner optimist:

- Notice if you tend to think of setbacks in terms of "always" and "never." Those two words are a sure sign you're thinking like a pessimist. Consciously decide to believe instead that setbacks are temporary, based on changing circumstances. Things will be better tomorrow.
- Some people can remain productive even when they're experiencing a setback in one aspect of their lives, such as their career or an important relationship. Others make their crisis mean that their whole life is falling apart. Work on seeing setbacks with proper perspective. How is your setback limited to just one area of your life? What other areas of your life are going well? Proper perspective creates hope.
- Focus on the things you did right each day, instead of what you did wrong. You'll find the positive side of the tally is much higher.
- Every misfortune is a challenge in disguise. Try to find the challenge in anything bad that happens, and use it as motivation to change a behavior or improve something about yourself.

Create Your Day Planner

PLAN TO BE UNSTOPPABLE! Tonight or first thing tomorrow morning, plan your next day's activities by filling out your Create Your Day Planner (see Appendix). If your energy is down or you feel discouraged today, recognize that your feelings are generated *solely* from your interpretation of something that happened in your day. Recognize that your situation is only temporary and instead focus on solving the problem.

 Something to Think About

In 2001, a 13-year-old Atlanta girl named Kenya Jordana-James founded *Blackgirl Magazine,* a new magazine aimed at promoting positive messages among African-American teenage girls, as well as offering insightful coverage of black history, culture, lifestyles, and entertainment from a teen perspective. Her first big challenge: landing an interview with hip-hop superstar Lauryn Hill, something even major media had trouble doing. What chance did a 13-year-old newcomer have? With an optimistic attitude and some support from her family when she started to get discouraged, *plenty*.

"It took six months to get the interview with Lauryn Hill. Sometimes I would call her three times a day. And then I would call two weeks later and I was like, 'I don't want to call this lady any more, she doesn't want to do the interview.'

"So I talked to my mom and said, 'Ma, she's not returning my calls, she's not picking up, she's not doing this, and she's not doing that.' And my mom said, 'Well, if you want the interview, you'll continue to call her.' So I continued to call. Finally after months of calling and e-mailing, I got the interview and it turned out to be very successful."

Day 13:
"Girlfriend to Girlfriend:" Make Structure Your New Best Friend

Today's Affirmation: To make any change in my life, I simply look for a support structure that keeps me accountable and literally forces me to take the step I've committed to taking.

This week, we've looked at the specific behaviors that will enable you to achieve your goals. A crucial part of changing any behavior is developing a support structure that keeps you accountable as you incorporate these new behaviors or habits into your daily routine.

A structure can be defined as anything that creates accountability and supports your efforts to produce a specific result. Structure can include a range of activities, from simply writing a plan for the day to making a commitment to a friend to follow through, from hiring a work-out trainer to finding a buddy to partner with for this challenge. Having or not having a proper support structure can make or break your ability to follow through and achieve your goal. If you build the right structure, it can become almost impossible for you *not* to follow through!

I follow this strategy *constantly* in my life. If I'm struggling to follow through on a particular goal, I always ask myself, "What structure can I create to hold myself accountable to my goal and to enjoy the process?"

Asking yourself this question is a great way to direct your focus on solving a problem, instead of fighting it. By answering that question, you can discover the leverage and support infrastructure you need to virtually force yourself to stick with your plan.

Discovering a Perfect Support Structure

Last year, I decided that I wanted to become more physically active. While I was already consistently going to the gym three times a week to lift weights with a trainer, I wanted to increase my cardiovascular exercise. It wasn't something I was eager to do, but I knew that, like lifting weights, it was something I needed to do for my overall fitness. My personal trainer had provided a wonderful support structure to ensure that I got into the gym consistently, even when I didn't feel like it. So I began looking for a structure to support my new goal.

A friend told me about "Team in Training" (TNT). This organization trains people to complete a marathon in exchange for raising money for the Leukemia and Lymphoma Society. While I never had the goal (or desire, for that matter) to run a marathon, I was drawn to the idea immediately. After attending TNT's orientation, I was hooked. They showed a powerful video of leukemia survivors and friends and family members who had been impacted by this dreadful disease. They were not victims, but rather individuals who were proactively raising money to help researchers find a cure by participating in marathons and half marathons across the United States.

I knew I had found the perfect structure to support my new goal of becoming more physically active—a group of caring, action-oriented individuals in a supportive environment, training for a marathon and raising money for an important cause. It was perfect! A bonus was that I would receive expert coaching and train every weekend with other people, many of whom had completed marathons before. If they could complete a marathon, so could I—even though I hadn't run since my college days (and I use the word "run" loosely).

So how does TNT train individuals who in some cases haven't run a single day in their lives to complete a 26.2 mile race after only 4 months of training? It's literally one step at a time. TNT's primary objective is for every team member to complete the marathon without injury, so they focus on helping people develop endurance and prevent injury. That means slowly building up your distance and speed.

Depending on fitness level, newcomers can join the running team, the run/walk team, or the walking team. I joined the run/walk team. We started by training in intervals, walking for three minutes and jogging one. Slowly we were able to increase our time and distance.

Miles of Persistence

Throughout my training, I fluctuated between feeling strong while I ran to feeling as though my legs had lead weights attached to them. There were aches and pains, fatigue and mental battles. And as the mileage on the weekends increased, so did my *lack* of enthusiasm for getting up at 5:00 on a Saturday morning to begin the training. By the time we worked up to 21 miles, training took 5 hours. Let's face it: Doing something you *love* for five hours can be overkill. Imagine doing something that at times feels like pure torture for 5 hours.

What kept me going was the fact that I *had* to follow through on this commitment! I had made a promise that I would complete this marathon—not only to myself, but to my teammates. There were many Saturday mornings when I really felt like staying in bed. But quitting was not an option. Once I got to the training course, I was surprised to hear that my teammates had gone through the same mental battle that I had. Yet we all showed up. We were in this together. And once we got started every Saturday morning, we actually enjoyed the process and were proud of our accomplishment.

After 4 months of training, my teammates and I successfully completed the Honolulu Marathon. Having a structure to ensure I followed through was integral to this accomplishment, and it's a strategy that I've continued to apply to virtually every area of my life. Whenever I want to make a change, I always look for support or accountability to literally *force* me to show up. And if one structure doesn't work, I find another that will.

Identifying Your Support Structure

I often have the pleasure of hearing from women who have completed the Unstoppable Women Challenge. I think the following letter from Susan vividly explains the power of a support structure:

UNSTOPPABLE WOMEN SUCCESS STORY

"I've started at least 20 exercise programs in the past, but I've always quit before seeing any results. I felt like a failure and had basically given up on the hope of getting into shape. When I heard about the Unstoppable Women Challenge, I decided to give my goal one more try because I felt that a 30-day commitment was doable. I committed to walk 100 miles over 30 days. This was a huge stretch for me, but I believed that I could do anything for 30 days.

"Every morning I got up 2 hours earlier to get in my walk. There were many mornings when I didn't feel like walking. But I committed to walk with a buddy and had to go. I got myself motivated by focusing on the stories of unstoppable people who had achieved amazing results in their lives. I felt if they could accomplish their goals, surely I could walk every day.

"Each day I tracked my progress in the Create Your Day Planner and was thrilled to see I was moving one step closer to my goal. I have never walked every day in my life. Yet each day I was inspired to do a little bit more toward my goal. I was so inspired that I accomplished my goal in just 21 days! I've already set my next goal: I'm going to walk 300 miles in 90 days. This is something I never would have even considered in the past. I now know that I am in control of my life and have the determination to accomplish whatever I set my mind to. The Unstoppable Women Challenge has literally jumpstarted my life."

—*Susan Meehan*

While Susan certainly has an unstoppable spirit, she also made some smart choices and built a support structure that would nearly guarantee her success. Instead of walking alone, she committed to walking with a buddy who would motivate and support her (and for whom she did the same). She also tracked her progress in her Create Your Day Planner—an activity that both inspired her and kept her accountable. No wonder Susan achieved her first 30-day goal and is now working on an even more ambitious one!

Of course, creating a support structure is a huge benefit no matter what your goal. For example, suppose that your goal is to create an outline for a book you've been dreaming of writing. Unfortunately, you've been procrastinating lately and haven't made much progress. It always seems that something more urgent demands your attention. You may decide that to complete the outline, you'll need to spend one hour every day working on it. What structure can you create to ensure that you follow through on this goal? Perhaps you might schedule the hour for first thing in the morning, and you might decide that you won't take any personal calls during that time. You now have a structure to help you follow through on the behaviors that will lead to the successful completion of your outline and ultimately, your book.

Structure Equals Success

As you're striving toward your 30-day goal, pay attention to what's working and what's not. If you're not consistently taking action, identify a more effective structure to ensure that you follow through. As Betty Ford said, "You can make it, but it's easier if you don't have to do it alone." Here are some tips to ensure you have the support you need:

Plan your day. People constantly tell me that simply planning their day has been *the most significant structure* they've integrated into their lives to help them achieve their 30-day goals. Proactively determining what needs to be done provides clarity and eliminates the potential for procrastination.

Work with a buddy. Experience has shown that having a buddy is one of the most important components to the program, because creating accountability is critical to reaching goals. People who have fully committed themselves to this process and their buddy have created amazing results in just 30 days. Give yourself the edge and work with a buddy.

Brainstorm new structures if the ones you have in place aren't working. If you're not consistently taking action toward reaching your goal, the problem could be that you don't have an effective support structure. Brainstorm new support structures you could put in place to ensure that you follow through on the behaviors necessary to achieve your goal. If that structure doesn't work, keep brainstorming until you find one that does.

Get online support. Go to **UnstoppableWomen.com** to meet other women who are participating in the challenge. As a bonus, clients have developed all sorts of creative ways to support the changes in their lives, and you can find many of these strategies listed on the Web site.

However you choose to do it, take advantage of the power a support structure can give you. The stronger your support structure, the more unstoppable you become.

Day 14:
Week 2 in Review

Welcome to the end of Week 2. It's time to check in and acknowledge your progress so far and identify any areas where you need help. Before you complete your Week in Review form, I'd like to ask you a few questions.

First, how do you feel about your progress so far in the Unstoppable Women Challenge? Are you very satisfied with your results? Dissatisfied? Somewhere in the middle?

If you haven't seen the progress you'd hoped for, don't listen to lies your voice of fear may tell you—that you're not good enough or disciplined enough, or that you don't have the time or ability to successfully complete the challenge. It's *not true*!

With each step you take, your life is slowly being transformed—even if it might not be obvious to you right now. By completing the Unstoppable Women Challenge, you absolutely will not be the same person as you were just 30 days ago. New possibilities will emerge. Even if things don't work out exactly as you planned, so what? You are in action and have gained invaluable new insights on what works for you and what doesn't, so next time, you can have a new, more effective plan.

Second, how would you rate your overall motivation level this week? Has it been high? Medium? Low?

To increase your motivation, you simply need to refocus your attention back to your purpose for participating in the Unstoppable Women Challenge. Your purpose is your driving force and will keep you going when obstacles threaten to stop you. Go back to Day 2 and review your "why" for participating in this challenge. Connect fully with *why* you set this goal and the deep satisfaction you will experience when you have achieved it. Think about how achieving this goal will positively impact other areas of your life. Feel the joy and excitement you'll experience by honoring your commitments to yourself today to make that goal a reality.

And remember, our emotions drive our behavior, so fully connect with the pleasure of achieving your goal and the pain of failure—what it will cost you if you don't achieve your goal. Use these emotional triggers as motivation to help you take consistent action.

The Week in Review Form

Complete the Week in Review form (see Appendix). After you've completed the form, review it to see if you can notice any recurring issues that are stopping you. Is there a disempowering belief or unproductive behavior that regularly shows up? Did you identify a structure that hasn't supported a new empowering behavior that you want to integrate into your life? If so, no problem. Just come up with another one.

It took me *years* to identify the right structure that enabled me to consistently maintain an optimum weight. I tried countless eating plans and exercise programs until I found the right one for me. Did this mean I wasn't successful all those years? No! Each failed attempt simply showed me what didn't work. And because I stayed with it, I have developed a plan that works for me. Perhaps in the future, my current program will require modification, but for now it's working. Use this process as a means to modify your approach from week to week. As you identify what is stopping you, you will be able to find better structures or resources to support your continuing efforts.

Day 15:
Draw On Your Creativity to Create Solutions

Today's Affirmation: I possess an abundance of creativity, flexibility, and imagination. Whenever I face any challenge, I connect with my inner knowing because I realize the solution lies within me. I am open and willing to experiment with new approaches in both thought and action and remain flexible with my plan to ensure I achieve my 30-day goal. There is always a solution. I am unstoppable.

Congratulations! You are now halfway through the challenge. You're making wonderful progress! As I'm sure you have experienced first-hand, to stay in action and achieve your 30-day goal, it's important to continuously re-evaluate your plan to identify what's working and what's not. Pursuing a goal is a constantly evolving process. Even the best of plans requires modification.

The path to success is not a direct highway, but a bumpy road full of twists and turns and occasional road blocks. The journey requires modifications and adjustments in both thought and action, not just once, but over and over. And that means you must be flexible and creative.

The story of Lyn St. James illustrates the vital importance of being flexible and creative as you strive to reach your goals—over 30 days or 30 years. Lyn prepared for years not just to be a race car driver, but also to be a businessperson. Early on, she realized that to compete with the big boys, she'd need a major corporate sponsor. But companies couldn't have cared

182

less about *her* racing ambitions. They were only concerned with selling products, and if she wanted their support, she would need to learn how to use her skills to help them do just that.

In addition to taking driving classes, Lyn also took courses in business, working hard to perfect her sales pitch and learning what she could do for the customer. Her success is testament to the power of charting your course and then modifying it as needed to overcome the inevitable obstacles along the way.

Unstoppable Woman:
Lyn St. James's Story

Women don't race cars. They don't get their hands dirty in the pit or take apart and reassemble high-performance engines. They don't compete in professional racing against men. And if they do compete, by no means do they ever, ever win.

That was the mindset that Lyn St. James faced—from the pro racing community and her own family—from the time her mother took her to her first Indianapolis 500 in 1966. From that day on, Lyn was hooked. She wanted to race cars against the best drivers in the world. But the best drivers in the world were men, and they sure didn't think women belonged behind the wheel of a Formula 500. As with so many other pursuits, professional racing was a world that didn't think women belonged—unless they were fetching coffee in the pit area.

To achieve her dream, Lyn would have to accept rejection as part of the price of her pursuit, learn from failures and modify her plan when necessary, and educate herself in the fields of racing and business. And in her 15-year quest to build her career as a professional racer, that's exactly what she did.

An Early Love Affair with Cars
Lyn grew up in a home of car lovers. Her mother was physically disabled as a child and felt a special freedom sitting behind the wheel of a car. "A car gave my mother mobility and feeling of power," recalls Lyn. She passed on her love of cars to her daughter, and they would often take long weekend drives together. When Lyn's mother taught her to drive at 15, she also taught her how to "feel" a car, to listen to its noises and understand its smells.

Later that same year, Lyn entered her first auto race, a drag race at Elizabethtown, Indiana, on a dare. Amazingly, she took first place—but her mother was not pleased. Racing cars, she said, was not for well-bred ladies. Ladies kept house, wore makeup, and played piano. "She told me that I had made a serious mistake and that I would never do that again," Lyn says. But even though she obeyed her mother's wishes for more than seven years, the seed had been planted. Lyn wanted to be a racecar driver, and ultimately nothing was going to turn her aside from that dream.

The Beginnings of a Plan

For the next few years, Lyn worked as a secretary and taught piano, but she never lost her love for the smell of fuel, the vibration of suspension as a vehicle moves over the road, and the competition of a race.

Things began to change in 1970, when she married John Carusso, owner of a consumer electronics business and an auto parts business—and a fellow car fanatic. After they moved to Florida, they bought a Ford Pinto for John to compete in at regional amateur races. Lyn was the "gofer" on John's crew, helping out around the garage and making lunches. The other mechanics didn't take her seriously—she was only the wife of the *real* driver on the team. They would send her on errands while they discussed racing strategies.

When John upgraded to a Corvette, Lyn inherited the Pinto, and a plan began to take shape. She would train, hone her skills, and begin racing. With John's support, she enrolled in the driving schools required by the Sports Car Club of America (SCCA). "The day I buckled myself into that car, I was 27 years old and yet I felt like I had been reborn. A surge of strength and desire stirred in me that I had never experienced in any other activity."

When her instructor virtually ignored her in class, she complained and by luck, they assigned her to the best instructor in the school. She was on her way.

Learning from Setbacks

Despite her enthusiasm, racing wasn't going to be easy. In her first race at the Palm Beach International Raceway, Lyn spun the Pinto into a pond. The accident was humiliating. But quitting was not an option.

"After losing control of that car, I had some time to think about my future in racing. After serious consideration, I knew quitting was not an option. I dug my heels in and knew I had to do it and I had to learn to do it well."

John gave her some pivotal advice: If she really wanted to become a professional racecar driver, she had to work on her craft tirelessly, learn from her mistakes and setbacks, and move on. Great advice, and Lyn made it pay off: She continued to refine her skills, and in 1976 and 1977 was the SCCA Florida Regional Champion and runner-up in the 1978 Southeast SCCA competition.

But behind this success, Lyn still faced a glass ceiling of chauvinism. Few sports are as dominated by the "good ol' boy" network. Even when Lyn was winning races, she found it nearly impossible to be taken seriously by her male team members. To them, she was still just John's wife, a woman playing around in a man's sport.

Things didn't improve when she and John divorced. No longer a team member, she would have to finance her own car, be her own manager, and find her own sponsors if she wanted to continue racing. Auto racing is the world's most expensive sport, costing tens of thousands of dollars per year even at the amateur levels. "No one said it would be easy," she says. "And like it or not, money is what makes our wheels turn."

And so Lyn learned the hard way about raising money to keep driving. Her first sponsor was a hairdresser in Oakland. Later she recruited local small business owners to support her. But if she wanted to race with the big boys, she needed big corporate sponsors. She began mailing letters to major corporations—and getting nowhere.

A New Marketing Angle

"After a few rejections, it didn't take me long to recognize that I was approaching this all wrong. Companies wanted to sell products and if I was going to get a sponsor, I needed to position myself as a marketing tool to help them do just that. Racing was a business and if I wanted to pursue it as a profession, I needed to learn the business side of the sport as well as the competitive side."

Lyn enrolled in an advertising class and subscribed to the major magazines in the industry, *Adweek* and *Advertising Age*. She read every book and magazine she could find on marketing, advertising, and sales, and took note of what other sports and celebrity endorsers were doing to help their sponsors. Then she did research to learn the effect the endorsement was having on a company's sales.

She quickly discovered a common theme in all of the successful endorsement and marketing campaigns: Every company needs something to set them apart from the competition. Now Lyn knew what her angle would be in getting a major sponsor. Women controlled about 75 percent of consumer spending decisions in the United States—and she was the *only* high-profile female driver on the professional circuit. Her gender would be her edge.

Sponsorship Is Job One

After reading an article about Ford Motor Company's attempt to attract the female consumer and their commitment to offer employment opportunities in nontraditional areas, Lyn began what would turn into a 2-year telephone and letter-writing campaign. She told Ford marketing executives: "What better way to attract women customers than to have a woman race car driver winning races in a Ford car?"

Great pitch. The response? A letter from the corporation's PR manager saying, in effect, thanks but not interested. However, the letter did leave the door open with one phrase: "Keep us informed of your progress."

That opening was all Lyn needed to persevere. Over the coming months, she contacted the people at Ford on a regular basis. Finally, Ford offered her a job at a car convention in Las Vegas, paying her $100 a day to stand in 100-degree sun and be a "product expert." Few people stopped to ask her questions, and she was tempted to write the trip off as a waste of time. But she didn't. She knew that in reality, it was one more stepping stone, a valuable foot in the door to the corporate sponsorship she needed. So she kept working to convince Ford that she was worth the risk.

After 2 years, in 1981, her persistence and savvy finally paid off: Ford Motor Company agreed to be her sponsor. With a major corporate backer removing most of her financial concerns, she was convinced she would finally make her mark on the racing circuit. However, the racing gods had another surprise in store for her. Without explanation, Lyn began losing races. Instead of impressing her new sponsor, she suddenly had to take drastic measures to keep Ford as her backer and was forced to travel a grueling 250-day-a-year schedule as a spokesperson and product consultant. Five long years passed before her next win.

Understandably, she began to doubt her ability and her plan. She had struggled to get a major sponsor but had never worried about her ability to win races—and now she was struggling to deliver a winning performance on the track! "I began to consider myself a total failure," she says.

New Plan, New Determination

An article about legendary NASCAR champion Bobby Allison pulled Lyn out of her funk. In it, Allison said he had gone through 17 different racing teams in 22 years in the sport. "I realized that I wasn't the only person going through this. It was simply the nature of the sport that drivers often race for many different teams," she says.

She returned to the track with a new attitude and a new plan to become the best driver on the circuit. In 1991, when Ford drastically reduced its overall involvement in road racing and dropped Lyn as a driver, she kept herself motivated with a huge goal: She announced she was going to drive in the Indianapolis 500.

The Indy 500 is the ultimate race car driver's dream. Now she just had to raise hundreds of thousands of dollars to make it come true. Undeterred, she began calling, writing, and making in-person pitches to more than 150 corporations. None of it worked. Her friends raised $10,000, but she needed ten times that amount. With only four months before the Indy 500, a personal acquaintance got her an appointment to make her pitch to J.C. Penney. At the Dallas office, Lyn met three female executives who understood the importance of what she was trying to do. "'I realized there was something there," says Gale Duff-Bloom, one of the executives Lyn met that day.

J. C. Penney agreed to invest in Lyn. The slogans of their *Spirits of the American Women* ad campaign appeared on her car, and she became a spokeswoman. The company would later confirm that their $250,000 investment produced $2.7 million in publicity.

In 1992, Lyn became only the second woman ever to race in the Indianapolis 500. While that would have been enough of an achievement, she excelled even further—finishing 11th and winning Rookie of the Year honors. She received her trophy to a standing ovation led by four-time Indy legend A. J. Foyt.

With the backing of J.C. Penney, Lyn became the first woman to become a full-time driver in the Indy Car World Series, entering six of 16 races in 1993. In her 20-year career, she set 31 international and national closed circuit speed records. For her accomplishments on and off the track, *Sports Illustrated* magazine named her one of the "Top 100 Athletes of the 20th Century."

Racing to Do More

Lyn has never been satisfied with simply being a successful driver. After all she had endured to improve her skills, build a team, find sponsorship, and triumph over male prejudice, she was determined to share both her experience and her good fortune. In 1993, she launched the Lyn St. James Foundation and Driver Development Program, which promotes safety and driver development for young women who want to become race car drivers. She also served as president of the Women's Sport Foundation. Later, she launched the Make A Difference campaign, donating some of her prize money to programs that offer opportunities to girls through sports.

Today, Lyn is a popular speaker, author of the autobiography *Ride of Your Life: A Race Car Driver's Journey*, and a sports commentator and spokesperson. She has been honored by many major women's organizations and publications for her courage and passion. She has even been a guest at the White House five times.

Never Take No for an Answer

Lyn's story represents more than sports success. Her sport of choice didn't want her, she struggled for years to find a corporate sponsor, and finally her hard-won driving skills threatened to desert her, yet she persisted. She had a dream and was willing to hang in there and modify her approach continuously to become one of the best racecar drivers in the country.

"I realized early on that the road to success is littered with rejection," she says. "If I had given up after all the no's I ever heard, I would have never made it in racing. Sure, rejection hurts, but it also provides you with an opportunity to learn, improve, and keep going. After my first dozen or so rejections, I finally realized that nothing in my life changed after someone told me no. Had I been scared of rejection, or if I hadn't accepted being turned down as a natural part of the process, I might never have learned to ask the right questions. You might get a thousand no's before you hear the first yes. But you'll never know until you ask."

> *"Early on, I discovered that the road to success is paved with rejection.*
> *No is not forever. No is only 'no' that day from that person. You can*
> *always go back to the same person tomorrow with new information.*
> *If you're committed and you're dedicated, you'll eventually*
> *find a way to turn that 'no' into a 'yes.'"*
> —Lyn St. James

⌒⌒⌒⌒ Unstoppable Action ⌒⌒⌒⌒
If You Can't Find a Way, Make One

As the story of Lyn St. James proves without question, success is no accident. Lyn invested countless hours of time and energy in her pursuit to become the best race car driver and the most savvy sponsorship dealmaker she could be—and the investment paid big dividends. She faced daunting, sometimes overwhelming, obstacles, but a key ingredient to her success was that she recognized what *wasn't* working and quickly identified a new approach. Her willingness to modify her plan when necessary kept her from being intimidated or giving up. In the same way, your creativity and ability to be flexible will enable you to stay in action during your Unstoppable Women Challenge.

When you're in touch with your creativity, you can think of unusual ways to work around problems, ways that align with your own skills and reflect your values. When you're flexible, you're able and willing to change and modify plans; you adjust to new circumstances and needs. Both mean you are willing to experiment with new approaches and fresh solutions.

The first step to renewing your creativity is to develop the inborn creativity that is already within you. You possess an abundance of creativity—enough to solve *any* problem that arises. The challenge is to keep your mind open and flexible. Your mind functions like a muscle; when you don't use it, it loses its ability to perform.

The following exercise is a powerful tool to help you flex your creativity muscle. This exercise will help you apply more creativity and flexibility to any obstacle you might be facing. Take a moment to think about a particular obstacle that is a concern to you and perhaps threatening to stop you on your 30-day challenge. Then answer the following questions:

1. Who? (*Who* has information or resources I need, *who* should be involved, *who* can help?)
2. What? (*What* end result do I want, *what* resources do I need, *what* do I need to know?)

3. When? (*When* does it need to be resolved?)

4. Where? (*Where* are potential resources?)

5. Why? (*Why* does this problem exist and *why* is it important to resolve?)

6. How? (*How* will I find the resources and *how* will I know when the problem has been solved?)

By applying these questions to any obstacle you face, you will immediately become more flexible, creative, and better equipped to adjust your course. Complete this exercise, and identify a new solution to keep your 30-day goal in action!

Create Your Day Planner

PLAN TO BE UNSTOPPABLE! Tonight or first thing tomorrow morning, plan your next day's activities by filling out your Create Your Day Planner (see Appendix). And the next time you're faced with a seemingly insurmountable obstacle, use what you've learned today. Take some time to reflect quietly on new, creative solutions to the problem. As you reflect, don't judge your thoughts—simply let the ideas flow. Sometimes a brilliant solution can appear out of what might have first seemed outrageous or unreasonable. The more you flex your creativity "muscle," the easier it will become to find new, fresh solutions to problems.

Day 16:
Giving to Others Is a Gift to Myself

Today's Affirmation: My eyes and heart are open to looking for ways to be of service to others. As I expand my capacity to give, I expand my capacity to receive. When I give, I feel a sense of purpose and contribution that positively serves every area of my life.

Living a life of meaning and unstoppability always involves giving. Many of the classic religious and secular texts throughout history contain some variation on "Give, and it will be given to you." Think about that for a moment. Isn't it true that the people with the most love in their lives give the most love? The people with the most friends are the most friendly? A recent study by Stephanie L. Brown, Ph.D., of the University of Michigan in Ann Arbor even showed that seniors who give aid and support to friends and neighbors actually live longer than those who simply receive it.

That's why one of your tasks in the Unstoppable Women Challenge is to identify one way you can be of service to someone else every day. What you give doesn't have to be big. It might be a smile to a stranger, an offer of business advice, a financial donation to a cause you've been wanting to help, or a few volunteer hours at a community shelter. By sharing your talents, time, or money, you will become invigorated about your goal and your life because you will be making a difference in the lives of others. This creates wonderful feelings of satisfaction that will serve you well beyond your 30-day commitment.

TV host Larry King asked Dana Reeve, wife of the late paralyzed actor Christopher Reeve, if she ever got depressed about her husband being confined to a wheelchair. "Yes, of course," she said. "And when that happens, I immediately reach out to someone else who's hurting. Chris does the same thing when he gets down. In fact, we usually do it together. Helping others is a surefire way to help yourself."

Consider making a daily habit of giving to others. It doesn't have to take a lot of time and energy. By opening your eyes and heart, you will notice countless ways you can simply reach out to others. There is nothing more fulfilling in life than expressing your love for others. When you create a habit of giving, *you* are the greatest recipient.

You're about to read the extraordinary story of Verneta Wallace. The strongest impulse in her life was to give, so she followed it. Without a cent of financial support from the government, working within a system that often treated those in need with cruel indifference, she became a loving foster parent to 109 children over 23 years.

Unstoppable Woman:
Verneta Wallace's Story

Her parents had been foster parents when she was a child, so Verneta Wallace was aware of the enormous responsibility it is to become a foster parent—but she also knew the enormous difference good foster care could make in a child's life. She and her husband David debated the idea very seriously. After all, they already had two young children. But they also knew they could make a real difference.

"We thought we could put a little spot in their heart so that for the rest of their lives they knew someone thought they were really great kids. It was unconditional love," she says. "We went into it fully aware that we would not always have the sweet little kid who would say, 'Oh, thank you so much for taking me.'"

Finances were an issue. Verneta and David were people of modest income, and when Verneta went to Catholic Social Services to inquire about being a foster parent, she learned that she would receive no monetary help from either the state or the Catholic Church. She and David decided to accept the challenge and try to make it happen using their own income.

Year One
At age 24, Verneta became a foster parent. Her commitment was tested right away; the first child she was given was a 10-year-old hearing impaired boy. "He was just learning sign language and I had a minimal amount of training, so we learned together," says Verneta. "The rewards were many. He learned to sign and speak. It was so exciting to see him learn things."

That same year, she also discovered the hardest part about foster care: helplessly standing by while your foster child, the child you loved like your own, is sent back to an unstable environment. "It was always difficult when children were sent to an environment we felt was not healthy for them or where they would not be valued," she says. This possibility was always in the back of her mind, so she gave as much as she could while she had the chance.

There were also moments with children whose parents were drug addicts, abusive, or neglectful that touched Verneta's heart. "This little girl was five years old and she had on boy's undershorts. Not panties that little girls would have but shorts," Verneta recalls. "So I took her to the store and I said, 'You need to have a dress to wear to church.' I let her pick out her dress [as well as some other clothing for little girls], two of these, four of those. You know, the kind of things that our children take for granted. And she was absolutely ecstatic. She said, 'Oh, you mean I get a dress of my own and I get to pick it out myself?' That's the kind of stuff that breaks your heart but makes it worthwhile."

On Call 24 Hours

Verneta and David opened themselves up to taking in babies and emergency cases, such as infants suffering from fetal alcohol syndrome who needed round-the-clock care. They also took in pregnant girls who were planning on giving up their babies. They would stay for a few months, deliver, sign the necessary paperwork, and be gone.

As she became known as someone who never refused a child, Verneta began to take in a non-stop flow of children who needed a safe haven: troubled, bitter teens who had bounced from foster home to foster home; younger children shell-shocked from abuse; and babies waiting to be adopted. Soon she was on 24-hour call to be able to take in a baby at a moment's notice.

Of course, in addition to special care, babies also require special supplies, which can be very expensive. Still, Verneta trusted that everything would work out. "I had no clue where I was going to get anything," she recalls. "But word got around at church and then it was, 'Oh, I have a bed or I have this . . .' People would give us clothes that their children had outgrown, or toys. We hit a lot of garage sales. We were always rearranging the budget."

"No Way to Console Them"

As the years passed, the children continued to come. The Wallaces cared for as many as three at a time, some with physical disabilities. There were the Inuit children from Alaska who needed special meals that Verneta had to learn to make. Most heartbreaking of all, though, were the crack babies suffering through withdrawal.

"It's awful. There is nothing to give them to help them overcome their addiction," she says. "They just have to go cold turkey and go through withdrawal. They've got the little tremors and little shakes and their little chins would shiver. And that harrowing cry . . . there's no way to console them." Verneta learned to live in the moment, to attend to the needs of these children without worrying about the reasons they had the need.

Over the years, she also took great pride in the fact that she never neglected the needs of her own children. "I never missed a school concert, play, or baseball game," she says. Her one concession to her family was that she never took in a child the same age as her own children. She reasoned they didn't need the competition.

A Mother's Rage

One of the greatest challenges for Verneta was visitation day. She was obligated to bring the child she was fostering to the very person who caused the child's estrangement—whether it was by drugs, abuse, or neglect. Often the mother, dealing with her own shame and guilt, would lash out at Verneta and personally attack her. They assumed that she was judging them for their poor parenting. Perhaps at first, Verneta did feel a certain resentment toward these parents. After all, she was dealing with the consequences of their actions. But soon she began to understand that these parents, though severely lacking in coping skills, did the best they could. She allowed them to vent their frustration to a point, then she'd let them know where she stood.

"I'd say, 'Let me just tell you a few things about me. I am not here to take away your child. I can see that you love your child and that you want this child back in your life,'" Verneta recalls. Still, she spent a great deal of time biting her tongue, taking verbal abuse when she was the best parent some of these children had ever had.

There were other hardships, of course. Over the 23 years, Verneta figures she got about 5 hours of sleep a night. "With the newborn babies that are being taken away from their moms, you're probably up every 2 hours, 3 if you're lucky," she says. "And of course with a lot of these babies, it takes 45 minutes to change them and feed them and all that stuff. There was not a lot of sleep."

Love and Nothing Less

As time went on, friends told Verneta she was crazy for continuing to take in more children. She and David even got into an argument over continuing to take in infants. But she never flagged in her efforts to make a good home for troubled children. What kept her going?

"We made a difference in a child's life!" she says. "We knew that when we had a baby live with us that he or she wouldn't remember us, but children know when they are loved and we gave them that. With the older children, they knew they were safe and cared for and had their eyes opened to a world they didn't know existed."

Verneta admits that having few rights as a foster parent was challenging. "You don't know that you're going to fight the intense feelings I did," she says. "It wasn't like I wanted to keep the child. But I had invested time and a part of my life, and there was a part of me in that child. I've had more than one social worker say to me, 'You know, you really get attached to these kids, are you being healthy?' And I'd say, 'Yes, I'm being healthy for this child.' Did I have difficulty with children leaving? Yes. But I always knew that there would be another child who needed us."

From Foster Mother to Social Worker

Eventually, the lack of sleep took its toll, and Verneta and David agreed they would end their tenure as foster parents. They handed over their last baby for adoption to a grateful family in 1997. But that wasn't the end of Verneta's work on behalf of children.

"I became a court-appointed child advocate so that I could really get in there and advocate for kids and stick up for their rights," she says. "I could fight in ways I couldn't fight as a foster parent. For instance, sometimes kids were returned to their parents and shouldn't have been. As a foster parent you have no say, but as a court-appointed child advocate you have a voice. I may not save all of them, but if I can save one, I feel good about it."

A Wider World

Of course, Verneta couldn't help but be changed by the experience, by all the lives intertwined with hers and David's. She knows that in the true spirit of giving selflessly, she's gained much more.

"My world was pretty small," she says. "I knew people abused drugs and didn't take care of their children. But those people weren't real to me. But once I got into it, I saw that the person was a mama who had gotten into some really dumb stuff, but still loved that child. It gave me a greater sense that the world is not black and white. It gave me perspective. Sometimes it's nicer not to have to know that stuff, but it's reality. You can choose to walk away and pretend like it never happened, or you can whine about it, or you can get in there and do something about it."

Verneta has also shared those lessons with her own children, who she says have surpassed her. "My children have a better capacity for what this world's all about and what it needs to be," she says. "I don't know that I could have given my children a lesson like that in any other way."

Verneta gets letters from some of her 109 kids and has received invitations to graduations from others. Still others have been inspired by her to become foster parents themselves. Grateful parents still thank her for the time and love she gave their children. But the greatest rewards come from knowing how much she gave, and how much her gifts meant, as illustrated by this story:

"I can remember we got three children who we had for a week, and when they got ready to go back home, I told them that the judge said they could go back home and live with their dad. The little girl, who was five, said, 'We thank you so much for letting us come and live with you. We have had such a fun time.' Then she says, 'Where are you going to put the toys after we leave? I need to know in my head so that when my daddy messes up again and we come back to live with you, I'll know where the toys are.'"

"But her dad did not mess up. And when I asked her where her mom was, she said, 'Oh, she ran away, she left us. But we're looking for another one,'" Verneta recalls.

Verneta knew despite all the work, sleepless nights, and heartbreak, what she was doing was, in a small way, saving the world one child at a time. "It was never easy to give so much to so many children while giving my own family the love they deserved," she says. "But I never considered quitting. I found the strength in my heart to keep going because I knew I was giving these children something many of them had never had: unconditional love. I knew most would not remember me, but I also knew many would carry the imprint of that love with them. It was like giving a tiny piece of myself to each child to carry into their lives. Giving to them gave me the strength to keep going."

⤳ Unstoppable Action ⤳
Be of Service

The Jews whom Oskar Schindler saved from the Nazi concentration camps gave him a ring that was engraved with the beautiful Hebrew phrase, "He who saves one life saves the world entire." Verneta Wallace understood that by giving of herself to each child without thought for the consequences, she was finding her own strength—and creating a legacy of caring and love that would go out into the world.

By caring for children who were disabled or abused, Verneta also gained perspective. One of the most powerful tools for immediately putting our problems into perspective is to help someone with problems greater than our own. There is nothing like another person's misfortunes to make our own challenges seem less daunting. Giving to others not only distracts us from our own difficulties, but helps us find our own strength, much as Verneta did. It can lead us to a purpose, exorcise our own insecurities, and help us gain a new sense of mission and determination for our own transformation.

🖎 Find ways to give and be of service.

Not sure how to fit "giving back" into your everyday life? That's okay. You can define service and giving in any way that works for you. Possible next steps could be:

- Volunteer one day per month to assist a non-profit in your community
- Mentor a new employee at work
- Become a Big Sister
- Donate blood through the American Red Cross
- Help an elderly neighbor with some of their shopping needs
- Cook a meal for a family in need
- Join Habitat for Humanity and help build a home for a family in need

- Teach someone how to read
- Take the extra step "above and beyond" to provide services to a customer or find a solution to a problem outside your job description
- Make a phone call to someone who needs cheering up
- Sign up for a committee at your child's school or in your community
- Mentor a teenage girl who needs help

Commit yourself to reaching out today. When we give to others, we are the greatest recipients. As physician and writer John Andrew Holmes said, "There is no experience better for the heart than reaching down and lifting people up."

For additional ideas and ways to reach out to others and lend a helping hand, visit **UnstoppableWomen.com.** Not only will you receive helpful tips, but you'll also meet other women in the unstoppable community who have been able to integrate giving into their daily lives. Their results have been nothing less than transformational.

"If you want to lift yourself up, lift up someone else."
—*Booker T. Washington*

 Create Your Day Planner

PLAN TO BE UNSTOPPABLE! Tonight or tomorrow morning, plan your next day's activities by filling out your Create Your Day Planner (see Appendix). Be in gratitude today for the wonderful givers and mentors in your life who have reached out to you. Reflect on the contribution others have had in your life. Take a moment to thank those people who have offered especially helpful advice or support to you as you've been working toward your goal. And don't forget to thank your buddy for her support and encouragement!

Day 17:
Develop Your Inner Circle

Today's Affirmation: I am identifying role models and mentors who are models of possibility and hope for my life. I know that if they can succeed, so can I. I actively invest time and energy to develop and build a network of mutually beneficial relationships and am eager to support others in their efforts. When I focus on giving and being of service to others, people will want to give back to me.

Margaret Thatcher's childhood role model was her father, who admonished her to lead and never follow the pack. Gloria Steinem adopted Gandhi and Louisa May Alcott as her early role models. One of Golda Meir's role models was Eleanor Roosevelt, who the former Prime Minister of Israel called "the first lady of the world." Oprah Winfrey's role models were the heroes and heroines she read about as a child.

Unstoppable people throughout history have drawn inspiration, ideas, and strategies from role models. Likewise, great leaders from the past—those who achieved excellence in fields such as sports, literature, or science—and even fictional or mythological characters have served to inspire the business leaders, politicians, and other high-achievers of today. Role models and mentors are critical to many personal triumphs—and are particularly relevant for women looking to make bold new changes in their lives.

The reason is quite simple: We learn how to act by modeling ourselves after others. When we're children, how we walk, talk, eat, play, and dress is learned from watching our parents and older siblings. And when we're older, the lessons we learn from mentors, teachers, and bosses about such things as studying, work habits, goal setting, and communication set patterns that last our entire lives. Role models are central to how we learn to be human.

That's why for your Unstoppable Women Challenge (and beyond!), it's vital that you identify role models—people in your life or public figures you admire—whom you can emulate. When working to achieve any goal in your life, whether it's losing weight, starting a new business, or raising happy children, finding other people who have reached that same goal—and learning how they did it—is one of the most powerful strategies you can use.

The story of Zoe Koplowitz demonstrates the power of role models to inspire us, to drive us, to keep us moving forward toward new possibilities for our lives.

Unstoppable Woman:
Zoe Koplowitz's Story

Have you ever cut a workout short because it was too much effort? Or decided to skip a morning run because it was just too difficult to get your body moving? Think about how you would manage if getting your body moving every day took all the energy and will you could muster. The temptation to give up would be overwhelming, wouldn't it? That's why Zoe Koplowitz is so amazing. With every reason not to dream, with every excuse for saying, "This is just too hard," she didn't. Step by step, with the support of a "dream team" of role models and friends, she reached her goal—and continues to do so.

Struck Down at 25

Zoe takes pride in the title "slowest woman ever to complete the New York City Marathon." That's because she lives with the daily challenges of multiple sclerosis, the disease that attacks the central nervous system and severely hinders movement. Diagnosed at age 25, she never let her disease stop her from being a typical attitude-filled resident of the East Village. On crutches with her red hair flying, she's chased drug dealers out of her building and worked to protect her community.

"I've never seen myself as a victim of MS," she says. But January 8, 1988, she was running her moving company when she swallowed a large vitamin C capsule and began to choke. As she started to black out, her partner performed the Heimlich maneuver and saved her life. The brush with death turned her perspective completely upside down.

"When I came to," she said, "I thought it was such an insult that I wasn't going to die from MS but choke to death on a vitamin C pill." She decided that rather than surrender her mobility and her will to fight her disease, she would take them back. So, like the true original she is, she decided to do the craziest thing she could: run in the New York City Marathon.

Zoe Finds a Trainer

There was just one problem: she was in terrible shape. The immobility of MS had left her 60 pounds overweight, and she couldn't even walk down the street without her crutches. She had no concept of what it took just to make it through the 26-mile race, much less actually participate. She tried to train herself, but kept falling down and getting nowhere.

Zoe's neighbors responded to her efforts predictably: they looked at her like she was nuts. But Zoe realized that she was trying something that had never been tried before, so being thought crazy was inevitable. It never stopped her. "I came to realize that looking stupid is an inherent part of risk taking and goal achievement," she says. "My goal is to cross the finish line, not to look good." But clearly, if she was to make that happen, she needed some help.

Then someone told her about Dick Traum.

Traum had been an athlete and the owner of a computer business when a freak accident crushed his right leg between two cars, resulting in the amputation of his right leg below the knee. Fitted with an artificial leg, Traum decided he had to get in shape after a friend dropped dead of a heart attack in his thirties. But since no one had ever done distance running on an artificial leg before, he had to become a pioneer in the field. And by October 1976, he had completed the NYC Marathon in the entirely respectable time of 7 hours, 24 minutes. If anyone could help Zoe overcome the obstacles she faced, it was Traum. His name, after all, means "dream" in German.

So Zoe began training with Traum's Achilles Track Club, a running club exclusively for people with physical disabilities. "When I attended the first workout, I was overwhelmed. I had never been around people with disabilities and there was an entire group of people in wheelchairs, amputees, those who were blind—and they were all in training. It was a wake-up call for me. They proved that having a disability didn't have to define what I could do."

Zoe started her training with Achilles. She was assigned a volunteer who would do the marathon with her. The volunteer worked for a magazine and five weeks before the marathon, she found out that she had to work that day due to the presidential election. It would be impossible for Zoe to finish the grueling marathon without support.

Zoe and Hester

At the training sessions, Zoe had met Hester Sutherland. Hester's daughter was a wheelchair athlete and a member of the Achilles Track Club. Hester attended the training with her daughter and because her daughter's pace was much faster, Hester stayed behind and walked with the women who were much slower. Zoe and Hester struck up a friendship and after hearing about Zoe's predicament, Hester happily volunteered to do the marathon with Zoe. "I was relieved and grateful. The fact that we'd be on the road over 20 hours didn't bother her a bit," said Zoe.

Zoe began to depend on Hester for more than friendship. Hester is an RN and Zoe is a diabetic. "Every two miles we have to stop and take my shoes off to look at my feet for any type of sore or hot spot before it turns into a blister," she says. "An untreated blister can present great problems for a diabetic in distance walking." Hester also helped Zoe keep her pace. "I have a tendency to speed up and run with the wild horses when the crowd is cheering," she laughs. "Hester keeps me on pace, reminding me that the goal is to finish. She nags me about drinking water, she gives me Advil, carries needed supplies and provides invaluable support as the long hours continue and the going gets tough."

Nearly a Day on the Mean Streets

In April 1988, Zoe lined up with Hester by her side and with thousands of others to participate in her first marathon. She had no illusions about how long it would take her to cross the finish line. That wasn't the point. Her primary objective was simply to get there. She knew it would be a long, exhausting journey; she expected it to take her at least 24 hours to finish the course a champion marathoner could complete in over two. So she dressed warmly, in tights and a jersey, with a stuffed turtle she named "Flash, the Miracle Racing Turtle" around her neck.

"For me, the New York Marathon is a race and a metaphor," she says. "It's an opportunity to reach past where you'd ordinarily give up in real life. Once you finish a marathon, accomplishing what you think would be impossible, no one can ever say no to you again. You now know you have what it takes to go the distance."

When the race began, Zoe and Hester let the lead runners pass, then Zoe started her long, slow journey on crutches. She would speak to fellow marathoners along the way, touching them with her story and her determination. And she loved going through Brooklyn, with its close-knit neighborhoods and warm people. During this first marathon, she was stopped by a timeworn homeless man in one of the borough's poorest districts, who said to her tearfully, "When you cross that finish line, think of me. Cross that line for me, too, because you're all I got." She knew exactly what the man was saying: like others, he saw her as the embodiment of possibility. If she could complete the marathon, maybe there was hope for him, too.

Not that walking for more than 21 hours through the streets of New York City was without its dangers. It wasn't. After all the other competitors had finished or given up, and night had fallen, Zoe and her support team were still plugging away, and they found themselves in some of the city's scariest, most crime-ridden areas. But Zoe refused to leave the official marathon route, marked by a blue line. "Wherever the blue line goes, I go," she said.

Many people have asked Zoe why she takes such risks walking for hours after dark through New York's war zones. Here, her defiance shows through, as she refuses to be another city dweller cowed by street violence. "That's the course. If you're not on the blue line, you're not doing the course. People run away from their difficulties. This is my life," she says. "I have a right to be here and face whatever comes my way. If I give up once, then I will have lost something very special."

Over the years, her late-night journey has put her face-to-face with drug dealers and gang members. More than once, she's feared for her life. But more often than not, these hardened criminals have cheered her on, escorted her through gang territory, and protected her from other individuals. Once, several teen gangs who had seen her on the news handed her off, one territory to another, until she was out of the Bronx.

If the fear of street crime was bad, the physical toll on her body was like torture. All marathoners suffer, but Zoe was on the course ten times longer than a competitive marathoner. She endured tremendous punishment, but she endured. In the end, she finished in a time of 21 hours, 35 minutes. The finish line was empty of people when she crossed, but that didn't matter. In her heart, there was a celebration going on.

A Symbol of Hope

That was 1988. Since then, Zoe has completed 16 New York City Marathons, finishing dead last each time. Each has taken her longer than the last, and each has been the best race of her life. Over the years, the punishment on her body has gotten harder to bear, but Zoe has never quit. Part of the reason is that she's attracted an "inner circle" of supporters who, inspired by her courage and determination, pitch in to help her keep running:

• Hester has run all 16 marathons by her side.

• Her physical therapist, Louanne Sforza. "Louanne's constantly thinking about the next tool to help me continue," Zoe says. Whether it's Pilates, physical therapy, fitting her for a back brace, or using a battery-operated machine that sends electrical stimulation to her legs to interrupt the flow of pain, Louanne enables her to get to the finish line.

• Friends and strangers have assisted her along the way. "I have friends who come out and walk with me for a couple of miles or a couple of hours," she says.

• A community of Zoe supporters has developed over the years. "Complete strangers, children who are now teenagers who heard about my story through their school, bring their family, friends, and neighbors to meet me every year," she says. "We all have cell phones and everybody is called to report my progress and my location so they can meet me with with noisemakers to cheer me on."

• The world famous New York City Guardian Angels, a community-based safety patrol program, has assisted Zoe in almost all of the marathons. In 2004, 15 guardian angels joined her through an entire half-marathon. "They taught us the power of keeping your word," she says. They're there if it rains, snows, walking through drug deals, or whatever circumstance. When they give their word, they're there."

The Accidental Heroine

That outpouring of love and support is enough for Zoe, but it's not enough for others who admire her. In the process of her racing odyssey she's become a spokeswoman and heroine, though that's not what she intended. In 1991, she was chosen to receive the Multiple Sclerosis Society's Special Achievement Award, and she continues to be a beacon of hope for people with MS and other debilitating diseases.

Zoe Koplowitz personifies the unstoppable spirit. She has written her autobiography, *The Winning Spirit; Life Lessons Learned in Last Place* and speaks to corporations, sharing her story of achievement in the face of obstacles. But for Zoe, the true reward is how her efforts have inspired so many others. "Over the years I've become a symbol of endurance for people," she says. "I get letters all year long. I carry them with me when I run. What I do is a metaphor for life, just like the marathon itself. It means you can get somewhere by putting one foot after another." Zoe Koplowitz is living proof that it's not where you start that counts. It's where you finish.

"No one is an island. Life is a team sport. If I was out there by myself, it not only wouldn't be fun, it wouldn't be possible. Being part of the team makes everyone better. And with will, determination, and a little help from your friends, anyone can complete their own 'life marathon.'"
—Zoe Koplowitz

Unstoppable Action
Cultivate Mentors and Role Models

As the story of Zoe Koplowitz shows, mentors can show up in the most unexpected places. The key is to find role models who speak to you personally, to whom you can relate. Just as the members of the Achilles Track Club understood the challenges faced by Zoe, if you identify with where your role model is coming from, you'll be able to translate his or her experiences to your own life.

Where do we find such people? There are two types of role models, *indirect* and *direct*. An indirect role model is a person you have never met, but know about. Oprah Winfrey has said that the heroic figures she read about in books were her role models, showing her the "open door" in her life. The women in this book are powerful indirect role models. Their stories prove what's possible.

Direct role models are people you know, from a coach to a mentor, a minister to a parent. Finding a direct role model is important because you can talk to this person and learn from his or her experience.

Find your role models.

How much we achieve may boil down to the quality of models we choose to emulate. For inspiration as you continue working toward your 30-day goal, create a Gallery of Unstoppable Role Models. To create your gallery, identify three or four individuals who have already achieved the result that you want to achieve. Look at the things they do that resonate with your lifestyle: how they communicate, their work ethic, and so on. Learn as much as you can about their methods of thinking and planning, their strategies, and their insights for overcoming obstacles.

Don't let the fact that you may not know these people personally stop you. If they've written books, take the time to read them. If they're giving a lecture at a convention, sign up and attend. If they've written articles, study their writing for insights into what enabled them to be a success.

When things aren't working "according to plan," draw strength from your role models. Remind yourself that they have been where you are and they prevailed. So can you.

A Place to Connect

If you're looking to connect with other women who are joining the Unstoppable Women Challenge, a great place to find them is at **UnstoppableWomen.com**. Every day, positive, motivated, courageous women like you gather here to exchange ideas, share encouragement, and tell their success stories. Step into the Unstoppable Women Challenge Forum, share your insights with others, and draw strength from others who've gone before you or are on the same path. Together, we can make incredible things happen.

Create Your Day Planner

PLAN TO BE UNSTOPPABLE! Tonight or first thing tomorrow morning, plan your next day's activities by filling out your Create Your Day Planner (see Appendix). Identify an area where you would like to learn more as a result of this Unstoppable Women Challenge. You might want to take your consulting business to the next level, become a recording artist, or develop a new product for the Internet. Who could provide the needed expertise? List as many potential resources as possible. If it is someone in your company, approach that person. Talk to your inner circle, and ask them if they know anyone in that field. Usually, each name you get will result in another referral until you meet the person you need to meet. If all of your leads eventually become dead-ends, do some research. Identify those who have written recent articles about the subject. Write each of them a letter with your questions or use e-mail, which provides swift and easy access to all sorts of individuals from college professors to corporate presidents. Ask these people for possible referrals or suggestions for other resources. You have nothing to lose, and each step will bring you closer to your goal.

Day 18:
Life's Greatest Risk Is Taking No Risk

Today's Affirmation: Making any change in my life requires risk. Risk is the fuel behind all growth and greatness. To overcome any fear, I prepare as best I can and then plunge into the very thing that scares me most. By taking risks, I build confidence and continue to grow and develop. I am willing to take a risk on me over these 30 days and beyond. I am unstoppable.

To live fully is to risk. There is no reward in playing it safe. Whether you want a healthier body, a more rewarding career, a better income, or a stronger relationship, you can't get what you want by just hoping it will happen. You have to act, risk failure, take a chance.

Even something as simple as making new friends requires a risk. To meet new people, you have to take the risk of introducing yourself and showing interest in them. They may or may not reciprocate the interest. That's the price of putting yourself out there. But without the risk, you're alone watching reality television.

If you want a raise at work, you'll have to take the risk of standing out, of doing more than your current job description. Your manager may not notice, but unless you risk the effort, you're not likely to break through to the next salary level.

The same principle applies to the Unstoppable Women Challenge. By committing to make a change in your life, you risk the possibility of "failure." Perhaps your breakthrough goal is to get a college degree, but the idea terrifies you. You're afraid of facing your kids if you don't do as well as you'd like, of looking foolish or even stupid. You have a deep yearning to do it, but you feel immobilized by fear.

How do you decide whether your goal is worth the risk? How can you evaluate whether or not to move forward? In his book *Failing Forward*, John C. Maxwell says that "risk must be evaluated not by the fear it generates in you or the probability of your success, but by the value of the goal."

That's great advice! Everything in life involves risk. The question is whether or not your goal is worth that risk. How important is it for you to achieve it? You can spend your time worrying about everything that could go wrong and talk yourself out of doing anything. Or you can muster up the courage to take a single step. The choice is yours.

I'll promise you one thing: Taking a risk to do something that matters deeply to you is far better than settling for where you are today and always wondering, "What if?" One of the saddest ironies of life is that people who abandon their dreams and take what they perceive to be an easier, safer path ultimately suffer far greater pain by never striving for their dreams. One of the most gut-wrenching, agonizing moments a person can face is looking back on a life full of regrets.

Take a Bold Step

The Unstoppable Women Challenge is about facing your fear head-on and being willing to take a chance on yourself This is your time! You can choose to live your life fully, or you can hide inside with the doors locked.

Millard Fuller, founder of Habitat for Humanity, says, "Most people tiptoe through life hoping to arrive safely at death." In their efforts to minimize risk and find the "safe" path, they don't really live.

Canadian singing sensation Loreena McKennitt was willing to bet on herself because she believed in her Celtic-inspired music even when no one else wanted to support it. Her decision to put up her own money to release her first CD stemmed from the belief that she had a unique voice and vision. As you'll see, the risk paid off enormously, giving McKennitt the kind of independence and influence most other artists only dream of.

Unstoppable Woman:
Loreena McKennitt's Story

After a career of nearly two decades, you could say Loreena McKennitt is on top of the world of Celtic popular music: nearly 13 million albums sold, a catalogue of six studio CDs and one double live record, a fan base that spans the world, with multi-platinum sales from Turkey to New Zealand. And enough awards to fill a room.

But Loreena's story isn't the typical music fable about an artist toiling in the clubs until one day, like magic, she gets discovered by a promoter and—wham!—she's got a contract, an entourage, and a Pepsi endorsement contract. Yes, Loreena toiled—in dinner theaters and lounges throughout her native Canada. But her "big break" came not from some promoter, but from herself. She risked everything on her talent, and her success has rewarded not only her, but the people of her community to whom she gives so much.

Performing on the Streets
As a young woman, Loreena had her eye on veterinary school, but she was always drawn to music. Of Irish and Scottish heritage, Loreena wrote music that tended toward those styles—the delicate, plaintive, ethereal strains of Celtic song and story. In 1981, she moved to Stratford, in Ontario, Canada, where she acted, sang, and wrote musical scores for the local Shakespeare festival. In the meanwhile, her passion for Celtic music grew, and when she was let go from the festival, she knew what she had to do next.

"In 1985, I borrowed money to record my music," Loreena says. "It was a compulsion to document my own musical interpretation of the music I loved." Her parents loaned her money—originally earmarked for her college education—to pay for the production costs, and she went into a studio and recorded her first nine-song record, *Elemental*. She then made 30 cassettes, gave a few to friends, and thought, "Now, what am I going to do with the rest of these?" Thus began her days of busking.

For those who don't know, a busker is a street performer. Loreena would travel to Toronto on a Friday night, set up with her Celtic harp at the St. Lawrence Market around 6:30 on Saturday morning, and play until 1:00 P.M. On Sundays, she'd play at the harbor. The money wasn't bad—"When the weather was good, I'd make $600 to $800 in a weekend"—and she was slowly building a reputation as a performer. She would continue her street playing on and off for four years.

"I lugged my harp in my car or flew across Canada, playing in lounges, and started building a concert career," Loreena says. Sometimes it was in libraries, church halls, and town halls. At her concerts, she'd sell her cassettes out of her car. "From time to time, there was an issue of being stigmatized by the perception that this was a fancy way of begging," she says. "I remember seeing a friend of mine from Winnipeg whom I hadn't seen for many years, emerging from the back of a crowd of people with tears running down her face, saying, 'Oh, Loreena, has it really come to this?' I replied, 'Well, thankfully it has,' as I tucked my booty away."

Opportunity Knocks, She Knocks Back

Loreena's future was certainly affected by an offer she received in 1988. Polygram, a major music label, came calling. They wanted to do an artist development deal and were ready to kick in $10,000 of seed money to get Loreena's music heard more widely. So in November, she went into the studio and recorded three songs, and added the classic tune "Greensleeves" as a fourth.

But when she went to the Polygram offices in January, 1989, to talk about their plans for her record, they were perplexed. "They said they had heard my music and that it was very nice, but they didn't really know what to do with it," she says. Loreena's response floored them. "I was determined to release my next recording the next year. So I said, 'No problem,' and offered to buy the recording back from them," she says. She offered to repay the $10,000 in $2,000 installments. This was utterly unheard of. "The woman in the Business Affairs Department practically fell off her chair," Loreena says. But Polygram sold her the recordings, and three of them went on subsequent CDs. Loreena laughs at the experience. "I had a plan before I ever met with them," she says. "I was going to continue, regardless."

True to her word, that very same year Loreena recorded her third album, *Parallel Dreams*, and saved enough money to take herself, three band members, and a two-person crew on a 30-city Canadian tour. She received some of her touring budget from the Canada Council for the Arts and paid for the rest herself. A 30-city tour is a grueling effort for any performer, but Loreena didn't have the support of a record label managing the details. She was responsible for every logistical detail: travel, accommodations, brokering contracts with promoters, media and publicity, sales, and so on. This was a huge undertaking for a self-taught artist who had been in the business less than four years. It was also her school of hard knocks, and the lesson was "Sink or swim."

A Business Education

Music is a glamour business, right? Not when you're pulling yourself up by your proverbial bootstraps and struggling every day for survival, as Loreena was. Her crash course in the nuts and bolts of the music industry meant starting her own label, Quinlan Road, named after a rural road in Stratford. It was hardly a "glamour" job: She ran the business from her kitchen table and sold records by mail order. "When the album came out, I had to start with the basics, including getting a receipt book and learning about taxes," she says. "I'd be sitting alone at my kitchen table, packing up cassettes, writing out receipts, because I couldn't afford any help. In 1989 I started making money—and in 1990 I moved the office out of my home."

While doing the 30-city tour, Loreena would call managers of record stores specializing in folk or alternative music, telling them she was coming to town. Then she'd roll up to a store on her bicycle or in her Honda Civic, cassettes under her arm, trying to get them to carry her record on consignment. "Sometimes, I'd send them my music ahead of time, but I would always let them know when I'd be in town and when my concert was being held," she says.

The experience, along with her exposure to music industry people who seemed to only want to make a fast buck, made Loreena determined to stay in the music industry on her own terms. "I decided that if my career plateaus and I have to teach piano, I'll reevaluate at that point," she says. "I decided to go with the process as long as the quality and the scope of my experience improved. That way, music would choose me, rather than me it."

Building Her Own Success

Loreena's national tours were starting to build a following, and people were now going into record stores and asking for her CDs. Interestingly, the record companies started changing their tune. No longer were they saying, "We don't know what to do with this music." Now they were interested in producing her music.

But Loreena had worked hard and smart and didn't need the support of a major recording label. "At this point, I had secured a great attorney who knew the inside of the music business," she says. "He told me, 'You've developed the capacity to finance your recordings; 99.9 percent of recording artists have not been able to do that. Because of that, you don't have to settle for [record company] terms. We can approach them from a whole different perspective." So she did.

Warner Music Group in Canada was the only label that acknowledged and respected the fact that she had developed to the point where she could bankroll her own recording career. As a result, they gave Loreena all the creative autonomy she wanted—and a royalty rate that was so high it was unheard of. They handled marketing and distribution, but left total creative control to her. Loreena thrived. "I delivered to them a finished album and artwork," she says. "We've gone from 35,000 record sales in 1989 to over 13 million today, and I've built an infrastructure to manage that."

Giving Back

Loreena still lives in Stratford, and besides managing her career, she spends much of her time giving back to the community that nurtured her. She is restoring local buildings, has founded the Falstaff Family Centre, and has a foundation that donates to many causes worldwide.

Loreena looks back on her experience and realizes that while she lived a hand-to-mouth lifestyle for several years, every success built upon the next. "I remember as recently as 1989 having to borrow money from my family to pay the rent," she says. "It was very lean through those years. And yet within a few years, I went from borrowing money from my family to making over $100,000, paying off my tour, the studio, my mom—everything."

True Passion Is Worth Any Risk

To some observers, it may appear that Loreena McKennitt is an overnight sensation. But she'd laugh at the idea. In reality, she's been working, studying, practicing, saving, researching, and learning for nearly 20 years, making progress one step at a time. In the end, she was willing to do what many people won't: take the risks to follow her passion.

Was the result worth that risk? Was it worth living hand to mouth, the pity of friends, the struggles on the road, the indifference of music executives, and the endless hours of learning the business, with no guarantee of success in the end? Loreena would tell you that not only was it all worth it, she had no choice. To follow her true passion, she *had* to accept the risk. And in risking, she felt truly alive. The risk was *part* of the reward.

Because Loreena was willing to bet on herself when no one else would, she has become one of those most fortunate of people: able to live doing what she loves, on her own terms, giving the world a gift of music and receiving infinitely more in return.

⌒‿∽ Unstoppable Action ∽‿⌒
Acknowledge Fear, Prepare, and Then Act

Loreena McKennitt knew that to succeed on her own terms, she needed more than musical talent and passion. She needed to educate herself about the music business. So she developed a step-by-step plan to become a savvy music businessperson: running her fledgling label, figuring out how to do media and publicity, and learning about taxes, agents, and contracts. By taking things a step at a time and preparing along the way, she reduced her risk of failure and kept herself from becoming overwhelmed.

Were there times when she was fearful? You bet. Fear is a natural reaction to change. It's the number one reason people hesitate to start anything new, opting instead for the way things are—safe, comfortable, and familiar. It's important to realize that everyone experiences fear when venturing into unknown territory. It is a natural response. The difference between stoppable and unstoppable people is their response to fear. Unstoppable people acknowledge fear and manage it by confronting the cause and determining how they can prepare for the challenge ahead. They decide on certain actions that will enable them to feel as competent and confident as possible.

As women, we tend to be more uncomfortable with risk than men are; there are two major reasons for this difference. First, we have significantly lower levels of testosterone, the hormone behind aggressiveness, competitiveness, risk-taking, and high sex drive. Second, women have historically been trained to revere security, not risk.

Columbia University's Carol Dweck, Ph.D., one of the world's leading researchers on emotional development, says that women fear risk because they fear making mistakes. "Women take less risks because they don't want to expose their inadequacies. They see inadequacies as permanent deficiencies rather than things that can be learned over time."

For example, when a woman is applying for a job and is asked if she can do something she knows little about, she'll say no, Dr. Dweck says. On the other hand, men say, "Sure," meaning, "Sure, I can learn." They don't want to expose inadequacies. Many women, particularly bright women, see inadequacies as permanent deficiencies rather than things that can be remedied. Often, women will not think of the learning that will take place on the job and how they can grapple with that as time goes on, but will instead focus on the skills that they lack and the gap between what they know now and what they need to know.

As young girls, many of us were perfect and got a lot of praise for being good little girls. And it becomes a standard that we can't live up to and we're afraid of falling from that standard.

Let's take a lesson from the men. If we want to move into new territory and make a change in our lives, it's important to let go of the expectation of needing to know everything up front. This is unrealistic and holds us back. My personal strategy for approaching any new undertaking has always been to prepare thoroughly. Whether I'm giving an important sales presentation or speaking in front of a large audience, I never "wing it." Initially, the task may seem intimidating, but the more prepared I am, the more confident I become.

To overcome fear, we must prepare as best we can and then plunge ourselves into the very thing we fear most. Only by taking risks can we build our confidence.

Finally, don't be surprised if you don't get initial support from others when you take a risk. Philosopher Arthur Schopenhauer said, "All truth goes through three steps. First, it is ridiculed. Second, it is violently opposed. Third, it is accepted as self-evident." Schopenhauer asserted that only 3 percent of people ever embrace a new truth during the first two stages, when their lives can be truly transformed. Ninety-seven percent wait for the self-evident stage, when embracing the new idea is safe and socially acceptable. Unfortunately, by then it's too late for any real opportunities.

By taking a risk, you are refusing to let fear create regrets for you. Instead, you are opening yourself to a world of new, exciting opportunities.

Is the risk worth the reward?

Are you experiencing fear and anxiety about your ability to achieve your breakthrough goal? Perhaps you're been putting off a particularly daunting step you need to take to achieve your 30-day goal? Take some time to think about what concerns you the most about this step. Acknowledge your fear—but don't stop there. Brainstorm some ways you could prepare to take this step. Preparation is the key to taking fear out of the unknown. Of course, you'll never be able to foresee everything that *could* happen, but by preparing for the most likely scenarios, you'll feel more comfortable. Then go ahead and plunge yourself into the thing you've been fearing—remember, the first step is the hardest! And once you've taken the risk, you'll be on your way to reaping the rewards.

Risk is the fuel behind all growth, all greatness. I've coached people who didn't achieve their 30-day goal in 30 days, but still said it was the most transformational experience of their lives. Why? For the first time, they had a plan and understood the mindset necessary to make real changes in their lives. They were in action! That is success! If we focus on what we gain through the process of trying and risking and see how we've grown and learned, we win.

Create Your Day Planner

PLAN TO BE UNSTOPPABLE! Tonight or first thing tomorrow morning, plan your next day's activities by filling out your Create Your Day Planner (see Appendix). Think of one thing you could do today that would force you to face something that causes you discomfort and thereby strengthens your unstoppability muscle. Maybe it's having an honest conversation with someone you've been putting off, but you know it must be done. Or maybe it's calling a prospect you think has been avoiding you and asking for their business. Or perhaps it's signing up for a class that you'd love to take, but you've been too afraid to commit to taking the course. Overcoming fear requires that we plunge into the very thing that makes us afraid so that, in the end, our fear will be eliminated. Start welcoming the chance to risk. Risk makes us feel alive, makes things possible. And each time you take a risk and face your fears, you are one step closer to achieving your goal for this 30 days and beyond!

Day 19:
Persistence Draws Assistance

Today's Affirmation: I will stay in action until I achieve my goal. As I continue to move forward, I will attract the people and resources that will support me in reaching my goal. Rejection is not personal but is a natural part of the process. I am resilient and will not stop until I reach my goal. I am unstoppable!

"No." Those two little letters strike fear into the hearts of us all. The word is inescapable. Everyone experiences rejection at some point. Whether you're rejected during a sales call, after a job interview, over an idea you presented to the PTA, or by a man you want to date, rejection is a natural part of life. The good news is, it's not fatal. "No" doesn't necessarily have anything to do with you personally. Perhaps your product wasn't the right fit for that particular company, the employer was looking for different qualifications, your idea was great but the timing wasn't right, or the man wasn't ready for a relationship. Who knows? The reasons could be endless. But the reasons aren't nearly as important as the "meaning" *you* attach to the rejection. How you interpret "no" will determine your outcome—whether you move forward with invigoration or quit from discouragement.

Nell Merlino certainly experienced her share of "no"s. But she proved that rejection is not the end of an exciting journey, but the beginning—if you persist. In doing so, you will not only succeed, but draw others to your support.

Unstoppable Woman:
Nell Merlino's Story

April 28, 1993, was a work day like any other, except for all the little girls. They were everywhere—walking with their mothers, hand-in-hand with fathers in business suits, riding the subway looking alternately serious and tickled to death. What was going on?

The answer is Take Our Daughters to Work Day (TODTWD), an event that's now annual, national, and cherished by parents and daughters alike. But as popular as it is today, it took an uphill fight to make it a reality. As with all revolutionary ideas, TODTWD had its doubters. But Nell Merlino was not one of them. And gradually, her persistence attracted the help and belief of others.

Boosting Girls' Self-Esteem
In 1992, a study had shown, rather alarmingly, that as young girls approached adolescence, their self-esteem dropped dramatically. The Ms. Foundation for Women asked Nell, an experienced activist and entrepreneur, to develop some new way to bring this disturbing phenomenon to the nation's attention.

Rather than focus on the negative, Nell hoped to create some event to boost the self-image of young girls. She reflected on how exciting and inspiring it had been for her as a small girl to watch her own father at his job. That fond memory triggered a simple, yet powerful, idea: One day each year, adults would take their daughters to work with them. She believed this would offer the girls strong role models to help boost their self-esteem.

You would think such a simple, positive idea would immediately be embraced by everyone, but that wasn't the case. Nell's idea would take a lot of work and determination before the detractors were convinced.

Meet People Where They Live
Nell's first task was a big one: raise $400,000 to publicize TODTWD and make people aware of it. In addition, she had the daunting task of convinc-

ing all the doubters, including the chair of the board of the Ms. Foundation, that it would succeed. At every corner, someone was telling her it wouldn't work. Some said the program wouldn't address the underlying causes of poor self-esteem, while others insisted that parents and corporations simply wouldn't participate because the idea was far-fetched. Others worried that what young girls saw at major corporations—the often lower-level jobs held by women—would discourage them, not elevate them.

Nell's answer to the naysayers was that you need to meet people where they are, whether it's a restaurant or a blue chip company, and demonstrate that any place can be an environment for change. "Change will *never* happen if you don't put it out there," she says. "We can't just ignore the problem and hope that it will just go away!"

The skeptics' next gripe was that the idea wouldn't work in small cities outside the major metropolitan areas like New York City, without a multi-million dollar marketing and PR campaign. The project didn't have the budget or staff to launch such a comprehensive campaign, but Nell was confident it wasn't necessary. She believed her idea had grassroots appeal, and that it would hit parents in an emotional way. She also knew the power of the media and suspected that if editors embraced the story, the country might, as well.

A Wall of Negativity

Nell and her team went on a crusade, bombarding the press with information about TODTWD. After an article about the event appeared in *Parade Magazine*, the Ms. Foundation received 10,000 letters, most of them from women talking about their own self-esteem problems as girls and encouraging the organization to move forward with such an important event. The letters were Nell's first proof that she was on the right track.

But oh, the doubters. They were legion. As Nell's team virtually single-handedly fought to create ongoing press coverage of the event and spread public awareness, she encountered group after group who dismissed it:

• They approached the nation's major school systems to request that girls receive excused absences from school for TODTWD, arguing that the girls would learn many lessons about life from that one day in the real world. Still, many school systems refused.

• Nell was surprised to find so many companies unwilling to participate, arguing that the girls would simply bother their parents at work and would learn nothing.

• A prominent educator called the idea a "waste of time" and argued that the girls would be better off in school.

• Some opponents cried foul, saying that boys would feel discriminated against. The Ms. Foundation countered with the fact that boys generally understand that their futures are tied to the pursuit of careers, something many girls do not. They even developed a history of gender inequity in the workplace to explain why TODTWD would be important for girls.

Despite the outcry, Nell knew the idea was a winner. It would take young girls out of their environment, open their eyes to the wider world, and expose them early to greater possibilities for their lives. But first, she had to convince the naysayers, a task that required her to keep fighting with bottomless persistence.

A 24/7 Advocate

Nell became a full-time TODTWD advocate. She started every day at dawn, hitting the phones. She arranged meetings, kept her small coalition on track, and supplied the media with a constant flow of information, and this in the pre e-mail days! She also organized a group of volunteers to help respond to all of the letters and calls received in response to the *Parade* article. Sometimes the volunteers didn't show up, and Nell and her soon-to-be husband stayed up all night stuffing envelopes.

Faster than she could have thought, a year passed. From February 1992, when she had delivered her five-page proposal to the Ms. Foundation, to April 1993, she had worked tirelessly to build support for TODTWD. Now her months of work and planning were over. But had they made a difference? Had people embraced the idea? She would know soon.

Girls on the Front Page

Nell was a nervous wreck, but she managed to fall asleep. On the morning of April 28, 1993, she woke at 5:30 A.M., turned on the television . . . and saw a little girl doing the weather report. "I was sitting there by myself, sobbing," she recalls.

TODTWD had taken hold. On the front pages of virtually every major American newspaper and featured in the leading reports of major TV news programs were young girls—girls of all ages and races, accompanying their mothers and fathers to work. Girls traded pizza futures on the floor of the Chicago Mercantile Exchange. They tested astronaut gear at NASA in Houston, they "supervised" workers in the Tennessee Valley Authority, and much, much more. In Nell's words, for one day, young girls were "visible, valued, and heard."

In the decade since that first TODTWD, nearly 71 million Americans have participated in the event, including employees at banks, law firms, investment companies, and other traditionally male-dominated businesses. Nell believes that when girls see themselves in a hard hat or judge's robes, they get a vision of what's possible. "People want fairness," she says. "And they want to show girls a world of what's possible."

Persistence Continues

Thanks to her endless persistence, Nell Merlino's much-maligned brainstorm has become a cherished part of American life. But she's not done. Today, she heads up a program called Count-Me-In for Women's Economic Independence. It's a national nonprofit organization that makes small business loans to women who can't get money from banks. It's just one more way Nell is trying to change the world, to create opportunity—and a vision of possibility—for women of all ages.

"A lot of issues sound so huge that people feel overwhelmed. But if you have
faith in your ideas, and you give people a more positive way
to express their feelings, they'll jump on it."
—Nell Merlino

⌒⌒⌒⌒ Unstoppable Action ⌒⌒⌒⌒
Refuse to Take Rejection Personally

Some will.
Some won't.
So what . . . Next!

Through Nell's story and the stories of other unstoppable women, we have seen that rejection comes with the territory when we're selling anything, whether it's a project, a product, an idea, or ourselves. Everyone isn't going to "get it" or be interested in what we're offering. So what! When we accept that "no" is a natural part of the process, we can easily move past each rejection until someone does say yes.

✎ Remind yourself that rejection isn't personal.
Whenever you're feeling discouraged about experiencing rejection in your life, *stop*. (There's that word again!) Rather than sinking into depression, immediately go back to your ABC's (see Appendix). Identify the meaning you're attaching to the "adversity," which in this case is rejection. If you're feeling down, you are clearly interpreting it in a way that is disempowering to you.

For example, let's say you share a project idea with a friend and explain that you'd like her to take part in it with you. But despite your excitement, she's less than enthusiastic about the idea. A typical reaction might be to become discouraged and start questioning the viability of your project. Instead, stop and dispute your belief. What other ways could you look at your rejection that will energize you and keep you moving forward? There could be countless reasons why this project might not work for your friend at this moment, including the timing or circumstances. When you change the meaning of the word "no" from being personal and permanent to simply a temporary situation that has nothing to do with you personally, you will immediately shift from despair to taking the next step.

When you treat rejection as just another hurdle and continue to persevere in your progress toward your goal, you will eventually attract others who want to help you. Other unstoppable people admire determination, will, and fortitude. If you hang in there long enough, you'll find assistance appearing from all directions—and your goal getting closer by the day.

Create Your Day Planner

PLAN TO BE UNSTOPPABLE! Tonight or first thing tomorrow morning, plan your next day's activities by filling out your Create Your Day Planner (see Appendix). Think about the rejections or setbacks you have already overcome during this Unstoppable Women Challenge. I'll bet just getting started was tough, and maybe you felt some resistance from family or friends who doubted your ability to achieve your goal. But you took that first step, and you're now well on your way to achieving it. Whenever you start to doubt yourself or someone tells you "no," read over your list of victories in your Create Your Day Planner to remind yourself of the great progress you're making.

Something to Think About

Michele Hoskins's recipe for success came from her great-great-grandmother's honey cream syrup. But persistence was the major ingredient. She won a $3 million contract with Denny's after calling them every single week for 2 years straight.

"At the time I got the idea to market my honey cream syrup to Denny's restaurants, they were known as the worst company to do business with for minorities, and they were experiencing a lot of bad press and discrimination suits. I was a woman and a minority, and I made a great syrup, something they sold a lot of. I believed that they needed me as much as I needed them.

"Each Monday morning at 10:30, I'd call their corporate office. Over a period of time, everyone in the organization knew I wanted their business. The receptionist would say, 'Michelle's on the phone. Who's talking to her today?' I talked to a lot of people, all promising to get back with me, but they never did. I spoke with the receptionist, secretaries, people in the diversity department, procurement, product development, sales— anyone who would listen.

"They really didn't know what to do with me, but they continued to take my calls. After two years, they got a new CEO, Jim Adamson, who restructured the company. He was very interested in making Denny's a diverse organization and improving their reputation. He had heard about my story and asked, 'Why aren't we doing business with this woman?'

"I ended up getting business from their diversity division and doing what I set out to do, not only delivering syrup to their 17,000 restaurants, but helping their image by becoming their poster child for diversity.

"The funny thing was that at the time I was approaching them, I was a small manufacturer in Chicago making syrup locally. I wasn't remotely prepared to manufacture and deliver my syrup to more than 17,000 restaurants. But I thought once I got the business, I'd figure out how to do it.

"I've learned that anything the mind can conceive can manifest through hard work, perseverance, and faith."

Day 20:
"Girlfriend to Girlfriend:" The Spirit of One Unstoppable Person Benefits Us All

A year and a half after my first book, *Unstoppable*, was published, my life took a significant change in direction. My marriage of 20 years ended. My husband had been my college sweetheart, and I fully intended to be married for the rest of my life. This experience shook me to my core and shattered the essence of my identity as a woman. I had *never* considered the possibility of becoming single, yet that's exactly what had happened.

My emotions were all over the map—fear, self-doubt, and despair. One day when I was feeling particularly down, I called my dear friend and mentor, Millard Fuller, and he told me the story of a man who had experienced a similar situation. When Millard was practicing law before founding Habitat for Humanity International, a man came into his office and said that his wife had just left him, taking the children with her, and he no longer had a reason to live.

Millard drove the desperate man to the home of an elderly woman who had no electricity, was going blind, and had leaks in her roof. On top of all that, the neighborhood gang routinely stole her monthly social security check from her mailbox. Millard told the man, "Before you kill yourself, I thought I'd introduce you to someone who has *real* problems."

Moving Through Hardship

Seeing what other people endure in their lives has great power to give us perspective on our own. I have had the great privilege of meeting courageous women who have experienced greater difficulties than I will (hopefully) ever know. Yet they had the courage to move forward in their lives. And because they did, I knew it was possible for me, too.

One year after my separation, I began the research and writing for *Unstoppable Women*. I was still healing from the divorce and found it extremely difficult to spend time writing virtually in solitude to complete the book. I felt unsettled, incomplete, and in pain, and I soon realized that my greatest task was to first become whole as a single woman. This process felt like an endless journey of reflection, reading, praying, meditating, and literally challenging many lifelong beliefs.

A year later, I re-read the biography of Joni Eareckson. I had read her story while I was in college and was extremely moved by her life. In 1967, Joni Eareckson was a young and vital teenager, just 17 years old, when she was in a diving accident that snapped her neck and turned her into a quadriplegic. In the harrowing months that followed, she was introduced to a world of tubes, machines, and a Stryker frame—a long, sandwich-like canvas on which she lay face up and then was flipped face down every few hours to prevent pressure sores. There were also many operations.

Fear, pain, heartache, and depression set in for Joni, capped by an overwhelming feeling that she had been deserted by God. Filled with anger, Joni stubbornly resisted occupational therapy. But her attitude began to change after meeting Tom, a young ventilator-dependent quadriplegic who was even more paralyzed than she was. Despite this, he had a positive attitude and allowed the therapist to work with him. Because of his example and the love and prayers of family and friends, Joni became open to new possibilities for her life.

After years of rehabilitation, she learned not only how to function in the world, but has also created possibilities for her life that are unfathomable for most of us. There isn't enough space to list all of her amazing accomplishments in these pages, but here are just a few:

• She is an accomplished and collected artist, painting with a brush between her teeth.

- She's written more than 30 books and has traveled to 35 countries.
- World Wide Pictures produced a full-length feature film, *Joni*, in which she starred as herself.
- She writes and records *Joni and Friends*, a daily five-minute radio program, that is heard over 850 broadcast outlets.
- She founded *Wheels for the World*, which has collected and refurbished more than 14,000 wheelchairs and shipped them to developing nations where physical therapists fit each chair to a needy disabled child or adult.
- A national columnist and highly sought-after speaker both in the United States and internationally, Joni has received countless awards for her accomplishments, courage, and contribution to the world.

After re-reading her book, the message was clear. If Joni could write more than 30 books and accomplish everything she had without the use of her arms or legs, *maybe* it was possible that I could get my *second* book finished.

As Tom had been a model for Joni, Joni became a model for me. Her story showed me the contrast between my own troubles and someone with *real* obstacles, and it became the impetus for me to once again move forward with writing my book. I have since had the privilege of meeting Joni in person and told her how her story had a pivotal impact on helping me move forward in my life.

No matter where you are in your life and what pain or challenges you may have experienced, you can heal and become whole. Allow each one of the women you meet in this book to be your models of possibility, as they have been for me. Congratulate yourself for having the courage to try. And whenever you feel like your strength is depleted or that you cannot take another step, reread the stories of these women. Draw strength from their strength. It's astonishing what the spirit can endure and what we can achieve, simply through the power of believing in ourselves—and never, ever giving up.

Day 21:
Week 3 in Review

Welcome to the end of Week 3. Great job! You are doing what most people are not willing to do. You're in action! So many people talk and dream about making changes in their lives. You're not just talking about it, you're doing it. Congratulate yourself for your successes.

Review your daily victories over the last 3 weeks. Every day you take a single step to make a change in your life and to help someone else is a *huge* victory. Celebrate the fact that you are taking charge of your life. These victories are proof that you are making progress. Even if you haven't achieved the results you'd hoped for thus far, if you continue to stay in action, you cannot fail.

And look at who you're becoming in the process. Savor the great satisfaction of knowing that you honored your promise to finish what you started. You are developing powerful habits and a foundation that will serve you in making any change you desire for the rest of your life.

The Week in Review Form

Complete the Week in Review form. (See Appendix.) Pay particular attention to anything that could stop you in your final week. Perhaps you need to increase your communication with your buddy. Have you been reading your story every day? Are you consistently writing down your one step? Notice areas where you have slacked off and see if that has impacted your progress. If so, finish strong. You are approaching your final week. Make this next week your best ever! Do whatever is necessary to successfully complete this commitment to yourself. You deserve it. Be unstoppable!

Day 22:
Love Is the Answer, but *Forgiveness* Is the Key

Today's Affirmation: I practice forgiveness on a daily basis. I don't take things personally, and I give others the benefit of the doubt. I acknowledge the healing power of forgiveness and actively choose to forgive, knowing that I cannot forgive myself unless I am willing to forgive others. Each time I forgive, I do it for myself, demonstrating the ultimate act of self-love.

Imagine that your life is a busy airport, with you as the air traffic controller. Now let's look at your control screen. On the best day, it's chaotic with departures and arrivals. But there are some planes that never seem to land. They circle and circle endlessly, taking up space and multiplying stress.

These planes are your unresolved grievances. They hover, but they refuse to land. With them buzzing in your personal space, you're forced to work harder. They distract you, exhaust your resources, and cause accidents. Unable to forgive or let go, you try to keep your grievances aloft, creating stress and risking burnout.

This is a scenario that Dr. Fred Luskin, director and cofounder of the Stanford University Forgiveness Project, uses in his latest book, *Forgive for Good*, to describe the toll that unresolved grievances take on our lives. As the analogy shows, harboring our injuries robs us of precious time, energy, and the ability to move forward in our lives.

And here's some interesting news: Research has shown that forgiveness is good for our mental and physical health. Having the ability to forgive seems to reduce depression, defuse anger, improve spirituality, enhance emotional self-confidence, and help people live with greater peace.

Forgiving does not mean being a doormat, simply condoning or forgetting injury. Nor does forgiving mean that it's wrong for you to feel hurt and angry. As Dr. Luskin says in his book *Forgive for Good*, "Forgiveness is the feeling of peace that emerges as you take your hurt less personally, take responsibility for how you feel, and become a hero instead of a victim in the story you tell."

This last point is the most important: When we forgive, we stop being a victim of our past. That includes forgiving *ourselves*. It means giving ourselves a break when we fail to meet a goal or come up short in being perfect. We choose to move forward with purpose, instead of looking back with resentment.

If you doubt your ability to forgive others or yourself, please read the story of Aba Gayle Orr. You'll see the incredible power that forgiveness has to transform lives, not just for the forgiver, but the forgiven. If she can forgive, perhaps we all can.

Unstoppable Woman:
Aba Gayle's Story

"I'm sorry, but your daughter, Catherine, is dead."

The police detective's tone was calm and matter-of-fact, the words of someone accustomed to delivering catastrophic news. "She was murdered," he continued, " . . . stabbed to death."

The news slashed through the pit of Aba Gayle's stomach like a razor and left her in an agony of sudden grief. Her mind reeled as her world was instantly turned inside out. "This simply cannot be!" she thought. "Catherine was so young, so beautiful, so full of life! *How could this happen?*"

It was a senseless and mindless act. A young man, Douglas Mickey, under the influence of drugs, killed his best friend, Eric, and 19-year-old Catherine, just because she was there.

"I have to remain calm," Gayle told herself. "None of this is real. Soon I'll wake up and the nightmare will be over." But she knew it was real. Afraid to cry because someone would hear her, she stepped into the shower, she recalls, "and with the water full blast, I *screamed* and *screamed* and *screamed!*"

Time of Darkness
So began an 8-year period Gayle calls her "time of darkness." She found herself debilitated by her overwhelming rage, hatred, and thirst for revenge against Douglas Mickey. With her anguish and fury buried inside her, it often took all she had to get through the day. "My rage permeated my entire being and impacted everything I did, including my relationships," she says. "All I wanted was revenge for the death of my beloved child."

Stuck in a deep pit of hate, Gayle had no idea how to escape, or if she ever would. She had absolutely no support system, no faith in God, no church or community to comfort her. Her family was moving on without her. She felt like one of Dante's damned sinners, trapped in an inescapable hell of guilt, grief, and darkness.

Waiting for Execution

Some hope of release came from the legal system. In 1982, Douglas Mickey was arrested, tried, convicted, and sentenced to death. The district attorney assured Gayle that when "the monster" was executed, she would find some peace. But like all death penalty cases, it would take years for Mickey to reach the gas chamber.

The day couldn't come soon enough for Gayle. But after 8 years scarred by an obsessive lust for revenge, she couldn't continue to live like this. "I had become a workaholic and would fly off the handle at the slightest thing. It was a very lonely, dark, and bitter place." She knew she needed to do something to start healing her soul. Her first step was to take a simple course in meditation. For the first time, she was able to sit quietly, momentarily silencing the bitter voices in her head.

As her mother's health failed, Gayle moved in and took care of her, and together they attended Unity Church in Auburn, California. Gayle had hoped this would bring some peace into her mother's life, but what it actually did was provide the revelation that would help Gayle finally release her rage and change her life. She discovered the church bookstore and began studying the teachings of the great religious leaders. "I learned that I am a beloved child of God," she says, "and that all of us are here to love each other without exception. We are all one in spirit."

A Quest to Forgive

Watching a video at the church, Gayle saw a Jewish Holocaust survivor explain how he was able to forgive not only the German people, but even the concentration camp guards who had killed every member of his family. She began to think that, maybe, there was another road to peace: forgiveness.

Yet as much as Gayle wanted to forgive her daughter's murderer, she couldn't let go of her rage and anger. She continued searching for a way to release her bitterness and explored the concept of forgiveness with her study group.

One day, a friend sent Gayle a newspaper clipping stating that an execution date had been scheduled for Mickey. Outraged, Gayle called San Quentin. "How dare you not invite me to his execution?" she screamed to the press secretary at the prison. "If anybody has a right to be there, I do as the mother of the murdered child!" The press secretary informed Gayle the news clipping was incorrect; no execution date had been scheduled. She told Gayle she could write a letter requesting that she be notified when a date was set. Gayle wrote the letter, intending to mail it the next day.

After hours of study, prayer, and discussion with her class that evening, Gayle felt that her heart might be open enough to "perhaps" forgive the man who killed Catherine. But when a classmate suggested that Gayle actually let the murderer *know* of her intent to forgive him, she was shocked and enraged. He deserved no such thing!

A Letter and Moment of Healing

Shaken, Gayle drove home. During the trip, a distinct, utterly compelling voice spoke in her mind. "It said, 'You must forgive him, and you must let him know.'"

She didn't sleep that night. Instead, she typed a letter to the man who had murdered her child. She began by telling him who Catherine had been, about her loveliness and how special she was. She told him how Catherine's vicious death had brutalized her family. She told him she had hated him, had wanted him punished to the fullest extent of the law—but that her feelings had changed.

As she wrote, Gayle was surprised to discover that she *could* forgive Mickey. "What I've learned is this," she wrote. "You are a Divine child of God. You are surrounded by God's love, even as you sit in your cell. The Christ in me sends blessings to the Christ in you." She ended by saying that she was willing to write or visit him if he wished.

Gayle says that this amazing letter of absolution did not come from her head, but from her soul. "I didn't create it, it just flowed," she says. "The 'writing and visiting' part was not my intellect working. I don't know *where* that came from!"

As she mailed the letter, something happened, suddenly, without warning. It was a moment that had eluded Gayle for 12 years. "I can still feel the shivers going up and down my spine, remembering the little click that the mailbox made as I dropped the letter inside," she says. "All the anger, rage, and lust for revenge simply *vanished*. And in its place was the most incredible feeling of joy and love and total peace.

"I was in a State of Grace," she continues. "I knew in that holy instant that I did not need to have anyone executed for me to be healed. I *was* healed! And now I could get on with my life!"

God on Death Row

Released from grief and venomous hate, Gayle didn't care if Mickey responded to her letter. He did. In a heartbreaking letter of his own, he expressed sorrow and remorse, and gratitude for Gayle's forgiveness. In the letter, Gayle learned about a young man who had turned to drugs to escape a life of endless pain. His mother committed suicide when he was 16; 6 months later his father remarried and his older brother committed suicide.

Gayle could tell the young man had been searching for his own answers for years, studying Carl Jung and becoming a self-taught psychotherapist. He wrote, "The Christ in me most gratefully accepts and returns blessings of Divine Wisdom, Love, and Charity to the Christ in you." He also wrote, "I would gladly give my life this instant, if it would in any way change that terrible night."

Against the advice of her friends and family, Gayle paid a visit to Mickey on death row. As she stepped into the visiting area, she was shocked. "I didn't see a single 'monster' in that room," she says. "It was filled with ordinary-looking men sitting with their grandmothers, wives, children, ministers. Everywhere I looked, I saw the face of God."

Mickey and Gayle talked and cried for more than 3 hours. She came to realize something she could not have seen while steeped in her victim's need for revenge: The night he took Catherine's life, Mickey had lost his own.

Leaving San Quentin, Gayle knew she had to make others realize that the inmates there were men, not monsters. "I knew that if the State of California ever executed Douglas Mickey, it would be killing my friend," she says.

A New Name, a New Mission

Gayle now spends many hours writing and visiting death row inmates, in what she calls her "mini-prison ministry." As part of Murder Victim Families for Reconciliation, she is a powerful voice for forgiveness and against the death penalty. She is even working with Mickey's attorneys to spare him execution. Asked by reporters if some people have committed crimes too horrible to deserve compassion, she responds, "I don't deal with their crime. I deal with the God-spirit within them. That is the Truth of their being. It is the Truth for every one of us."

When Gayle turned 60, she gave herself a gift: She changed her name to Aba Gayle ("aba" means "joyful heart" or "one with God"). It is Aba Gayle Orr whom hundreds of death row inmates—as well as thousands of capital punishment advocates, opponents, and journalists—have come to know and respect.

Gayle suffered a mother's worst nightmare: the murder of her child. She *was* a victim. But after years of trying in vain to fill the abyss inside her with hatred and vengeance, she listened to a voice telling her to forgive. Through faith and love, she made the astounding, valiant choice to forgive, and was healed and made whole at last.

> *"By all definitions, I am a victim, for I am the mother of a beautiful young daughter who was brutally murdered. But I have learned that there is another way to live and that I have a choice. I chose to stop being a victim, and my path to freedom has been forgiveness."*
> —*Aba Gayle*

Unstoppable Action
Practice Forgiveness

With an incredible act of absolution and forgiveness, Aba Gayle Orr freed herself from the hatred, anger, and resentment that had blighted her life for 12 years. In a situation where no one could have blamed her for going to her grave hating Douglas Mickey, forgiveness allowed her to move forward, granting her the grace and vision to change her life and the lives of others.

Some will argue that the offender doesn't deserve forgiveness. But that's a trap. Forgiveness is about neither the offender nor the offense; it's about *you* moving forward, not punishing yourself for what can't be changed.

Forgiveness is not condoning unkindness, nor does it mean reconciling with someone who has treated you unjustly. Forgiveness is becoming responsible for how we feel. Even though we experience great pain, we are able to find peace and move on in our lives. After being mistreated, abandoned, or cheated on in a relationship, we may not forget, but forgiveness takes away the power of the misdeed. We learn to take painful experiences less personally.

How many people do you know who are angry and hold grudges about something that happened years, even decades, ago? Whether it was an offense by a parent, relative, neighbor, spouse, co-worker, or friend, they won't let their grievance go. These people think their anger gives them power, when in fact they are victims of their past. *The past cannot be changed.* Forgiveness means recognizing that truth and moving toward the future.

The Four Stages of Becoming a Forgiving Person

In his book *Forgive for Good,* Dr. Luskin says that the ability to forgive is a skill that once developed can be drawn on in any situation. He suggests that there are four stages to becoming a forgiving person.

Stage One: We experience a loss or betrayal and are filled with hurt and anger. We blame the person who wronged us as the cause of our pain.

At this point, we're not considering that we have a choice about how to respond. We're just feeling wounded by the offense.

Example: You're angry that your business partner wants to dissolve your partnership for reasons you don't feel are justified. You feel angry and blameless in the situation. You tell others how you were wronged and how poorly your partner handled things.

Stage Two: After a period of being upset, we begin to see how our anger isn't serving us in our lives and relationships, so we take steps to see things from a different point of view. We may try to see the experience from the other person's perspective or simply minimize the importance of the situation.

Example: After calming down, you talk with your partner in an effort to understand her perspective. You realize that if the business isn't working for her, she has every right to take a different path. You're now able to appreciate your partner for what she has brought to your business and value the friendship you have developed.

Stage Three: We have experienced the power of forgiveness and choose to quickly let go of grievances. We reflect on past encounters of forgiveness and the peace and joy we experienced. When we notice grievances forming, we quickly challenge the "story" we attach to the situation. We realize that the extent and duration of our pain is largely up to us. We can choose to minimize the time we are upset and how quickly we move forward.

Example: Instead of taking your business partner's decision personally, you recognize that she is human, with the same needs as you. Understanding the power of forgiveness in a relationship, you quickly choose to move forward and not stay in "hurt feelings" mode. You both become less attached to "being right" or to your interpretation of what this event meant.

Stage Four: Dr. Luskin believes this is the most difficult yet the most powerful stage, and I agree. This is where we operate from a place of forgiveness in our daily lives. We take things less personally. We know we are responsible for how we feel and rarely take offense. We don't condone unkindness, nor are we doormats. But we understand that people are not perfect, and that this means they will hurt us at times. We understand that we also are not perfect and that everyone, including ourselves, operates primarily out of personal self-interest. How, then, could we not offer forgiveness to others, for behaving at times in selfish ways?

Disappointments and wounds occur in all relationships, including long-term stable marriages, loving families, and great friendships. In Stage Four, we understand that hurt and conflict in relationships are common occurrences. We strive to make peace. We give others the benefit of the doubt. We understand the healing power of forgiveness and actively choose to forgive on a daily basis.

✎ Who do you need to forgive?

Make a list of the people in your life toward whom you feel anger and resentment. While it may be difficult at first, acknowledge that anger and resentment are holding you back from fully living, loving, and creating an unstoppable life. Look at your list and identify at what stage of practicing forgiveness you are with each person. Make a decision to move past your anger and let your grievance go. *You do this not for them, but for yourself,* demonstrating the ultimate act of self-love. I am not suggesting that this is easy or that it will happen overnight. But, like Aba Gayle, make the decision today to start the process. As you begin to practice forgiveness as a way of life, you can invest your energies into solving problems, rather than taking offense and playing the role of a victim.

Of course, sometimes the person we most need to forgive is ourselves. There comes a time when we're disappointed in ourselves for not honoring our commitments, for not being "perfect." When we feel this way, it's vital that we forgive ourselves, commit to doing better in the future, and move on. Nothing productive ever comes from self-hatred and condemnation.

Make a list of areas where you're judging yourself. What do you need to forgive yourself for? Practice the four stages of forgiveness on yourself.

If you find yourself getting "stuck" in anger and having a hard time forgiving yourself or someone else, try the following tips:

- Speak with people who have forgiven others and think about what you can learn from their stories.
- Read books about forgiveness to learn how others have forgiven in difficult situations.
- Recall times that you have hurt others and needed forgiveness.
- Write a forgiveness letter to yourself or to someone you need to forgive.
- Cultivate an attitude of gratitude for your life.
- Ask yourself, "Who would I be without this resentment or anger?"
- Practice forgiving for one minute at a time. Becoming a forgiving person is a habit we can develop, so start with the little annoyances in life.

For example, imagine you're at the grocery store, in the express checkout lane. The lane is supposed to be limited to customers with 10 items or less, but there's someone ahead of you with 15 items. Notice your thoughts and judgments about this person and the feelings they produce. You could be annoyed that this person isn't following the rules and is slowing down the "express" lane, you could complain to the person behind you about the selfishness of this customer's behavior, or you could stop and use this circumstance as an opportunity to forgive. If you have trouble letting it go, recall a time when you didn't follow the rules or perhaps acted in a selfish manner. That gets me every time. Many times we judge others for the very things we've done in the past.

Create Your Day Planner

PLAN TO BE UNSTOPPABLE! Tonight or first thing tomorrow morning, plan your next day's activities by filling out your Create Your Day Planner form (see Appendix.) Reflect on a time in your life when you were forgiven for a grievance someone had against you. Connect with how it felt to be forgiven and the joy you experienced knowing any resentment toward you was fully released. Start flexing your forgiveness muscles by consciously practicing forgiveness toward others tomorrow. And remember, when we forgive, we do it for ourselves.

Day 23:
Surround Yourself with People Who Lift You Higher

Today's Affirmation: I surround myself with people who encourage me to play bigger in the world and who recognize my brilliance. I am building a support team of people who are positive and encourage me in my efforts to create new results in my life. Together, we are unstoppable!

It's hard enough to stay positive and keep the faith in the day-to-day pursuit of our dreams. When we associate with negative or unsupportive people, it becomes almost impossible. Unfortunately, it's difficult to eliminate all of the negative people from our lives because they may be those closest to us—a parent, spouse, sibling, or even best friend. And since these people have history with us, they'll typically remember how we've succeeded or failed in the past. They may simply not be able to think of us in terms of what's possible. The saying "A prophet has no honor in his own home" couldn't be more true.

We all need to create a support team and an environment that provides love and encouragement. Sometimes, those who are closest to us aren't the best people to do that. In that case, we need to find someone who can.

Jean Renfro Anspaugh had long sacrificed what she truly wanted in order to live up to the expectations of others. But when others' wishes for her began to be an albatross around her neck, she did what any unstoppable person must do: She built a support system that helped her change her life.

Unstoppable Woman:
Jean Renfro Anspaugh's Story

For most of Jean Renfro Anspaugh's life, she did what other people expected of her. She was the good girl who never caused any trouble. After she graduated from college with a liberal arts degree, her family encouraged her to "get serious" and get a real degree. Her sister was a lawyer and her mom worked in the court, so getting a law degree seemed like the sensible thing to do—for someone else. But because Jean didn't value her own desires at the time, she went along and took the LSAT and was accepted to a law school in Sacramento.

She'll never forget getting off the plane in Sacramento. It was 100 degrees and she weighed 315 pounds. She hated it. But she bought a house and settled in anyway. Then one night, she got what she describes as "The Calling."

The Collapsing Chair

"I was sitting on my favorite lounge chair on the patio of my house in Sacramento and my mother, as usual, was telling me what I should be doing with my life and how my weight was getting in the way of *everything* I needed to do. When she went into the house, my chair collapsed underneath me. I sat on the concrete floor screaming. That was a defining moment for me. I reached the point where I just couldn't take it anymore."

The collapsing chair woke Jean up and made her realize that she had to do what she had always wanted to do, no matter how much heartache it would cause, no matter who told her she was crazy, no matter what sacrifices she had to make. She was going to find a way to lose weight because she was worth it. But she knew she couldn't do it alone. Nor could she depend on her family and friends to be her support group.

Boot Camp

Jean asked her parents if she could borrow money to sign up for the world-famous Rice Diet, the Duke University program with the reputation of being the Marine Corps boot camp of diet programs. They refused. They told her to just use her willpower, or jog a few miles a day. Instead of giving her hope, their "help" deflated Jean. She knew that if she were serious about losing weight, she would have to surround herself with people with the same mission. So she sold her house and everything she owned. Her parents and friends called her crazy. Her professors at law school tried to talk her out of it. But there was no turning back.

Jean threw her belongings in her car and drove to Durham, North Carolina. She didn't have enough money to stay very long, but she was determined to make this critical change happen no matter what she had to do. "I believed that my pilgrimage to Durham would be as magical as visiting the castle at Disneyland and the doctors at Duke would waive their magic stethoscopes and cure me of my obesity. What I found when I turned off the exit into the city of Durham was anything but magic. It looked like a dump." On top of that, it was 97 degrees—uncomfortable for a thin person, unbearable for an obese one. She checked into a cheap motel that had special rates for "Ricers" and prayed they had air-conditioning.

They did. On her third day, she went to the diet clinic with two other dieters. They immediately felt united by their cause and pledged to each other that they would let nothing stand between them and a "thin" future.

A Like-Minded Community

When Jean arrived at the clinic, she was stunned by all the fat people. "I had never seen so many fat people before and they were wearing shorts and halter tops, something I would have never dared to consider. Bare bellies and rolls of fat were hanging out everywhere and no one thought anything about it. Here I fit in. I was like everybody else."

The Rice House is not a live-in facility and provided no housing for the dieters. Since Jean couldn't afford to stay in a hotel the entire time, she moved out of the hotel in the hopes of finding cheaper housing. She was willing to sleep in the car, if that's what she had to do. Fortunately, she found inexpensive accommodations, and something more. Her landlady, Mrs. Ethylene, had been renting to Ricers for more than 40 years and was an expert on diets, dieters, and doctors. If Jean ever needed help or had questions, Mrs. Ethlylene was there.

"In Durham, I was with my own kind," Jean says. "I was no longer alone in my struggle. Thousands of people had come here before me. I felt at peace with myself and my body and for the first time, I could relax and be me. I didn't have to have the best personality, or be the smartest to compensate for my obesity. It was liberating."

She could now focus on what was important: getting healthy and losing weight. She didn't have to worry about thin people judging or ridiculing her. People like her, who had first-hand experience with the struggles of getting thin, surrounded her.

Finding Patterns in the Weight-Loss Wars

With the expert advice and support of the Rice staff, Jean lost 70 pounds after four months. But she was also out of money. Rather than leave Durham without reaching her desired weight, she convinced the doctors at Duke to give her a job and pay her in reduced medical fees. They agreed and hired her to work to develop a database with profiles of the dieting patients. To further subsidize her stay, Jean also worked as a waitress and dishwasher at the Rice Clinic. The job enabled her to interact with many of the patients, and as she did, she found comfort in their similarities and hope in their differences. While everyone had a different story, the reason for being at Duke was always the same.

While collecting information for the database, Jean was struck by the different people from all over the world who were fighting weight problems: Supreme Court justices, athletes, actors, celebrities, and regular folk. "Research indicates that 95 percent of the people who lose weight will regain it within five years. I was determined to be among those 5 percent but I had no idea how to make that happen. By talking to successful dieters, I hoped to learn their secret. I was committed to finding the cure to my own struggle with obesity," says Jean.

To get her answers, she began to interview men and women at Duke who were fighting the battle against obesity. In a year, she collected more than 1,000 stories and identified specific patterns that enabled successful dieters to defeat their long-time battle of the bulge.

First, she learned that overeating and diet had nothing to do with knowledge. All the know-how in the world will not make you thin. What worked for successful dieters was their ability to leverage the power of pain and pleasure when making food choices. Successful dieters were able to fully associate with the pain of living as an obese person, and subsequently they chose a piece of fruit instead of a piece of pie.

Others didn't look at what they were doing as a diet but as a prescription for health, happiness, and spiritual healing. The buddy system was also effective.

Jean was not only gaining new awareness and insight into a challenge that had plagued her for years, but she was also continuing to lose weight. When she decided to put the collection of interviews into a book, she simultaneously created a new future—even a new identity—for herself. She no longer defined herself by other people's standards. She wasn't ever going to be a lawyer; she was a writer.

When she announced to her family that she was writing a book, they were dumbfounded and told her that nothing would come of it. She wrote the book anyway and called it *Fat Like Us*. Before the book even hit the shelves, *60 Minutes* called for an interview. And since the book has been published, Jean has gotten calls from numerous celebrities, thanking her for it. She is now a professional speaker and folklorist. Most important, she is her own woman.

Jean arrived in Durham a lost soul looking for hope. She left a newly empowered woman with a mission: to give a voice to the millions fighting the lonely, bruising battle against obesity. But it wouldn't have been possible without the love and support of the community she found. With that support, she's become a source of hope for others. Through her Web site (www.fatlikeus.com), her workshops, and her speaking engagements, she helps thousands of others walk the same path she's walked.

Ironic, isn't it? She went to Durham to lose. But she ended up gaining so much more.

> *"To lose weight or achieve any goal, it's critical to get support from like-minded people. It's hard to feel like the odd one out and a support group offers a shared identity, feedback, and positive reinforcement to keep you on track. You can do it alone, but it's a lot easier if you don't have to."*
> —Jean Renfro Anspaugh

Unstoppable Action
Create a Support Team

The story of Jean Renfro Anspaugh is a clear example of how surrounding ourselves with supportive people provides a powerful structure for creating change in our lives. While it may not be practical to drop everything and move across the country as Jean did, it is important that we spend time with people who provide encouragement and support us in our efforts to lift ourselves higher.

Do you have that kind of support team in your life? Do you have a community to rely on, where you gain and give support and encouragement? To successfully complete this Unstoppable Women Challenge and move on to even bigger changes, it's important to surround yourself with people who understand the road you're on and encourage you to continue.

The first step in building your support team is to assess the people in your life. This is important because the people you spend the most time with not only play a role in furthering or hindering your goals, but they're also the people you tend to emulate. Researchers at the University of California at Berkeley have demonstrated that associating with successful people improves performance and increases the chance of success. Conversely, associating with unsuccessful or unimaginative people is counterproductive.

✎ Rate the amount of support you get from those closest to you.

In your journal, make a list of the 10 people who are most involved in your life. This could include a spouse, children, co-workers, neighbors, or friends. Next, rate them from 1 to 10:

- 10 = Someone who makes you feel great about yourself, builds you up, and is totally supportive of your goals.
- 1 = Someone who discourages you, tears you down, or provides no moral support.

After making your list and rating the people, add up your ratings and divide by the number of people on your list to get an average rating. If your average score is 5 or below, half your time is spent with people who drain your positive energy and discourage your dreams. Your goal should be to raise that average to an 8 or 9.

Even though you can't eliminate some people from your life, you can minimize your interaction with them. You can also set up boundaries for what is acceptable feedback regarding your goals. If there are certain subjects that you feel are off limits, tell them so. Don't allow yourself to engage in conversations about your goals with people who you know will provide negative feedback. If they can't provide balanced feedback, don't have the conversation.

At the same time, you can offset any negative influence by associating with people who encourage you and provide a positive example. This is your support team.

Make the Most of Your Relationships

To create the best possible support team, try the following tips:

• Build more relationships that nourish and restore you—with a coach, buddy, spiritual advisor, mentor, or role model. Spend time with people who will hold you to a higher standard.

• Pay less attention to relationships that make it easy for you to maintain the status quo. Some friends will always tell you what you want to hear and let you get away with failure. Spend your time with friends who understand your goal and will help you grow.

• Terminate negative relationships—those focused on gossip, complaining, or making excuses. They aren't a good investment of your energy.

• Intentionally open yourself to meeting new people.

• Get buy-in from your family. If you can help your family members see how your goal directly benefits them, you'll get more of their support. For example, if you're going back to work, you can point out that the money you make will help pay for a nice family vacation.

• Continue to support your buddy. Share your daily insights and draw strength from each other. This not only provides accountability structure, but it makes the process more fun and enjoyable.

• Finally, use the support you have been given to help someone else on their journey. By building relationships based on mutual support for

---

UNSTOPPABLE WOMAN SUCCESS STORY

"I successfully completed the Unstoppable Women Challenge and achieved the best month in sales in the 8 years of my business. But the most exciting part of my story is how the Challenge impacted my relationship with my 12-year-old son. Alex has a heart condition, and he wanted to do something for someone else. The American Heart Association sponsored an event called 'Jump Rope for Heart,' and Alex decided to participate. He set the astronomical goal of raising $1,500.

"When he told me of his goal, I immediately thought it was well beyond what was possible for him. In the past, I would never have supported him in setting such a lofty goal, but because I was taking part in the Unstoppable Women Challenge, I decided to encourage him instead and let him go for it.

"Alex asked me to drive him around to local businesses so that he could ask managers and employees to sponsor him. I thought this would be a complete waste of time and wanted to suggest that he instead call a few family members and ask for a donation, but again, I was reminded of the Unstoppable Challenge and how anything really is possible, so I agreed.

"Alex spent 2 hours telling business owners what he was doing and asking for their support. Later he wrote letters and e-mails and made phone calls. I was amazed at his boldness and determination.

"He didn't achieve the goal of $1,500, but he raised more money than any other kid in his school—almost $300. Alex said, 'Mom, I would never have done it if you hadn't encouraged me to do it.' It was a powerful experience for both of us, and the biggest eye opener I have ever experienced in my life. The Unstoppable Women Challenge has transformed both of us."

—Christal

each other's goals, you'll both benefit. I think a lovely example of this is the story from Christal on page 255, who took what she learned during the Challenge and used it to encourage her son.

Look for Support from Nontraditional Sources

When we think about our support team, it's natural for people like our spouses, girlfriends, and sisters to come to mind. But you can also find great support in other, less-obvious places. Check out the following leads:

• **Nonprofit organizations:** Identify a nonprofit that compliments your purpose and passion. Volunteer for a committee. By giving your time and resources, you'll make a difference in your community and meet great people you might not have ordinarily have come into contact with. Their ideas, creative energy, and support can help you notice new opportunities or paths you might not otherwise have considered.

• **Professional associations and conventions:** People from all over the country gather at industry conventions to share ideas, methods, and techniques. These meetings offer an excellent place to make new connections and meet top achievers in almost any field.

• **Your place of employment:** If you are currently working for a company, don't miss an opportunity to maximize your existing resources. Think of opportunities that you could develop more fully. What special projects could you volunteer to lead? Whom do you admire in your company, and how can you learn from them?

• **Personal coaches:** Personal coaches work with all types of individuals to help them define and achieve personal and career goals. You might consult with a coach on anything from starting a business to improving your backhand in tennis.

Create Your Day Planner

PLAN TO BE UNSTOPPABLE! Tonight or first thing tomorrow morning, plan your next day's activities by filling out Create Your Day Planner (see Appendix).

Do you want to know my motto? Here it is:

"I refuse to be around people who don't recognize my brilliance."

I firmly believe that we all have our distinctive brilliance to contribute to the world, and life's too short to be around people who just don't "get it." As your support team develops and you become more confident, you'll be able to handle the barrage of naysayers and obstacles. Be selective about whom you spend time with, and treat negative influences like the plague! Negativity works like poison in your bloodstream; if you give in to its power, it will weaken your confidence and kill your drive and enthusiasm. Your goals and your life are too important to let that happen!

Day 24
Trust Your Inner Knowing

Today's Affirmation: My uniqueness is my strength. My skills, passions, and gifts are like no one else's. I have unique qualities to contribute to the world, and I follow my inner guide even when it's contrary to what the experts might say. I trust my inner voice and intuition. As I stand tall in who I am, I give permission for others to do the same.

Do you ever feel a little different from most people, that you don't quite fit into a particular niche? If so, don't feel bad because you don't "fit in." Celebrate it. Turn your uniqueness into a strength. Your skills, strengths, passions, and gifts are like no one else's. So why should you conform to someone else's idea of what you should be? You shouldn't. Instead, turn your differences into assets. The world is full of extraordinary women who have done just that.

Today, Aretha Franklin is hailed as the Queen of Soul. But when she signed a deal with Columbia Records in 1961, they tried to turn her into a pop jazz singer. Franklin was less than enthusiastic. In 1966, she went to Atlantic Records and focused on soul, and her career began to soar. She was one of the first women to actively steer her own recording career. Her mantra with producers was, "If you're here to record me, then let's record me, not you." As a result, she earned R-E-S-P-E-C-T.

Another woman who didn't quite fit in is Oprah Winfrey. In the early days of her career, Oprah was fired as a TV reporter because she broke the cardinal rule of journalism: She openly sympathized with the unfortunate people she interviewed. When she started crying while interviewing a woman who had lost seven children in a tragic fire, she lost her job.

What's more, when Oprah was 22 and a new anchorperson, a group of men in suits sat around a table and suggested that she change her name to Suzie! They told her, "No one will ever be able to pronounce or remember Oprah. Besides, Suzie is friendlier."

To stay true to herself and to keep her media career going, Oprah came to realize that she would have to create her own venue. She worked hard to launch *The Oprah Winfrey Show*, a talk show with a heart and a hand extended to people in need. Today, Oprah is a one-woman media empire worth billions.

Imagine what would have happened if either of these women listened to popular opinion! People look at what has worked in the past, and they'll encourage you to conform to a tested formula. But your uniqueness might be a whole lot more interesting than any formula.

To some, Sarah Morris's physical disability must seem like an overwhelming obstacle. But to Sarah, it's just part of who she is, part of what makes her unique. While her body remains limited, her soaring, unstoppable spirit has helped her turn her unique circumstances into an asset, providing her the time to add to her knowledge, refine her journalistic skills, and turn her greatest passion into a professional career.

Unstoppable Woman:
Sarah Morris's Story

Sarah Morris loved the Los Angeles Dodgers. Lived them, breathed them, hung on every inning of every game like it was life or death. The team was her passion, and she had one dream: to cover the Dodgers for a newspaper. Forget that she never took a course in journalism, hadn't attended a live game since age eight, or, for that matter, never had a paying job. To add to the list of strikes against her, she had an even greater limitation—cerebral palsy, which made it impossible for her to use her hands to write.

Sarah ignored it all. She knew that if she were to achieve her dream, she would have to do things differently than most.

Growing Up with Baseball

Baseball had always been a part of Sarah's life. Her grandfather was a big Dodgers fan, and her favorite activity at her high school in Pasadena, California, was as the baseball team's statistician. The work kept her involved in school activities and with the game she loved. But she wanted more.

Dependent on disability income, with no money for special computers or training, Sarah knew she had few prospects. But despite the limitations of her body, there was nothing wrong with her mind. She wanted to write about the one thing she loved: the Dodgers, a team she loved for its tradition and its courage in breaking the color barrier with Jackie Robinson. But how to get such a job?

Creating Her Own Opportunity

Rather than accept her limitations, Sarah decided she would create her writing opportunities by designing and publishing her own Web site. And so Sarah's Dodger Place was born, a fan site where Sarah would publish her own insightful comments and critiques of the Dodgers' performance, good and bad. Here she could be a sportswriter—without pay, but doing what she loved.

She spent endless tedious hours typing her stories by pecking away one key at a time with a stick attached to a headpiece—the same way she entered the code for her Web site. She put in at least five to six hours per day writing her stories that virually no one but her mother would read. Yet she was delighted. She was published. Because her cerebral palsy made it difficult for her to speak, she had honed a unique writing voice backed by her vast knowledge of the team and the game. And those words were finally out there for others to read.

Two Writers Meet

One of the nation's best, most outspoken sports columnists, Bill Plaschke gets a ton of e-mail. But Sarah's stood out. In it, she blasted him for a recent column on the Dodgers, vehemently disagreeing with some of his points. "This person was extremely passionate, yet very informed about the Dodgers and I rarely get both. It was one of the best e-mails I'd ever received. She knew what she was talking about."

That began a correspondence that included dozens of e-mails. Bill learned that Sarah was 31, lived in Texas with her mother, and was a passionate Dodgers fan. Eventually, he told her she should take her knowledge and writing skill and work for her local newspaper. Sarah e-mailed back saying she couldn't because she was handicapped and had to type with her head. Bill was suspicious. He sent her another e-mail saying that shouldn't stop her and asked if he could call her so they could talk about it. Sarah e-mailed back, "You can't call me. I can't talk."

Now Bill was sure something was up. "I found it very hard to believe that this terrific writer was tapping away one key at a time, unable to use her hands or her voice. I thought she was just hassling me." He had no way of knowing that she had to use a head pointer to type on a computer that would read back her work to her. What would take an average person one hour to type, took Sarah five. But Bill was intrigued and willing to investigate further.

So when he was in Texas to cover the Lakers, the cynical journalist went to see Sarah Morris for himself. "Sarah sent me directions to her house that were two pages long listing every little farmhouse and dirt road along the way. As I turned down her driveway, I saw through the weeds four or five wheelchairs sitting outside the house. I knew this must be the place. Her mom met me at the door and welcomed me in. There was Sarah, this frail little body sitting in a wheelchair with this huge giant smile. I thought, she really does exist."

For the final proof of her situation, Bill asked Sarah to show him how she typed with her head. "When I saw her type the words that appeared on the screen, I felt sick and ashamed of myself. All this time I didn't believe her."

Blue Days
Astounded by Sarah's talent, knowledge, and sheer determination, Bill wrote a candid, heartfelt column about her in the *Times*. It not only attracted attention from readers who besieged the *Times* to hire Sarah, but also caught the eye and heart of Ben Platt, manager of the Dodgers.com Web site. Further encouragement came when Dinn Mann, editor-in-chief for the parent site MLB.com, called Platt and suggested that they hire her. Platt made an offer, and Sarah accepted her first paid writing position.

Today, the woman who bleeds Dodger blue is a leading columnist for Dodgers.com.

Her mother, Lois, says that the opportunity to write and learn has changed Sarah. "She's becoming more independent every day," she says. Sarah, speaking through her mother, says, "It's hard work, but I love it."

Bill, for one, remains inspired by the young woman who first called him on the carpet for his column. "Sarah Morris symbolizes that part of us all that dares to dream—to embrace life without limitations and to realize everything that's possible if we have the courage to try."

That's success, one letter at a time.

Unstoppable Action
Celebrate Your Uniqueness

Sarah Morris could have been excused for giving up on her dream in the face of enormous physical disability. But she didn't. She followed her own path, one that she could not have negotiated had she depended on the need for approval from others. She trusted that she had a unique voice and a unique perspective on the team she loved, and she worked tirelessly to bring that voice to others. Her uniqueness—her dedication and love of the Dodgers despite her limitations—proved to be a great asset.

Research indicates that average, or "normal," people produce average, or "normal," results. It takes an "abnormal" or unique person to create, innovate, or do things differently. The people who stand out from the pack always do it their way. People like Susan Powter, the peroxided fitness guru who wanted to "Stop the insanity!" or Judge Judy, who gave new life to the dying court show genre. They stood out because of their unique style and were successful because of it.

People will always try to fit you into the mold they think is best. I've had publicists, media consultants, friends, and associates suggest changing all sorts of things about me, from adopting a "hipper" look to changing the way I sign my name.

It takes courage to not only hold true to your uniqueness, but to embrace it, knowing that many will not "get it." That's okay. As your uniqueness opens new doors for you and your appreciation of who you really are expands, you'll see that you have a unique way to express yourself in this world . . . a way that no one can duplicate.

Let your inner voice be your guide.

Take a moment to list at least 10 things that you believe are unique about yourself. Perhaps it's your outlook on life, your sense of humor, your mission, or the way you really listen and make a person feel special. Celebrate your uniqueness and acknowledge these gifts that make you special.

When people offer suggestions that you change something, listen to your inner voice. Does their advice have merit, or is your unique style a truer reflection of who you are? Follow your own vision, despite what others think you are supposed to do. Don't try to be like someone else, because you'll only be second best. Honor your authenticity. Stand tall in who you were meant to be. People will beat a path to your door if you let your uniqueness shine.

> *"Never sell your soul, because nobody can pay you back. Ever.*
> *To me, being your whole self, your true self, is as much a part of*
> *success as anything else. I am who I am. I have my own style,*
> *and it has freed me to bring my whole person to work. . . . If you can't*
> *be yourself at work, find a different workplace. If you feel you are*
> *constrained or selling your soul or leaving a part of yourself behind, then*
> *you aren't performing to your potential and should go somewhere else."*
> —Carly Fiorina, chairman and CEO of Hewlett-Packard

Create Your Day Planner

PLAN TO BE UNSTOPPABLE! Tonight or first thing tomorrow morning, plan your next day's activities by filling out Create Your Day Planner (see Appendix). There is no more powerful guide for your life than your intuition. If you're facing a situation that you're uncertain about, take a few moments to be still and meditate. Listen to your inner knowing. Follow your inner guide even when it's contrary to what the experts might tell you.

Something to Think About

As long as Nia Vardalos could remember, she wanted to be a performer. She figured that as long as she took the right classes, worked hard, and auditioned for every part, her talents would eventually be recognized.

Unfortunately, Hollywood doesn't judge actors on talent alone. And in 1996, when she moved to Los Angeles to be an actor, the harsh and often unfair reality—that talent often takes a back seat to appearance—slapped her in the face. After months and months of badgering her agent and waiting to be sent out on auditions for the upcoming sitcom season, her agent finally leveled with her: "You're not pretty enough to be a leading lady, you're not fat enough to be a character actor, and you're Greek. There's nothing I can do for you."

Nia decided to write and produce her own one-woman show. "Don't make it too ethnic," everyone told her. But she ignored them and wrote about what made her laugh the most, her wacky Greek family. She found a small theater in Los Angeles and debuted *My Big Fat Greek Wedding*.

Over the next year, word of mouth spread about the show. Film producers started to turn up. Some wanted to buy the idea, but only if they could change it to *My Big Fat Italian Wedding*. No deal. Nia stuck to her convictions. But she was running out of money fast.

With her last cash, she decided to run an ad in the *Los Angles Times*, hoping to attract a wider audience. Jackpot. Rita Wilson, who is Greek, came to the show, loved it, and returned with her husband, Tom Hanks. When Wilson mentioned to Nia that the play would make a good movie, the always prepared Nia handed her the screenplay. Hanks and Wilson pitched the idea to several studios, but they always got the same response: They loved the script, but didn't want Nia.

Convinced it could be a success, Hanks and Wilson ended up producing *My Big Fat Greek Wedding*, which was made for $5 million and starred Nia Vardalos. The film has broken box office records, raked in more than $200 million, and become the highest-grossing romantic comedy ever. And its success is all due to one woman who refused to be denied her chance to bring her unique vision to life.

Day 25
Don't Mistake Success for Failure

Today's Affirmation: I define my success. It is not determined by whether or not I reach my goal, but whether or not I continue to take one step forward no matter how many times I fail. If I do not quit, I simply cannot fail. I am unstoppable!

S low and steady wins the race." It's not glamorous, but it's true. The tragedy is that most people never even get in the race, and many of those who do hope that success comes easily and swiftly. When it doesn't, they're out of the race, before it really begins. What they don't realize is that *the decision to be unstoppable is never made just once. It is made moment by moment, again and again.*

Setbacks are inevitable. In fact, they're evidence that we're doing something. The more mistakes we make, the greater our chance of success. Failures indicate a willingness to experiment and take risks. Unstoppable women have learned that each failure brings wisdom and insight that will take them one step closer to achieving their dreams.

When we focus on one unstoppable moment at a time and stay the course, the end result will take care of itself. Margot Fraser can attest to that firsthand.

Unstoppable Woman:
Margot Fraser's Story

"Women will never wear these things!" Not the first words a budding entrepreneur in the footwear business wants to hear. The year was 1966, and those were the words of Tom Jackson, owner of Jackson's Booterie in Santa Cruz, California, to Margot Fraser. The "things" he was reacting to with such horror were a pair of strange, earthy-looking sandals that seemed to spring from the town's counterculture. Later on, they would be called Birkenstocks.

Although Birkenstocks today have a worldwide following, back then people derided them as ugly, often starting with the phrase, "Why in heavens would you ever . . . ?" But slurs did not daunt Margot Fraser, an unswerving, German-born Californian. Modest and mellow (like her shoes), Margot just shrugged off the criticism and kept on going. "I thought, this cannot be," she says, "because I like the shoes so much. I wear them. I am their customer and there must be more like me."

Putting Her Best Foot Forward
In 1966, Margot was an independent dressmaker who suffered from chronic foot pain. While visiting her native Germany, she heard about a shop in Bavaria with a shoe that could help her. So she went, and the shoe turned out to be made by a 200-year-old company named Birkenstock, which had only started mass-producing this anatomically correct sandal the year before.

Margot bought a few pairs of the stocky, odd-looking sandals, and after three months of wearing them, "I looked down at my feet and said, 'My God, my toes have straightened out!'" she recalls. Her first thought was that she *had* to let other women know about these shoes. But there was a problem. In 1966, women expected their footwear to be beautiful, not comfortable. Looking for comfort in a shoe didn't even enter into the minds of most American women. Fraser believed that women had suffered long enough in pointy, high-heeled shoes, and she knew she could win their hearts (and feet), *if* she could get them to try the shoe.

Unfortunately, she didn't know the first thing about business or sales. However, one of her greatest strengths has always been an ability to live with uncertainty. "I don't have all of the answers," she admits, "but I can live with the questions because you never know what will happen from one day to the next."

Margot decided to sell Birkenstocks out of her home. And even though she received a less than enthusiastic response from retailers and health food stores, she kept plugging along. In 1967, she paid $100 for a small exhibit booth at the Association of Health Food Stores Show in San Francisco. She recalls, "Our display consisted of a few pairs of sandals sitting on a table." Not exactly eye-catching, but it was a start. Margot believed if anyone would be interested in trying her foot-friendly shoes, it would be women standing behind the counters all day in the healthy products business. So she told the women at the show that they didn't have to buy anything . . . *just try the shoes on.*

One woman was interested in the Birks, but her husband snapped, "What do you want to buy those ugly things for?" The woman bought a pair anyway and wore them throughout the three-day show. At the end, she found Margot and said, "You may have something here, because I can *feel* the difference." She bought three more pairs and began selling them out of her San Rafael health food store. Margot was on her way.

Shoe Business
Not long after, Margot went into partnership with the business in San Rafael, and Birkenstock Footprint Sandals, Inc., was born. "We started this company in a way everyone said could not be done," she recalls. "Luckily, I didn't *know* this was true, or I might have gotten cold feet. We had no business plan and started with $6,000 borrowed from the Crocker Bank with my partner's credit. I didn't have any credit. I was divorced and couldn't even get a gas card." Such was life for an unmarried woman in

the 1960s. But Margot *did* have open credit with the German manufac-
turers, so with the partner's credit and her connections, the business took
off—at the speed of drying paint. No matter. A beginning is a beginning,
and slow and steady. . . .

A health food store rented Margot office space for $25 a month.
One of her first vendors in 1972 was a college student, Melanie Grimes,
who sold the shoes from her dorm room. Grimes still remembers Margot's
refreshing attitude toward business. "When I eventually opened a store of
my own and ordered 87 pairs of shoes," she says, "the shipment arrived
with a letter from Margot saying, 'If the shoes are not for you and your
customers, please send them back for a full refund.' That letter is still on
the wall."

As is the case for all entrepreneurs, challenges were never in short
supply. When Margot attended a regional shoe show in a motel near the
San Francisco Airport, she didn't have a single customer for two days.
People stuck their heads into the hotel room, rolled their eyes in disbelief,
and disappeared. "You weren't supposed to leave the show before it was
over," she says. "But I thought, 'I'm getting out of here!' I packed everything up and left by the fire escape." But amazingly, people whom she had
never seen called her after that show, and one became the catalyst for the
first Birkenstocks store.

Step by Step

Slowly, organically, the funny-looking, really comfortable shoe started
catching on. News of it spread by word of mouth. The hippie movement
made them the footwear of choice for the counterculture. Shops opened
selling nothing but Birkenstocks. Retailers in the Bay Area opened
Birkenstock accounts. Just as slowly and steadily, Margot expanded from
California to Chicago to New York. "Our company grew by word of
mouth. People had friends or relatives who also had shoe stores in a different part of the country, and that was how we grew."

It took 10 years for Birkenstocks to go on sale from coast to coast.
But Margot has always been comfortable doing things the right way and

letting success come at its own pace. "I believe in taking deep breaths and going with the flow," she says. "I managed to live on very little for the first few years. Patience is a big part of it. I think many people just give up too soon, and they don't stick through the self-sacrifice."

Today, nearly 40 years after that first rude awakening with the Santa Cruz retailer (who, by the way, later signed on and is now a very strong dealer), Margot, now a 60-something grandmother, has built Birkenstock Footprint Sandals, Inc., into a 200-employee company with 100 licensed specialty stores and 3,000 retail accounts—step by step, store by store, account by account. She sells more than two million pairs of shoes each year, which means a lot of happy feet. It's also confirmation that her initial instinct was right: Comfort sells.

Margot gives her employees much of the credit for her success, so she's made them pretty comfortable as well, selling them 100 percent ownership of the company.

Through it all, Margot Fraser has remained modest, steadfast, and sincere. "I never really tried to succeed," she says. "I always had a good product and I believed in it, but I was only interested in doing things right and building relationships with my customers." Her approach remains the same today, and she uses her wealth and influence to promote better working environments for all laborers, encourage the formation of more women-run businesses, and wipe uncomfortable shoes off the face of the earth.

"No one took me seriously, and before they knew it, we had a pretty good company. No one bothered with us. And it's easier to ask for help as a woman. They don't expect you to know too much!"
—*Margot Fraser*

Unstoppable Action
Redefine Success

Your success is not determined by whether or not you reach your goal, but whether or not you continue to take one step forward, no matter how many times you fail.

As we've seen in Margot Fraser's story, success doesn't happen overnight. It is a process. An old adage says, "The arrow that hits the bull's eye is the result of a hundred misses." I'm sure everyone in this book would agree. It's through adversity and failure that we ultimately win. Being able to see failure as an opportunity for learning and improvement is critical to becoming unstoppable. People who can't bear a moment of failure have doomed themselves to mediocrity, for they'll never be able to push themselves past a point that is uncomfortable or unfamiliar. Yet it is beyond that point where success dwells.

It's important to remind ourselves that failure is an event, not a person. If you don't achieve your 30-day goal, does that make you a failure? If you don't get a promotion at work, does that make you a failure? If you get married and then divorced, does that make you a failure? Of course not!

Failure doesn't characterize who you are. It is simply an event that happens to you. And when you continue to move forward, despite difficult experiences, you have already won!

Turn failure into a valuable gift.

Turning failure into a gift requires objectivity and may take some practice. A great exercise to provide insight on how your "failures" may ultimately serve you is to think about a major setback you've had in your life. Now that time has passed and you can objectively evaluate the experience, list specific ways in which you ultimately benefited from this setback.

For example, most people would see getting fired as a major setback. But after some time has passed, they can look back on that situation and find the gift. Perhaps that "failure" gave them the push they needed to find a career they really love. Without that event happening, they would never have left the security of their position to branch out into other areas.

The next time the outcome you had hoped for doesn't transpire, look for the gift. Ask yourself the following questions:

1. What can I learn from what happened?
2. What am I grateful for about this experience?
3. What are the potential benefits of this experience?
4. What is the best way for me to move forward?

Commit to finding the gift in any setback. Not only will you gain from each experience, but the combination of your commitment, courage, and faith will be the greatest triumph of all.

> *"Mistakes are part of the dues one pays for a full life."*
> —*Sophia Loren, actress*

Create Your Day Planner

PLAN TO BE UNSTOPPABLE! Tonight or first thing tomorrow morning, plan your next day's activities by filling out Create Your Day Planner (see Appendix). Chances are, not every step you've undertaken in your Unstoppable Women Challenge has gone smoothly. You've probably made some wrong turns, hit a pothole or two, or even pursued a path that turned out to be a dead end. The key, though, is to keep on moving, to not let these setbacks end your journey. If you're still wincing from the disappointment of a setback and feel that you've gotten stuck, take some time to think about how you can make a "U-turn." How can you turn this experience around so it becomes a plus, something from which you can learn a valuable lesson?

Something to Think About

Without the perseverance of one very determined lady, women might not even have the right to vote. Like other women of the late 19th and early 20th centuries, Susan B. Anthony found it intolerable that half the U.S. population—the female half—was denied the right to exercise the most basic duty of citizenship: voting. But unlike many others, she did something about it.

Anthony and many other supporters of women's suffrage went from house to house, braving abuse and slammed doors, trying to spread the word about the importance of giving women the vote. "After each rebuff (which often included snide remarks about who did and didn't have husbands) the women simply trudged on to the next street, the next row of houses, the next grudgingly opened doors," Rheta Childe Dorr wrote in *The Woman Who Changed the Mind of a Nation*.

In spite of verbal taunts, being pelted with eggs and garbage, and being burned in effigy, Anthony continued to lead the campaign for more than 50 years. She was the driving force behind suffrage conventions and campaigns for voting rights. As Lynn Sherr, author of *Failure Is Impossible*, writes, "She arranged everything from flowers to furniture on the suffrage programs; personally raised huge amounts of money; wrote hundreds, sometimes thousands, of letters a year with suggestions, requests, and outright orders to both friends and strangers; in short, she almost single-handedly maintained a sprawling army of very diverse women who were united only in their desire for the vote." Despite setbacks, she refused to think of her efforts as failure.

About the inevitable opposition, Susan B. Anthony told her supporters, "Take your stand and hold it. Then let come what will, and receive blows like a good soldier."

Ironically, Anthony did not live to see her victory. But she was victorious. In 1920, fourteen years after her death, Congress ratified the 19th Amendment to the Constitution, giving women the right to vote. Through her perseverance, Susan B. Anthony had given American women not only the right to vote but an unstoppable role model for justice.

Day 26:
Stand Up and Be Counted!

Today's Affirmation: Every day I show up and take action, I am proving to the world that it's possible for someone else to do the same. I continue to grow as I step into my greatness. Each time I take a stand for my inner truth and beliefs and show love and compassion to another person, I improve myself and set my spirit free.

Bishop Desmond Tutu once said, "It is important that people know what you stand for. But it is equally important that they know what you won't stand for." How often do we witness injustice in the world but remain silent because it doesn't directly impact us? Or see inequities and unspeakable acts of violence broadcast on the news and feel helpless to make a difference?

It is easy to understand why we often feel that our voices don't matter. After all, we're each just one person. What can we do? But we never know how our actions are impacting those around us. At the very least, by standing up for something we believe in, we are fighting the good fight and setting an example for others to do the same. In the process, we earn a greater sense of self-respect and pride.

Sherron Watkins, a former Enron vice president, was simply doing her job when she discovered a serious breach of ethics at her company. With uncommon bravery, she chose to stand up for what was right, even though she knew it might end her career. She wrote a letter to CEO Ken Lay warning him that the company's accounting methods were illegal and a recipe for disaster. When she was proved right and Enron went bankrupt in 2002, Watkins became the star witness for the Congressional subcommittee investigating the financial fraud, and ended up on the cover of *Time* magazine with the caption, "The Year of the Whistle Blower."

Watkins didn't set out to become a public figure. Yet she risked her privacy and her livelihood to do what was right. Similarly, Senator Patty Murray has become known as a woman willing to stand up for her convictions. She has devoted her political career to making a positive difference in people's lives. In fact, that career began because she saw an injustice and didn't fade into the background and let it continue. A political novice, she acted, and with the strength of her convictions, she made change happen.

Unstoppable Woman:
Senator Patty Murray's Story

Patty Murray didn't get into politics because she was part of a powerful political family or a veteran activist. She got into politics because she was trying to be a better mom. And because she stood up to be counted, she has changed the lives of families from coast to coast.

With a degree in recreation from Washington State University, Patty enrolled in a community college course that taught parenting skills, hoping to learn some new ways to interact with her two preschool-age children. "One day, I went to class," she says, "and the teacher announced, 'We're not going to have this class anymore. They've discontinued funding.'"

Shocked, Patty learned that the Washington state legislature in Olympia had made the decision to cut program funding. Outraged, she piled her two kids in the car and drove 72 miles down to the state capitol and started asking questions. She talked to lobbyists, legislative staff, and others about the effects of such decisions on families. Then came a further outrage: A state legislator told her that her voice made no difference. "You're just a mom in tennis shoes" were words she would always remember.

Full Force into Politics
Patty's response to that dismissal changed everything. "I drove home very angry. Who were they to tell me that my voice wasn't as important as the opinion of these guys in suits?" she says. She vowed to herself that they were not going to force her to walk away from this. So she started making phone calls to the teachers and parents from the same community college course at campuses all over the state, telling them what was going on.

"I did what every woman with a couple of kids would do," she says. "I got on the phone and called my girlfriends. I was able to put together an extensive network by simply asking them for the names of friends of their friends." Calling and networking occupied Patty from early morning until late at night, as she simply did what came naturally to her.

In three months, she had turned 15,000 parents into the Organization for Parent Education—and then turned them loose on the state legislature. They wrote letters, signed petitions, held marches . . . and got the program funding restored! It was a sweet victory. Patty had proved that "moms in tennis shoes" could make a difference. She recalls, "That taught me a great lesson. You can complain about what people are doing, or you can do something to change it." She chose the latter.

A Different Voice

The funding victory wasn't enough for Patty. She learned how one person, truly committed, can change things. It was the early 1980s, and her son was about to start kindergarten. Patty wanted to know who was making the decisions about his school, so she visited the school board. She was surprised to see five older adults who were nice but who were all retired, with no children in school. "I thought, 'Who on this board understands little kids? Who has a real investment in how our school district is run?'"

She looked around the room and thought if she didn't do it, nobody else was going to. So she decided to run for the school board. She lost by 300 votes, but when the winner died three months later, she was appointed to fill his term. She ended up staying for several years and eventually became school board president.

This position led her to the Washington State Senate, where she lobbied tirelessly on behalf of her school board and education issues. Patty tried to get her voice heard by talking to senators and representatives, yet she watched in frustration as the policies most important to her as a school board president and mother were not registering on the Senate floor.

"One day while sitting in the gallery, I was looking down on the senate floor and I saw a lot of old bald heads. It struck me that perhaps the reason my voice wasn't being heard was because the policies and legislation that were passed were, again, by people who didn't have small children. I realized that the only way I could make a difference and make my voice heard was to be on that senate floor," she recalls.

Patty was told by the "experts" that she had no chance. "I had no money and no political background," she says. "But I wanted to show people that they could do this, too. It's not an elite club in politics. This is a democracy. We need different voices, we need different perspectives, and no one should be told they can't do this."

Outrage

Patty's fierce determination gave her an unquenchable need to prove the naysayers wrong, and her outsider status gave voters a new choice. They took it. In 1988, she upset an incumbent who had been in office for 15 years.

She did it the same way she's done everything: with a little help from her friends. "My husband was great. My kids were great. They licked and stamped envelopes and put plates on the table for dinner when I was on the phone," she says. "By the time my kids were 8 years old, they knew how to do laundry."

Now a legislator, Patty had a chance to see how the system worked from the inside. She continued her crusade for the welfare of families and children, leading the charge to pass Washington's family leave law, one of the nation's first. But it was an event in the nation's capitol that sparked her next move.

She watched the Clarence Thomas-Anita Hill sexual harassment hearings and saw 14 older Caucasian men presiding and thought, "What have we done?" Patty thought it shameful that the highest lawmaking body in the land so poorly reflected the diversity of people in the country. So, almost on impulse, she decided to run for the U.S. Senate in 1992.

Capitol Hill

When they were told about her plans to run for the U.S. Senate, "the reaction from my friends was, 'Oh no, here she goes again!' The reaction from political insiders was that I could not succeed," Patty recalls. It was an uphill battle, like all the fights she has chosen. She was a nobody, pitted against a five-term Republican Congressman for the seat. She had no massive party machine to help her raise money, and she had no one with deep pockets or far-reaching influence in the corridors of Washington, D.C. She was a "commoner," given no chance of winning. Of course, that was the same thing the "experts" had said about her state senate bid.

What she did have was her burning conviction to stand up and be heard. "I didn't focus on the difficulty of the task," she says. "I focused on the end result and making a difference." And once again, Patty proved the doubters wrong. She was outspent dramatically, but she took 54 percent of the vote and was on her way to Capitol Hill.

Since that stunning victory, Patty has proved herself true to her initial convictions. She spoke up about the Tailhook Navy sex scandal at a time when women were still regarded as curiosities in the Senate. She has continued to work for the welfare of everyone from rural workers to college-bound students. She's chaired the Transportation Appropriations Committee. And she was instrumental in passing the federal Family and Medical Leave Act.

Through it all, Patty has remained the same fiery activist and unaffected mom, genuine and hardworking, uncorrupted by Washington. Terry McAuliffe, chair of the Democratic National Committee, says about Patty, "She is up and coming—one of the Senate's shining stars."

What keeps Patty fighting the good fight? She shares something her then-teenaged daughter, Sara, said to her one day when Patty came home fed up with the battles. "She asked me, 'What's wrong?'" Patty recalls. "And I said, 'It's just been one of those days and I'm wondering why I'm doing this and is it really worth it?' She just looked me in the eye and said, 'You're doing this so one day I can.'

"My daughter had said it best. I have to do this not only for myself, but for my daughter and the next generation of young women."

"Usually, when people tell you that you can't make a difference, they're afraid you will. When I die, I will feel proud if I was able to encourage other women to follow their dream."
—*Senator Patty Murray*

⟨———⟩ Unstoppable Action ⟨———⟩
Discover What Matters to You

"We must not, in trying to think about how we can make a big difference, ignore the small daily differences we can make which, over time, add up to big differences that we often cannot foresee."
—Marian Wright Edelman, founder, the Children's Defense Fund

Patty Murray didn't set out to be a senator and a leader. She simply saw something that she believed should be changed and followed her convictions and determination until it was. That path led her to the Senate, and may lead her higher still.

Through the Unstoppable Women Challenge, you are making a change in your life. And in the process, you are changing not only the way you see yourself but also how you see the world.

Like the unstoppable women whose stories you are reading, who are models for all of us, you too are becoming a model of what's possible. Every day you show up and take action, you are proving to the world that it's possible for someone else to do the same. And as you do, your image of who you are continues to expand. You're making a difference. You're not only improving yourself, but helping others do the same.

Identify what matters to you.

What are you willing to stand up for? Try to identify at least three areas that are important to you. If there's something you believe in, that affects your life or your community, write it down.

THREE THINGS I'M WILLING TO STAND UP FOR

1. _____

2. _____

3. _____

Once you've identified three areas that you aren't willing to compromise on, stand up and speak out. Don't sit on the couch waiting for someone else to act. Ask yourself, "If not me, then who?"

I'm not suggesting that you should risk life and limb or commit every waking minute to righting injustice in the world. What I am suggesting is that you start noticing what is happening around you and flex your unstoppability muscle. If there's graffiti near your home, get a crew of neighbors and wash it clean. If you see someone being treated in a racist or prejudiced way, speak out against it. If you think your city government has made a poor decision on an issue, write a letter to your local newspaper bringing it to the community's attention.

Doing this takes courage. It may mean going against popular opinion. Friends and family may try to talk you out of your convictions. But when we fight for our beliefs and follow our inner truth, we set our spirits free. As author and lecturer Marianne Williamson beautifully stated, "As we let our light shine, we unconsciously give other people permission to do the same. As we are liberated from our own fear, our presence automatically liberates others."

"Our lives begin to end the day we become silent about things that matter."
—Martin Luther King Jr.

Create Your Day Planner

PLAN TO BE UNSTOPPABLE! Tonight or first thing tomorrow morning, plan your next day's activities by filling out Create Your Day Planner (see Appendix). Take a moment to think about the people who inspire you. Consider people who are living today and those who have lived throughout history. Who has taken a stand that you truly admire? This will be a key insight into what is important to you. Maybe you recently read a biography or an article, or saw an inspirational film that moved you. Notice the qualities and causes that speak to your heart and think about one way you could express that in your life and community this week.

Something to Think About

Betty Williams says she's never met an "ordinary housewife," yet that's what most people dismissed her as when she began crusading against sectarian violence in Northern Ireland. Raised Catholic in the famously divisive region, she deliberately raised her family in a neighborhood of both Catholics and Protestants so they wouldn't absorb the same religious hatred that was ripping her country apart.

Sadly, the violence found her, when a skirmish in 1973 left a British soldier shot and dying at Williams's feet. She knelt beside the young man and prayed and was scolded by her neighbors because the boy was "the enemy." Three years later, her friend Ann Maguire's three children were killed when an Irish Republican Army vehicle plowed into them. Williams witnessed the tragedy, and it changed her forever. "I still don't know what happened inside of me that day," she says. "There was an explosion within. I just knew I couldn't continue to live like that."

She immediately went to work collecting signatures—6,000 in all, from Catholics and Protestants alike, demanding the end of the violence. She asked the local newspaper to print her phone number so people could call to offer help, a risky move in a violent time. She and Maguire's sister, Mairead Corrigan, knocked on countless doors and pulled the women of Northern Ireland together for a rally. Just four days after the deaths of the Maguire children, 10,000 women marched through the streets of Belfast. Williams would name her group the Community of the Peace People.

Just a few weeks later, nearly a quarter million people would pack Trafalgar Square in London at her behest to protest the violence in Ulster. It was the beginning of the peace movement in Northern Ireland, one that led directly to the Good Friday peace accord in 1998. For her brave efforts, Williams was awarded the Nobel Peace Prize.

Today, Williams lives in Florida, where she works as a university professor and coordinates a global program to protect children. She's never wavered in her belief that each of us changes the world in some way. It's up to us to decide what that change will be.

Ordinary housewife indeed.

Day 27:
"Girlfriend to Girlfriend:" Great Pain Requires a Greater Purpose

Part of your journey toward becoming an unstoppable woman is helping another woman create an unstoppable result in her own life. Why? Because the power of helping someone else transforms *our* lives. When we give without thought for what we'll get in return, we receive the true rewards.

I had the opportunity to test this theory firsthand. After separating from my husband of 20 years in December 1999, my son and I spent the holidays at my parent's home in Florida. During my visit, I was in deep pain and found myself with a great deal of time to think. After a lot of gut-wrenching introspection and many tears, I realized that while I couldn't control what was happening in my marriage, I could control how I lived my life. Then and there I made a vow to myself: The next Christmas season, I wouldn't be at my parent's house feeling sorry for myself. Instead, I would dedicate myself to doing something for someone else over the holidays.

Homes for the Poor Ease the Pain

In early January, I called Millard Fuller, founder of Habitat for Humanity International. I told him about what had happened and my desire to do a project with Habitat for Humanity. He had just gotten back from Nepal and told me about this majestic Himalayan kingdom, home to five of the seven highest mountains on Earth, including Mt. Everest. Yet it is also one of the poorest nations in the world. More than 90 percent of Nepalese families subsist on meager incomes from small-scale farming and often lack access to adequate sanitation or even potable water. Instead of being sent to school, children are sent to work in the fields. For them, their only inheritance is the same poverty they experienced in childhood.

A simple decent home—made of concrete blocks and a metal roof— is but a dream to most Nepalese families. Such a home not only carries prestige, but is also passed on for generations, securing future dignity and self-respect. I was struck by this contrast of abject poverty surrounded by incredible natural beauty, and I decided that I wanted to help. I began to realize the truth of the statement: "When you have a great pain in your life, you need a *greater* purpose."

The question became, "How many houses would I need to build to offset my pain?" Five? That didn't seem like enough. 10? No. 20? No. 30? Still no. Nothing seemed adequate until I reached the number 100! One hundred houses seemed bigger than my pain.

Off to Nepal

Not only had I never been to Nepal, but I'd never before raised money for a project such as this, and I had no idea how I would pull it off. But just having the purpose of helping 100 families invigorated me. It was much bigger than my circumstances. Whenever I started to feel self-pity or cry about what I had lost (and there were many of those times), I'd think about the Nepalese families who didn't even have a simple roof over their heads or a place to protect their children from the cold mountain nights. It kept my life in perspective.

That year, as I spoke and traveled across the United States, I was a woman with a mission. I shared the Habitat for Humanity Nepal project with anyone who would listen, including corporate leaders and audience members, asking for their financial support. With just $2,000, we could build a simple house for a Nepalese family that would be handed down to children, grandchildren, and great-grandchildren. And to my delight, the people I spoke to responded with great generosity: In 12 months, I raised all the money needed to build 100 homes. The following December, a team of 20 people went to Nepal, where we worked on the first three of the 100 houses in that project that were to be built over the next 2 years.

A Great Gift

One of the three families whose houses we were building was for a woman named Chandra Karki, who was supporting seven other family members, including her parents and her brother's family. Amazingly, all these people were living in a small one-bedroom shack. For 10 years, Chandra had saved money from her job at a cookie factory to purchase land, in the hopes of one day building a house. Without the help of Habitat for Humanity, it would have been many more years before she could have saved enough money to build a home.

Even though Chandra and I didn't speak the same language, we immediately connected. We soon discovered we had a lot in common. We were both single women buying a new home. I was buying my first house as a single woman, and she was buying the first house of her life. It struck me that even though we were living worlds apart, we were both experiencing similar emotions of excitement and nervousness.

On the last day of the trip, we had a ceremony dedicating Chandra's new house to her and her family. Emotions ran high for everyone, and it was difficult to walk out of that simple house, which had become a home to this loving family. As we were leaving, Chandra turned to me with tears in her eyes and said, "Thank you so much. Please don't ever forget me." And I thought, "How could I ever forget you? Helping you got me through the most difficult year of my life." It was *Chandra* who had given *me* a great gift.

That is the power of a purpose focused on helping others. When life happens, as it does to all of us, such a powerful purpose keeps us moving forward, getting our minds off of our problems and onto something greater. My purpose—my fundraising and my time in Nepal—turned what could have been one of the worst years of my life into one of the most precious and rewarding.

I want to encourage you not only to connect with a buddy and support each other to complete the Unstoppable Women Challenge, but also to find a way you can be of service to others. Make it a lifestyle, a way of being. What you do doesn't have to be big. There are simple ways to give, whether it's a smile to a stranger, a financial donation to a cause, volunteering your time at a community shelter, or mentoring a child. There are countless ways you can give every day if you open your eyes and your heart. In doing so, you will be invigorated about your goal *and your life* because you will know you are making a difference in the lives of others.

Day 28:
Week 4 in Review

You've made it to Week 4. Congratulations! Let's review your progress and success for this final week. You'll use this information to write your unstoppable story on Day 30.

The Week in Review Form

Complete the Week in Review form (see Appendix). Again, notice any recurring disempowering beliefs or unproductive behaviors that have come up for you this week. Don't judge them as good or bad. Be grateful that you are now aware of them and focus on the new behaviors and beliefs that you can incorporate into your life and into the next Unstoppable Women Challenge to move you forward.

Most people live their entire lives completely unaware of the sabotaging beliefs and behaviors that hold them back. Look at how much you've improved and the insight you've gained about yourself over the last four weeks. You truly are a different person today than you were when you started this journey. And that is definitely worth celebrating!

Day 29:
Continuing Your Unstoppable Journey: What's Next?

Today's Affirmation: By consistently taking action, I am part of an elite group of women with the courage and determination to complete the Unstoppable Women Challenge. Regardless of circumstances, I have consistently taken action and fulfilled my commitment. My story, along with the stories of the other unstoppable women in this book, is living proof that it's never too late to make positive changes in your life. I am truly unstoppable!

Congratulations! By making it to Day 29 and consistently taking single steps, you've placed yourself in an elite category. Countless others have started books or programs with the intention of changing their lives, but they never finished. They may have had the same enthusiasm or motivation that you had (or even more). But somewhere along the way, they lost it. Life happened, or they decided that the rewards weren't worth the effort. You didn't.

As you completed the challenge, you no doubt had to fight off some demons—disempowering beliefs and behaviors that have held you back in the past. Yet this time, you prevailed. I know that as a member of the human race, you encountered obstacles and faced the temptation to quit. Yet you chose to continue. You are now a different person than when you took your first step. No one can ever take that from you!

Regardless of the size of your goal, reaching it is a huge accomplishment. You have consistently taken action and fulfilled your commitment. So many women talk about their dreams, wishing they could accomplish this or that with their lives. But they just talk . . . or dream. You're doing it.

Your story, along with the stories of the other unstoppable women in this book, is proof that it's never too late to change your life.

There's Always Hope for the Future

Today, I'm going to briefly introduce you to a number of women who demonstrate that the best in life is yet to come. Later in their lives, they decided to cast aside limiting stereotypes and approach their futures with passion, hope, purpose, and love. As a result, they changed their lives—and often the world around them. We can all look to them for inspiration. They are proof that our futures hold wonderful possibilities, whether we're 22 or 82. For example, Mother Teresa was 55 before the Pope authorized her Sisters of Charity Mission as a papal autocracy. She went on to help millions of suffering people in the streets and slums of Calcutta and to become a global symbol for mercy, healing, and selflessness.

Ever think about entering politics and the world of public service? Golda Meir was 70 when she was elected prime minister of Israel, becoming the first female leader of a Middle Eastern state and a pillar in the early days of the peace process. Margaret Thatcher was elected Prime Minister of Great Britain in 1979 at the age of 54.

Do you secretly yearn to change careers? Studies by the U.S. Department of Labor suggest that the average person has eight careers in her lifetime. Lydia Bragger became a radio talk show host at age 69 and was still on the air when she turned 96. Ruby Hemenway began her writing career at 92, penning her first column for the Greenfield, Massachusetts *Recorder*. She even had cataract surgery so she could continue writing and is so concerned about falling behind that she's usually five stories ahead.

Ever think about starting a business? Stella Nicole Patri, 64, started her own book-binding business when she was in her sixties. She had always been intrigued by Japanese paper making, and in 1960 she decided to take an apprenticeship with the Italians, whom she felt were doing interesting work with book and paper restoration. When she received no response from Italy, she went on her own and met with the American cultural attaché, who got her an apprentice job restoring paper. Eventually, she opened her own book-binding shop, and she's been busy ever since. And what about the business that became the Mary Kay Cosmetics empire? That was started by Mary Kay Ash in 1962, when she was 52!

Don't Be Limited by Your Age

How can you contribute? At 100 years old, Josephine Dukes is still working and has no plans to retire. Five days a week, for four hours a day, the passionate centenarian is on the job in Oakland, phoning her roster of 35 senior citizens (most younger than she) to check in on them. With a personal touch, she makes sure that their hearts are warm, their refrigerators are cool, and their lives are A-OK.

Doris Eaton Travis, who resides in Norman, Oklahoma, is enjoying her third career at age one hundred. She started her career as a dancer and actress, with the Ziegfeld Follies. She then owned and operated one of the nation's largest chain of Arthur Murray dance studios. With her late husband, Paul Travis, she ran a Quarter Horse ranch, which she still helps to operate today. And at 88 years old, she became the oldest graduate of the University of Oklahoma, majoring in history. When Doris turned 100 years old, she said, "This is not the end, but a new beginning."

What new beginnings are awaiting you? What do you think it's just too late for? When Melanie Reid was a girl, her teachers told her parents she was mentally disabled. She lived with that label and her illiteracy until she was 51. Then she decided she wanted to learn to read, so she enrolled in the Harty Bible School in Pittsburgh, her King James Bible in hand. Today, 2 years later, Melanie is able to read to her 11 grandchildren.

I could go on and on. The inspiring, heartwarming stories of women of all ages who discover the unstoppable power within themselves seem endless. These women prove that it's *never* too late to pursue your true heart's desire.

⌒⟶ Unstoppable Action ⟵⌒
Leverage Your Momentum

What else is possible for you? You've laid the foundation. You owe it to yourself to continue this process, to fully develop and grow, to realize your full potential. Use this challenge as a beginning. Leverage the momentum you've created. The great news is that achieving your goals will get easier as you continue to raise your Unstoppability Quotient and integrate the empowering beliefs and behaviors into your life that will enable you to persevere through any obstacles. You now know you can do it . . . because you've already done it!

🖎 What's next? Continue your journey.

Take some time to think about areas you'd like to explore for your next Unstoppable Women Challenge. Perhaps you want to continue toward the fulfillment of a goal you started with this challenge. Review the goal you wrote down on page 21. Were you able to accomplish that goal in one Unstoppable Women Challenge? If not, you'll want to redefine your 30-day goal, then repeat the Challenge.

Perhaps you'd like to focus on a new goal. For her first Unstoppable Women Challenge goal, one woman chose to become consistent with her exercise program. The second 30 days, she applied these principles to develop her business. The third 30 days, she narrowed her focus and developed a marketing plan for her business. Again, return to Part One of the book. Reread the responses you wrote in the "What Do I Want?" chart. Review the areas in your life that you are interested in improving or changing. Then choose one goal that would literally jump-start your life and give you great joy if you achieved it over the next 30 days. Commit to it by writing it on the following page.

To build on the momentum I have created and to propel my life, career, relationships, or lifestyle to an even greater level, I commit to the following goal for my next Unstoppable Women Challenge

_____

_____

_____

_____

_____

Next, and as important, identify someone to whom you can give back during your next Unstoppable Women Challenge. As you no doubt experienced, when you make a conscious effort to reach out to others, your life becomes more meaningful and joyful. What other ways can you contribute? How can you make your experience with your buddy more fun and exciting?

Apply what you've learned to your next 30 days. Continue to take risks. You deserve to be everything you were meant to be. Don't let anything or anyone keep you small. Know that you are unstoppable!

Day 30:
Write Your Unstoppable Story

You thought it would never arrive, but you're here. Day 30. You *are* unstoppable! You have successfully completed your Unstoppable Women Challenge. You identified what you really wanted to achieve, created a step-by-step plan, and decided to "show up" every day to take action to make it happen. Your results demonstrate that anything is possible for you.

So what do you do next? First, *celebrate*! Reward yourself for your consistent effort. Why is it important to fully celebrate your success? Too often, as women, we focus on where we've fallen short. It's time to change that habit. If we don't take the time to celebrate our victories, we might overlook them completely. That wouldn't reflect the truth of what we've accomplished! If we want to continue to make progress, it's critical to recognize and commemorate each step we're taking to make positive changes in our lives. Refer to the "end of challenge reward" you created for yourself during Day 9 and follow through: give yourself the reward!

If you didn't successfully complete your goal, don't beat yourself up. Celebrate anyway! Focus on your accomplishments and on the areas where you showed up and took action. Congratulate yourself for the progress that you made! This is a process, and you can continue to build on the success you've already achieved. You have now laid the foundation to creating any desired change in your life, and that is definitely worth celebrating!

Secondly, it's time to write and share *your* unstoppable story by answering the questions on page 296. Again, what's most important is not what you achieved, but the progress that you've made. What did you learn about yourself during this challenge? What did you personally have to overcome to stay in action? What tools were most effective in supporting you in this process?

By answering these questions, you are uncovering the keys to your continued success. Use your story as a success imprint. You have proven to yourself that you can make change in your life by simply committing to taking a single step at a time.

Share Your Success Story with Others

It's important to share your success story with others so they can celebrate with you. Share your story with your buddy and celebrate each other's success. I also encourage you to share your story with the unstoppable community by visiting **UnstoppableWomen.com** and posting your success story. While online, you can celebrate with other challenge participants who have shared their success stories as well.

And finally, share your unstoppable success story with me. I am honored that you allowed me to be a part of your unstoppable journey and am eager to hear about your progress. Let me celebrate and acknowledge you for your unstoppable efforts. You can share your story by e-mailing your responses to me at Cynthia@unstoppable.net. Or you can photocopy pages 296 to 298, fill them out, and mail them to Unstoppable Enterprises Inc., P.O. Box 877, Agoura Hills, CA 91376-0877.

If you send me your story, I'll send you a *free* downloadable Unstoppable Women Challenge Certificate signifying your successful completion of the Challenge. It will serve as a visual reminder of your success. I'll also send you free daily insights to support you on your continued journey. (Make sure you include your e-mail address so I can send you the Certificate.)

I look forward to hearing your story and continuing our journey together. Never stop believing in yourself, and don't let anything stop you from creating the life you want *and deserve*!

May God continue to bless you, my new unstoppable friend.

Cynthia

Your Unstoppable Success Story

Name _____

E-mail (mandatory to receive the Challenge Certificate)

_____

Address _____

City_____ State____ Zip code _____

What was your 30-day goal?

_____

_____

_____

Did you achieve your 30-day goal? List specifically what you accomplished during the Unstoppable Women Challenge.

_____

_____

_____

What motivated you to participate in the Unstoppable Women Challenge? What were you no longer willing to settle for in your life?

_____

_____

_____

How do you feel about the progress you achieved by participating in the Unstoppable Women Challenge?

_____

_____

_____

What was the greatest benefit you received by participating in this program? How is your life different from when you first started the Challenge?

_____

_____

_____

_____

What's the greatest obstacle you had to overcome? How did you get past it in order to successfully complete your goal?

_____

_____

_____

_____

What was the greatest tool, support system, or reward you received that enabled or motivated you to complete your Unstoppable Women Challenge?

_____

_____

_____

_____

What's the most important limiting belief you had to change in order to successfully complete the Unstoppable Women Challenge?

_____

_____

_____

What's the most important disempowering behavior you had to eliminate in order to successfully complete your 30-day goal?

_____

_____

_____

_____

How did giving back to others impact your life over the last 30 days?

_____

_____

_____

_____

Would you recommend this program to others and why?

_____

_____

_____

_____

Afterword
The Unstoppable Women Movement

"Never doubt that a small group of thoughtful, committed citizens can change the world. Indeed, it is the only thing that ever has."
—*Margaret Mead*

By completing the Unstoppable Women Challenge, you are now part of a growing movement of women who are changing their lives for the better, one step at a time. My personal mission for the Unstoppable Women Challenge is to inspire *millions* of women to do what you have just accomplished: to commit to taking one step each day for 30 days to make a breakthrough change in their lives and to make a difference in the life of another woman.

The two guiding principles behind this book and program are the driving forces in my life and, I hope by now, yours as well. They are simply this: Help yourself and help someone else.

It is impossible to help others until you first choose to help yourself. By completing the Unstoppable Women Challenge, you have done that: You accepted responsibility for the results in your life and identified what you wanted to change. Then you worked tirelessly to make your life different from what it was when you started. Step by step, unstoppable moment by unstoppable moment, you grew stronger and more assured.

With your newfound strength, you are able to extend yourself and help someone else on their path. In doing so, you reap the greatest rewards. Giving to others makes your life richer and more fulfilling. The more you give, the more you receive. It is the law of the universe.

And because of the changes you have made in your life, you are now a powerful model for what is possible for others. Your success provides others with hope that they, too, can change their lives. Essentially, by helping yourself, you *are* helping someone else.

My deepest hope is that you will continue on your unstoppable path. As you continue to learn, grow, and make positive changes in your life, take what you have learned over the past 30 days and use it to help another woman in her life.

Imagine a world in which millions of women are committed to changing their lives and at the same time reaching out to help others. I have received hundreds of e-mails, letters, and calls from women who are doing just that.

The excitement is building, and *you* are an important and integral part of this mission and the Unstoppable Women Movement. Please let me know how I can continue to support you in creating an unstoppable life and in your efforts to support others on their journey. You can contact me by sending an e-mail to Cynthia@unstoppable.net or mailing a letter to Unstoppable Enterprises Inc., P.O. Box 877, Agoura Hills, CA 91376-0877. And don't forget to visit the online Unstoppable Women community at **UnstoppableWomen.com**.

Together, we can change the world, one step at a time.

APPENDIX

What Do I Want?

8 KEY AREAS	WHAT DO I *REALLY* WANT?
1. PHYSICAL Appearance Overall health Fitness level Eating patterns Exercise routine Optimal strength 　　and energy	
2. FINANCIAL Earnings, savings, and 　　investments Net worth goals Money management goals Financial security	
3. PROFESSIONAL Job satisfaction Passionate about career Advancement potential Education and skills to 　　develop	
4. PERSONAL Fun/adventure Vacations Rejuvenating activities Enough time for myself Environment and home	

WHAT AM I NOT WILLING TO SETTLE FOR?

What Do I Want? (cont.)

8 KEY AREAS	WHAT DO I *REALLY* WANT?
5. RELATIONSHIPS Family, spouse, children, parents, siblings Romance Friendships Finding a mentor Expanding my network	
6. MENTAL/ EMOTIONAL Personal growth Emotional stability Skills to develop Happy and whole Clarity on life's purpose	
7. SPIRITUAL Actively growing spiritually Regularly pray/meditate Spiritual community Regularly express love to others	
8. GIVING BACK— LEGACY Contribute to others Donate money to causes I care about Make a difference	

WHAT AM I NOT WILLING TO SETTLE FOR?

Converting Your Dream Into a 30-Day Goal

WRITE YOUR 30-DAY GOAL

_____

_____

_____

_____

Week One

	CATEGORY	# DAYS/WEEK
Step 1		

Week Two

	CATEGORIES	# DAYS/WEEK
Step 1		
ADD Step 2		

Week Three

	CATEGORIES	# DAYS/WEEK
Step 1		
Step 2		
ADD Step 3		

Week Four

	CATEGORIES	# DAYS/WEEK
Step 1		
Step 2		
Step 3		
ADD Step 4		

My ABC Evaluation

30-DAY GOAL:

_____

_____

_____

_____

ADVERSITY (TRIGGERING EVENT):

_____

_____

_____

BELIEF: (Disempowering Interpretation)	NEW BELIEF: (Empowering Inerpretation)
CONSEQUENCES:	NEW CONSEQUENCES:

Create Your Day Planner

COMPLETE THIS FORM EVERY MONDAY THROUGH FRIDAY DURING WEEKS 1 THROUGH 4.

DAY #:

30-DAY GOAL: Write your goal as if it's already happened.

_____

_____

UNSTOPPABLE STORY: Read the day's story and write the key learning insight (the chapter title) below.

_____

_____

_____

DAILY ACTION: List the one step you *must* take today to stay in action on your 30-day goal.

_____

_____

ADDITIONAL STEPS: Add an additional step ONLY if you have already consistently integrated the first step into your routine.

☐ _____

☐ _____

☐ _____

MEET WITH BUDDY: Speak with your buddy EVERY DAY and review your actions, what's working, what's stopping you, and one area of improvement you will focus on to stay in action on your 30-day goal.

COMPLETE BELOW AT THE END OF THE DAY

First, review the list above and check off all completed actions.

UNSTOPPABLE VICTORIES: Write down at least one thing you did that you are proud of that moved you one step closer to the achievement of your 30-day goal.

GIVING BACK: List one thing you did to encourage or support someone on their unstoppable journey.

Week in Review

WEEK #:

One Step:	How many days did you complete your one step?
	_____ days (# of days you took action) out of _____ days (total # of days per week your goal requires action)
Additional Step: **(Optional)**	How many days did you complete your additional step? (If applicable)
	_____ days (# of days you took action) out of _____ days (total # of days per week your goal requires action)

Reward yourself for the steps you are taking! Use the great feelings of success and accomplishment to propel you forward. You are creating *lasting* change in your life.

REWARD YOURSELF!

How can you reward yourself for your victories this week? List one or two things you will do to reward yourself for a job well done.

- _____
- _____
- _____
- _____
- _____

If you didn't complete your one step every day, your next step is to identify what happened. Refer to your daily sheets for last week and complete the following questions:

SPEAK WITH BUDDY:

How many days did you speak with your buddy?

_____ days (# of days you took action) out of 5 days

DAILY CHAPTER:

How many days did you read the daily story/chapter?

_____ days (# of days you took action) out of 5 days

DAILY VICTORIES:

How many days did you write down your daily victories?

_____ days (# of days you took action) out of 5 days

GIVING BACK:

How many days did you give back to someone else?

_____ days (# of days you took action) out of 5 days

What is the single most disempowering belief that stopped or threatened to stop you this week? (Refer to any ABC evaluation forms you completed this week.) What is the new belief you need to stay in action?

Old Belief	New Belief
Consequence	**New Consequence**

What is the single most unproductive behavior that stopped or threatened to stop you this week?

_____

_____

_____

What new BEHAVIOR do you need to stay in action this coming week?

_____

_____

_____

What STRUCTURE can you create to ensure you follow through on your goal?

_____

_____

_____

Adding the Next Step (Weeks 1 through 3)

To determine if you're ready to add an additional step next week, calculate your Unstoppability Quotient (UQ). If you've been successful at completing your current steps with 70 to 80 percent consistency, go ahead and add your next step. If you struggled to consistently take your current steps this week, consider repeating these steps next week. When you do feel comfortable with those steps, it's time to add in the next one.

CALCULATE YOUR UNSTOPPABILITY QUOTIENT (UQ)

_____ days (# of days you took your one step) divided by

_____ days (the total # of days per week requiring action) = UQ

Your Unstoppability Quotient for This Week = _____

Index

Underscored page references indicate boxed text.

D

CONTINUE YOUR UNSTOPPABLE JOURNEY WITH FREE RESOURCES FROM UNSTOPPABLE ENTERPRISES INC.

The *Unstoppable* Web site, www.unstoppable.net, offers free resources as well as tools and programs to help inspire, motivate, and encourage you to live a more enriched and fulfilling life. In addition, you'll have the opportunity to meet and engage other unstoppable individuals through our dynamic community.

To join our unstoppable community, simply go to the website and click on "Daily Insights." You'll receive daily email quotes, messages, and affirmations from author Cynthia Kersey. Additionally, you will receive exclusive notification of special networking opportunities in your area, announcements on upcoming conferences where you can meet other unstoppable individuals and continuing information on unstoppable publications, products and services that will assist you in your pursuits.

Giving Back

We also encourage you to participate in one of our Unstoppable Foundation *Love in Action* projects. The Unstoppable Foundation focuses on a wide variety of women-related issues including housing, education, health, and personal empowerment and provides grant and scholarship programs for individuals and non-profit organizations. The Unstoppable Foundation is a tangible vehicle for the *Unstoppable Women Community* to actively help people worldwide create a life of love, dignity, and empowerment.

For more information about the life-transforming projects the Foundation supports, visit www.unstoppablefoundation.org or write:

P.O. Box 877
Agoura Hills, CA 91376–0877

ABOUT THE AUTHOR

Cynthia Kersey is a best-selling author, speaker, and president of Unstoppable Enterprises, Inc. She is also co-author of several popular books and programs.

Ms. Kersey has spent more than a decade researching and interviewing hundreds of the world's greatest achievers and has applied her extensive knowledge of human potential in the development of effective, proven products and programs aimed at helping people dramatically improve performance, achieve success and enhance their quality of life. Cynthia's critically acclaimed first book, *Unstoppable*, revealed the secrets and traits of successful people and outlined a simple process that anyone can apply to create unstoppable results in their business and life.

Cynthia has appeared on hundreds of radio and television shows and is a radio personality in which her weekly *Unstoppable Moments* has been featured in markets across the U.S. and Canada. Her books and programs have received rave reviews from national opinion makers and readers alike, including Scott DeGarmo, former editor of *Success Magazine* who considers *Unstoppable* "this generation's *Think & Grow Rich.*"

Ms. Kersey's company, Unstoppable Enterprises, Inc. (UEI), www.unstoppable.net, provides tools, strategies, and resources designed to empower people to live unstoppable lives.

To find out more about how to utilize Ms. Kersey's services as a consultant, coach, or keynote speaker or to receive a brochure detailing other unstoppable products and services, please call toll-free at 888-867-8677 or visit UEI's Web site at www.unstoppable.net.

CREATE YOUR OWN UNSTOPPABLE SUCCESS STORY WITH PRODUCTS AVAILABLE FROM UNSTOPPABLE ENTERPRISES INC.

Unstoppable 30-Day Challenge

By Cynthia Kersey

Audio and TeleCoaching Program

Would you like additional support to help you successfully create the results you want and complete the Unstoppable 30-day challenge?

This comprehensive program skillfully combines an inspirational audio and TeleCoaching program designed to move you into action and take your life or business to the next level in just 30 days.

These powerful tools will support you in your Unstoppable 30-Day Challenge:

- **Unstoppable MENTORS.** Each day you'll listen to the true story of an individual who overcame great adversity to achieve a goal or dream. (Audio Program)
- **Unstoppable COACH.** Cynthia will travel this journey with you every step of the way. In **five one-hour conference calls,** Cynthia will coach you and other unstoppable participants through weekly challenges—giving you the insight and skills you need to successfully complete your Unstoppable 30-Day Challenge.
- **Unstoppable Challenge DAILY PLANNER.** A daily, proven, step-by-step daily action planner that will help you establish a breakthrough goal, break it down into 30 easy steps, and document your daily planning and progress.
- **Unstoppable TEAM.** Join other unstoppable people who are committed to completing the 30-Day Challenge. You'll benefit immeasurably through their support and accountability.
- **Unstoppable INSPIRATION.** Receive daily e-mails of insight & inspiration.

To join the Challenge, simply go to our Web site at www.unstoppable. net and click on "30-Day Challenge." Remember, the stronger your team, the more unstoppable you become. **Don't let anything stop you! Join us today!**

Unstoppable: 45 Stories of Perseverance and Triumph from People Just Like You!
By Cynthia Kersey
Trade Paperback Book
In this enduring book, you'll discover that ability, upbringing and financial backing are less a factor in success than the indefatigable human spirit—a spirit empowered by seven success characteristics nearly every unstoppable achiever possesses.

Your Unstoppable Journey
By Cynthia Kersey
Audio Program
An effective, enriching audio program and 80-page workbook that reveals powerful concepts you can use to not only identify your heart's true desire—but to achieve it! You'll also meet others who've traveled this road and can show you the way. In just 15 minutes a day, you'll learn how to develop *unstoppable* Purpose, Passion, Belief, Preparation, Team, Creativity, and Perseverance!

For more products and services from Unstoppable, visit www.unstoppable.net.